Teaching home economics

Mary Moon

Teaching home economics

Batsford Academic and Educational Ltd
London

© Mary Moon 1981
First published 1981

Reproduced from copy supplied
printed and bound in Great Britain
by Billing and Sons Limited
Guildford, London, Oxford, Worcester
for the publishers
Batsford Academic and Educational Ltd
an imprint of B T Batsford Ltd
4 Fitzhardinge Street
London W1H 0AH

ISBN 0 7134 1833 8 (cased)

Contents

Acknowledgment

My thanks are due to the many colleagues, former students and pupils in schools who have influenced my philosophy on education. I would also like to thank those who have kindly given permission for me to quote from their work, full reference to which appears at the end of each chapter.

Preface

The law requires that every parent in this country should send his child to school. What happens there fits him to take his place in a complex world. Survival in society depends upon the possession of the right knowledge and skills. To acquire these he needs the help of his teachers. During the eleven years of compulsory schooling a pupil will meet many teachers with varied interests, abilities and education. It is with their professional education that this book is concerned.

Part 1 sets the scene by looking at those schools which educate pupils from five to eighteen years. It is in these that a student teacher will one day teach. This part of the book illustrates that education is a continuous process from the primary, to the middle and high school years. At each stage the curriculum is designed to meet the changing needs of pupils as they develop physical, mental, emotional and social skills. The teachers who bring this about are prepared by their higher education and professional training. This is based on centuries of tradition and the experience of those who have gone before.

Part 2 examines in greater depth the framework for a teacher's role. It looks at the daily routine cycle of preparation, communication and evaluation. Beyond this lies the incomparable satisfaction to be gained in watching pupils develop from unawareness and incomprehension through knowledge, understanding and skills to reasoned action and creativity. Some notable teachers from the past whose influence is still seen in schools, universities, religion, government and commerce are looked at briefly. In education they have been responsible in part for developing a curriculum which forms the basis of pupils' studies today.

The end of the last century saw the introduction of statutory elementary education for all. This brought with it the establishment of professional training courses for teachers. The development of this is traced in Part 3. The training of teachers varies according to their destination. A brief review of past and present practice will guide prospective students in choosing wisely their own higher education and professional training. This is followed by some aspects of a student teacher's preparation for the teaching role. Home economics teachers are employed principally in the middle and high schools. Part 4 identifies their particular professional needs and discusses how these may be met. A knowledge of factors which influence learning in children, forms a significant part of a teacher's professional studies. Part 5 is therefore addressed to some of these factors. Finally, Part 6 looks at the school curriculum and the contribution which home economics can make in the primary, middle and high schools.

It is hoped that those who choose to read this book will enjoy it as they look at the many facets of student teachers, schools and home economics. For prospective students and student teachers in training it is hoped that a view is given of a varied, interesting profession which embraces men and women of intellect, culture and artistry. There is a place within it for teachers of many shades of scholarship and talent. For women the teaching profession still offers one of the most varied and highly paid careers. Attention is drawn as well to the growing career opportunities for home economists in industry, commerce and the social agencies. For many of these posts, professional training as a teacher is a bonus. Attention is drawn in the text to the close ties which now exist between home economists in education and industry, commerce and the social agencies. Not only do they now share common first degree courses, but their professional training courses have so many factors in common that they could be run in tandem.

It is hoped, therefore, that teachers in schools, further and higher education, will derive satisfaction from identifying with that which is familiar to them in the text and seeing their particular contribution in the context of an individual's continuing education.

Part 1

The school

1 Education begins at home
The pre-school years (0-5)

Education is a life long process beginning at the moment of birth. Five years elapse (or one fourteenth of the total expected life span) before an individual is exposed to statutory education within the school setting. During those five years he will have listened daily to the spoken word. For four years he will have used language himself and acquired a vocabulary of some two and a half thousand words. This allows a long gestation period prior to learning to read and write. In addition, the individual is the recipient of a bank of new experiences which, with repetition, consolidate through the medium of the sensory organs of sight, hearing, touch, taste and smell.

A passive receptor

Initially a baby is a passive receptor and his parent (mother) a captive teacher. First responses are limited and are of a purely reflex nature. For example, the new born infant is unable to fix his eyes upon an object, although the eyes are completely formed and the lids and pupils react to the stimulus of light. Only when the appropriate stage of maturation is reached will the individual be able to control and direct specific bodily functions. Knowledge of the appropriate age and stage at which it is possible to introduce new knowledge and skills is of great importance to both parents and teachers. As maturation progresses it is equally important that individuals themselves know and understand the potential limits of their achievement at differing stages of the life cycle.

An active learner

As maturation progresses the infant learns how to feed himself and how to control his immediate bodily functions. The family comprises his immediate world. He learns when to expect its members to sleep and wake. Soon he recognizes that certain personal tasks are performed regularly at given intervals, eg washing, dressing, eating and elimination. He learns that communication is achieved by facial expression, gestures or noise, eg smiling, crying or waving the hand. Later sounds are organised and speech begins. Now and later the ability to listen proves a powerful factor in both the quality and quantity of learning; for listening is the forerunner to understanding. Mobility is first achieved by crawling and subsequently by walking. The elements of self and corporate discipline emerge as the infant observes that approval is won by deference to those older within the family group, whether they be brother, sister or parent.

A bank of experience

The average child therefore who is about to enter school has a substantial experience already in walking, talking, listening, observing and living as a member of a family group. Depending upon the success or otherwise of these early experiences he will to a greater or a lesser degree have formed regular, disciplined, healthy habits. These will relate to eating, sleeping, exercising the body and relating without friction to those in the immediate environment.

And so to school

Entry to school will bring with it contact of a physical kind with those outside his immediate environment. It also brings contact with many familiar and unfamiliar learning activities and it is to those in the context of the primary school which the next section addresses itself.

2 The early years of education
The primary school (5-9)

The primary or first school is the most informal of our educational institutions. To the visitor they are bright, cheerful places with much evidence of the children's work about the reception area, rooms and corridors. There is constant ebullient activity among both staff and pupils which generates an invigorating atmosphere. One catches the infectious feeling of hope and optimism which cannot generally be experienced either in the middle or later years of schooling.

Small, intimate units

Primary schools are usually small, intimate units housing one hundred and fifty to three hundred boys and girls. These pupils attend full time. Some schools have a nursery unit attached which provides education for toddlers of three to five years. These children attend either in the mornings or afternoons but not full time. They move into the primary school at the beginning of the term in which they become five.

Parental interest

Often schools are centred in a particular community. In the last century this might well have been a village with the church, inn, shop and houses clustered close by. Now the primary school could be at the heart of a housing estate. Children often live close by and walk to school. Parents are encouraged to accompany their children for reasons of safety. This means that parents can usually be contacted easily when it is necessary. Often a positive relationship between home and school is readily established. Lack of parental interest and concern is less apparent when children are at this age.

The head teacher

Within the school the hierarchy is simple. The head teacher is responsible for the management of the staff, buildings and resources. Academic staff are appointed in consultation with the local education authority adviser (delegated to this task by the chief adviser) and the governors of the school. The head teacher is responsible for the professional and personal welfare of all staff. He enjoys a remarkable degree of autonomy in deciding the range and content of the curriculum. Staff work under his direction to fulfil his plans. The head teacher is also responsible for the academic and pastoral well-being of the pupils. This includes keeping accurate records of pupils' progress and health. The latter embraces vision, hearing, speech and physical state. It is often said that a school is only as good as its head. Truly when the school wins the approbation of the community he is praised. Conversely if the school is viewed with disapproval the head is blamed. In all contacts with the community outside school the head acts as liaison officer and speaks as its representative.

The deputy head teacher

The head teacher is assisted by a deputy. He supports the authority of the head in his dealings with both staff and pupils. As a member of the staff common room he is ideally placed to liaise between the head teacher and his staff. If the head is absent the deputy assumes his role and the authority which accompanies it.

Other posts with special responsibility

The sharing of areas of responsibility varies from school to school. Administratively there may be one teacher in charge of the nursery unit. Another may have oversight of the lower school which comprises the infant classes. A third teacher may have charge of pastoral and professional progress of probationary staff. The same person is usually responsible for all visiting students and liaison with their tutors. All three of these posts demand very experienced teachers and may be rewarded accordingly. Responsibility for specific areas of the curriculum may or may not be recognised. If they are, they may relate to subject leadership in English (including oversight of the library), mathematics, science, music, creative activities or physical education and games. Any of these could be linked to a responsibility for the pastoral care of boys or girls.

Grouping pupils

Individual staff have an almost total commitment to one class or group of children. Groups may be designated as reception, middle infants, top infants, junior I and junior II. Other names may be given to these groups, but they relate to a horizontal chronological grouping covering the ages five to nine years. Usually there is a flexible passage between the groupings. This is to allow for the wide range of differences in ability and rates of maturation within this age group. Some teachers believe that the infant years (five to seven) are better spent in vertical groupings. This means that each group contains infants with ages ranging from nearly five to seven years. A child admitted to such a group could remain with the same teacher for three years. Although acknowledging the sense of security and continuity which this could bring to a child, many teachers feel that chronological groups allowing for flexible movement are better for teacher and pupil.

The class teacher

When a child enters school the class teacher is a key figure in his life. He is given into the teacher's charge by his mother at the door. It is the teacher who helps him remove his coat, change his shoes and shows him to his own peg. He learns the symbol which will identify his peg and his drawer where pencil, paper, books and personal possessions will be kept. Through the day the teacher is constantly there in *loco parentis*. The teacher provides the adult hands which smooth the way in dressing and undressing for *PE,* at mid-morning and afternoon breaks, lunchtime and finally home time. The teacher soothes him when he is angry and admonishes when he is rebellious. She referees quarrels and comforts the injured. Apart from all these very personal activities she introduces the child to the wonders of the classroom and the infinite world to which it is the gateway.

The classroom

Each classroom or teaching area provides a highly structured environment which is carefully planned. Space is divided to provide a number of areas which when thoughtfully used will develop children's mental, emotional and physical talents. The volume and diversity of equipment, materials, books, toys, etc, and ensuring that it is put to the use for which it is intended demands skillful organisation and management by the teacher. There must be a place for everything and constant checking by both children and teacher ensures that everything is in its place. This gives pupils a feeling of pride and responsibility in recognising and maintaining an ordered environment. The key word is accessibility. Everything must be readily available for the individual pupil's use. Teaching methods depend very much upon individual tasks set and individual pupils completing them in their own time and at their own speed. Provision is made for different specific areas within the classroom.

The home base

This is usually carpeted and provides an area where children can be grouped together. They can sit comfortably on the floor at any time when the teacher wishes to speak to all of them. This includes morning and afternoon registration and during the school's quiet time when the teacher reads a story.

The stimulation area

This is the teacher's province where new ideas and interests can be introduced. It is changed frequently to encourage children to look to see what is new.

The creative corner

This provides materials for making and doing. Finished work is displayed here for all to see and admire.

Imaginative play

This area provides a wealth of clothes and accessories for dressing up. Here real and imaginery roles may be acted out. Puppets and a puppet theatre may be included.

Wet area

This provides opportunity for children to engage in tasks which are frequently not allowed at home because they are too messy. They can paint on newsprint or make sticky collage. Designs may be made with fruit and vegetable templates. Fingers, hands and feet can be used for designs needing greater impact. Clay can be kneaded, punched and pummelled. Water may be poured and boats sailed. Sand pies can be made and castles too.

Quiet area

Furnished with tables and chairs this area is used for practising the tool subjects of writing and number.

Book corner

The book corner brings together a display of books among which pupils may browse. Provision is made for comfortable seating for those who wish to linger.

Nature table

Both pupils and teacher contribute to provide a seasonal calendar of natural events. For example, bulbs may be grown and spring flowers arranged. Fruits and vegetables in season, gleanings from the harvest field and autumn leaves all serve to illustrate the continuity of plant life. Fish or small animals like the hamster or gerbil may be kept. These provide subjects for observation and generalisation on how the basic needs of living creatures can be met.

Display area

A pin board and table is needed for the display of children's written work, models and art and craft.

House corner

A Wendy house or curtained recess may include toy items of familiar household furniture and furnishings. This gives a home setting where pupils can act out their own or adult life styles.

The daily care of all these areas sets a formidable task for both pupils and teacher. For the pupils the organisation and management of personal property, shared books, equipment and materials communally held in trust, is a valuable part of their social education. It is therefore important that everyone participates on a fair and equal basis. Sometimes the class teacher with young pupils has a class assistant who will as part of her duties help both with the tasks and their supervision.

The school day

(i) Morning assembly

The day begins with assembly. These are lively and interesting. All staff and all children meet together to share in a Bible story, modern parable and the singing of hymns of praise. Notices of interest to all are given, eg if Jane has been awarded her first swimming certificate or John has returned home from hospital. This is part of a developing thread of learning to care what happens to others, ie to rejoice when they are happy and to offer support when they are under stress. The head, staff and pupils all play a leading role in these proceedings. Children learn whilst still uninhibited to take a central role without fear. Often a simple ceremony marked by a be-candled mock cake will take public note of a child's birthday. An open invitation is extended to parents to attend assembly on a given day each week. Many do, and may visit the classroom afterwards to see their child's work. It is very encouraging to see in school many parents, whose mother tongue is not English, participating freely in these activities. It should be noted that any parent not of the

Christian faith may elect to withhold his child from morning assembly. In practice few do. A more plebian value of morning assembly is to allow latecomers to filter in anonomously without fuss before classes begin. Since lateness of the child at this age is the responsibility of the parent this is both practical and humane.

(ii) The timetable

Timetabling in the primary school is very simple. It is bounded by the regular functional breaks of morning arrival, play times in morning and afternoon, lunch time and afternoon departure. Half an hour is set aside daily for a quiet period during which pupils are grouped together in the home base and listen to a story read by their teacher. This may precede lunch or afternoon home time. The classroom may be left at other appointed times to use shared communal facilities for PE, dancing, singing, television programmes, musical instrument practice, etc. During the rest of the day activities are organised by the teacher within the classroom.

(iii) Daily classroom activities

All children engage in writing practice and, as soon as is feasible, creative writing. A significant amount of time is spent in reading and in doing mathematics. Apart from this the day should give each child opportunity for playing, talking and engaging in group discussion. He should be able to explore and enlarge interests including making and creating. Adventures into literature, music, religious education, and history should be undertaken for their own sake. Healthy habits should be encouraged through practice. This may include adventures in home economics.

(iv) Teaching methods

Basic skills of reading, writing and number are practised daily both individually and in groups. Activities are varied and changed at twenty to thirty minute intervals.

Reading readiness

Pre-reading activities are given. When pupils are skilled in these reading begins.

Pre-reading activities include identifying and sorting shapes, colours and objects. These are counted and arranged in groups, eg

(a) Shapes.   Triangle   Circle   Square
3 yellow circles
4 yellow circles
Learning is reinforced by drawing these.

(b) Matching games, eg jigsaws or 'snap' type card games.

(c) Counting games. These are often sung, eg 'Ten green bottles hanging on a wall . . . . Nine green bottles . . . .'

(d) Listening to stories.

(e) Listening to and looking at illustrated stories whilst they are being read.

(f) Talking about pictures and illustrated stories. When a pupil is adept in the skills listed above the teacher knows that he is ready to begin reading.

A reading scheme

Reading schemes are many and varied. Each school selects the one which teachers feel to be most appropriate for their children. Schemes are comprised of a number of attractively presented books designed to be used in series. These are graduated in difficulty. First books in a series begin with a single word plus a picture representing it on each page. This gives way gradually to two words and two objects or people to be identified in each picture. As books become more difficult the text increases and the pictures become less dominant. When pupils can read fluently pictures become less and less important until they can do without them altogether.

Teaching reading

The teacher selects key words contained in the first book in the reading scheme. She shows these on large scale 'flash' cards one at a time to her group gathered in home base. At the same time she directs their attention to a large scale picture representing the word. Initially she may show six words and six pictures. Then she starts again at the beginning and checks to see which pupils can recognise the word without the picture. This is continued over a period of time, changing the sequence until pupils are familiar with the words. They then turn to the reading book and the teacher checks each pupil's progress in learning the vocabulary. When pupils are familiar with all the words in one book they move on to the next. After a few days in the reception class pupils are formed into groups according to the speed with which they acquire vocabulary. They are then taught in groups to enable the teacher to vary the degree of difficulty in the flash cards shown to each group. The teacher aims to check and record each pupil's progress each day.

Teaching writing

The teacher introduces the written word to a pupil first in large scale. She sits beside him and holds his forefinger and together they trace the line which the pencil will take. Then he tries to do it himself. When the teacher is confident that he knows the path she pins a piece of greaseproof paper over the template. The pupil then traces out the word with his forefinger and then attempts to follow the same path with his pencil. When proficient in this activity the teacher writes a word on a sheet of paper a little larger than normal. The pupil then seeks to reproduce this below. One word gives way to two until a short sentence can be reproduced.

As proficiency increases the teacher invites the pupil to dictate a sentence to be written. This gives way eventually to several sentences being written and later to the pupil constructing and writing his own sentences. This may be done with the aid of sentence building kits. With this method the pupil arranges commercially produced cardboard word cutouts into sentence formations and then copies them. Alternatively he can draw from his own known word store and supplement this with spelling assistance from the teacher. All pupils are encouraged to compile their own dictionary of words which they have used.

Early number experiences

Sorting, matching, ordering and counting have already been mentioned as pre-reading activities. They are also significant in early number experiences.

Sorting objects or things results in the individual seeing one or more sets of objects or things. Sorting requires the ability to discriminate and classify and leads on to progressive thought and decision making. Matching objects or things leads on to an understanding of a one to one correspondence. This in turn helps to reveal the notion of cardinal number. *Cardinal* numbers are those primitive numbers from which counting or reckoning begins, eg one, two, three, four . . . , as opposed to ordinal numbers. *Ordinal* numbers mark the position in an order or series, eg first, second, third, fourth . . . .

Placing objects in order of size helps pupils to understand in due course that numbers too may be placed in order of size or magnitude, eg 1, 2, 3, 4. When this understanding is reached the pupil may be said to be able to count. It is important to differentiate between counting and the mere recitation of numbers in sequence. Counting requires not only the ability to see things as individual articles but also to recognise them as members of a set, eg one, two, three, four, five toes, one, two, three, four, apples. Counting is not easy and pupils proceed in easy stages. They learn to say the number 'names' from one to five, five to ten and so on.

At the same time the concepts of more, equal and less are introduced. For example, three is one more than two and three is one less than four. This prepares the ground for addition and subtraction. It also provides the first clue for later use that multiplication is accumulated addition, eg two times four equals eight. Two add two, add two, add two also equals eight. The concept of 'equal' must also be fully understood. Young pupils often find difficulty also in comprehending that the number of objects in a group remains the same regardless of the manner of their grouping. For example, one may have four apples but three apples plus one apple or two apples plus two apples also equal four apples. However the apples are grouped the resulting number remains the same. This concept is referred to as the *conservation* of number.

The names given to symbols denoting numbers are *numerals*. These are used in everyday conversation both at home and at school. At school pupils will use these names orally during practical activities. Experience will also occur both in reading and writing them until total familiarity is achieved. The teacher observes and questions the pupil daily to estimate his knowledge and understanding of number. This progress is recorded. Progression in number follows a well charted, carefully prescribed path. Those wishing to know more will find a select list of books at the end of this chapter.

The role of play in learning

Play is the means by which young children come to terms with their environment and distinctive stages in it may be observed during maturation. During play children are able to work out feelings of pleasure, satisfaction, unhappiness, guilt, anxiety and frustration. When using materials like sand, water or dough, they are able to express feelings of aggression, frustration, hate or anger quite freely without hurting anyone. They can bang, pummel, make or destroy with impunity. Materials may be observed and compared noting both similarities and differences in appearance, feel, sound, smell and performance. Pupils ask and are asked questions which develop understanding and in time critical thought.

Solitary play

The earliest form of play is solitary. Initially it consists of exploring the body through touching and feeling. This is followed by a similar exploration of anything within reach. Thereafter the baby looks, listens and watches thus adding all the time to his store of knowledge and experience.

Spectator play

During the next stage in development the infant observes his mother and his family around him. Long before he can talk he watches his mother perform household tasks. Brothers and sisters are seen playing together or with toys, games, etc. Father is observed cleaning the car, digging the garden or playing darts. From watching others the young child now mobile, plays alongside others.

Parallel play (at school)

This stage in development is characterised by an apparent wish to be with other children and to play alongside them but not actually with them. It is important at this stage for the teacher to provide each individual child with his own materials. He may then carry out tasks identical to his neighbour without either sharing the activity or speaking to him. The development from this stage to the next is very gradual.

Partnership play

This is reached when individuals are able to share. Some children (and even adults) find it difficult to share with others. This stage in maturation can not be hastened. Teachers can help this along by providing situations in which it is fun to share, eg in the home corner, or on the rocking boat.

Group play

This is the final stage. By now the child has learned by experience to trust his fellows and may regard them as his friends. Group play is usually directed by an older person, eg child, parent or teacher. In school it is important to have sufficient equipment or apparatus to ensure that children do not have to wait too long before enjoying 'their turn'.

Using raw materials

The use of raw materials provides pupils with the opportunity to gain new knowledge and experience essential to normal development. Sand, water, paint, clay or dough may be used for this purpose. Initially pupils explore the new material and experiment with it using it for different purposes and in differing situations. The second stage involves repetition of some activities and practising these until successful control is reached. The third stage is illustrated by the ability to control the material in some form of creative work. Each stage proceeds in an unhurried manner to ensure a feeling of security. Hurrying may result in interest being lost. It may lead to a lack of incentive to improve skills and even to a refusal to work with a given material altogether.

The teacher's skill lies in giving new experiences using the same material or similar experiences using different materials. Careful observation will reveal the moment at which a more difficult activity or piece of apparatus may be introduced. The degree of participation by the teacher is important. It is important to know when to watch and when to listen. New words can be introduced when appropriate. This may occur quite naturally as a pupil embarks upon a positive description. Time is necessary for discovery to emerge naturally through unhampered play. If time does not permit actions to be repeated many times the discovery of what 'sometimes' or 'always' happens cannot be made.

As co-ordination between hand and eye and motor skills develop individuals can be given control over the choice of what to do in order to achieve a desired result. Pupils will then discover for themselves the link between 'cause' and 'effect'. The use of differing raw materials is important, therefore, not only as a means of developing muscular co-ordination and skill but also in widening language usage and in developing intelligence.

The curriculum

From the activities readily observable in primary schools it is apparent that during the early school years one cannot tease out 'subjects' as such. These activities serve to develop within the learner more than one or even many skills. It is hoped that by the end of the period spent within the primary school all children will be able to speak clearly, fluently and with confidence. This may be shown in the ability to converse both with other children and with adults. Pupils should be able to read and to enjoy and understand the text. Writing should be clear and legible in appearance and creative in content. Children should be able to count competently, carry out the prescribed mathematical processes, measure and solve certain mathematical problems using the principles which they have learned.

Social education

The role of play in learning has already been discussed. It also has a significant role in the social education of children. Play fulfils the need for adventure and co-operation. It enables the individual through experience to anticipate his own and the reactions of others in given circumstances. This should lead to an ability to control both feelings and actions. Social education gives opportunity to learn about one's self, one's family and children and families in other lands. Pupils learn about and from other children in the class and other key figures within the community. For example, each school may have its own community policeman. This officer is a frequent visitor and helps in promoting road safety and the avoidance of other dangerous personal situations. His photograph will be displayed in a prominent place so that all children may be made aware of his identity.

The boundaries of the classroom may be extended through the medium of stories, poetry, pictures, films and television. On a personal level opportunity is given for talking, listening, writing and reading. Through all these activities the basic exploration of the meaning of personal relationships begins.

Science and home economics

Early experiences in science link with those in mathematics and home economics. Pupils explore and experience new phenomena, materials, sounds, objects, ideas, etc. Encouragement is given for observing and recording carefully and accurately. This is done orally and by drawing and writing. Objects and materials are grouped and classified. Observations include size and shape, length, volume, weight, time, texture and proportion. The relationship of these individually and to each other is considered. Often small animals and plants are kept so that gradual change can be recorded in living things. Food and its relationship to life and health in both the plant and animal kingdoms is explored through a practical involvement. Plants are nutured and animals fed.

Pupils themselves study the qualities of natural foods, fruit, vegetables and nuts. Foods are sampled in a raw state and records are kept of observations on appearance, smell, taste and texture. The application of heat (and moisture) brings about changes in these foods which may make them more attractive and palatable. These experiments lead into early discussions on cooking methods, recipes and food preparation. Personal responsibility for one's health can and should be taught from the earliest class. This includes the acquisition of a wide range of food 'tastes'. Because children come from multi-racial and cultural backgrounds many nutritious, tasty and economic foods are not common on the home tables.

Food education and good dietary practice should be taught in the classroom and in conjunction with the midday school meal. Milk, eggs, cheese, fish and meat can follow fruit and vegetables as 'tastes' to be acquired. Along the way cereals will of necessity accompany many protein foods. By concentrating on a 'sensory perception' approach to fruits, vegetables, milk, cheese, eggs, fish, meat and cereals one can consolidate the knowledge and experience already being gained in the early years in basic skills. Furthermore, one can lay the foundations of healthy dietary practice. This can be accompanied by simple guidelines on cleanliness, sleep and exercise.

Aesthetic development

The primary school is usually the most consistently active of schools in the promotion of aesthetic appreciation. It is fostered (usually through play) by the preparation of materials in two or three dimensions using drawing materials, collage, simple printing (potato), tie dye, clay, paint, building materials, sewing, knitting and food preparation. Music and movement give scope for singing, dancing or playing a musical instrument (percussion, recorder, violin). The early years in school for all pupils are very active, physically, mentally and emotionally. These years are full and rich in experiences and rewards. It is not by chance that these schools rarely seem to be other than vital, happy places.

It is hoped that this brief sketch of some aspects of primary schools will fulfil two purposes. Firstly that it will provide a basis for a reasoned personal appraisal to be made during primary school visits in the early days of a student's professional training. Secondly, it can then be used as a check list for recalling what was actually seen during those visits when personal observations have to be recorded in report form. From the point of view of one's own development as a teacher it is important that one can readily discern the most significant features of one's learning.

These can be summarised

1 The early years in primary school are the second important stage in the child's learning cycle. The first being the pre-school years. Thus the primary school builds on the pre-school knowledge and experience.

2 The curriculum is designed to include knowledge, experience and skills known to be necessary for the healthy development and maturation of all children.

3 The curriculum is taught in a relaxed, informal, stimulating atmosphere and environment.

4 The timetable is flexible with the minimum of constraints.

5 Teaching areas are sub-divided to give a highly structured learning environment.

6 Learning is individual and self pacing.

The teacher's role

1 To provide an environment in which learning may flourish. This involves a continual renewing of environmental influences within the teaching area.

2 To observe, listen and respond.

3 To support, encourage and extend pupils' thinking.

4 To select appropriate experiences and materials and to plan for their use.

5 To record daily progress in reading, writing and number. To evaluate development in these and other areas.

Primary school teachers may be the most adept and flexible of all teachers when managing people, equipment and ideas. They often have large classes with vast amounts of equipment which is constantly used by individuals and groups in an ordered, carefully planned manner. Pupils are used to keeping the teaching area tidy in an astonishingly natural way. Prospective home economics teachers will do well to study such management methods.

The pupils

1 Pupils develop and mature rapidly within the first school.

2 Reading, writing and number are mastered.

3 Personalities develop so that pupils are ready to enter the middle school feeling secure, confident, able to make decisions whilst retaining the refreshing curiosity which characterises the very young.

It is with the middle school, its structure, staff, curriculum and pupils that the next section concerns itself.

Selected references and further reading

Ministry of Education, Children and their primary schools—a report of the Central Advisory Council for Education (Plowden Report), Vol 1, HMSO, 1967

Department of Education and Science, Open plan primary schools, Educational survey No. 16, HMSO, 1972

Department of Education and Science, Primary Education in England, a survey by HM Inspectors of Schools, HMSO, 1978

Department of Education and Science, HMI Series: Matters for Discussion, 9. Mathematics 5-11, A handbook of suggestions (that which should be taught to all children), HMSO, 1979

Lovell, K, *Educational psychology and children,* University of London Press, 1967

Lovell, K *An introduction to human development,* Macmillan, 1968

Parry, M *Sand play,* Arnold, 1976

Parry, M *Play with bricks,* Arnold 1977

Parry, M *Early years cookery,* Arnold 1978

Bruner, J *Under five in Britain,* Grant McIntyre, 1980

Pugh, G (edited by), *Preparation for parenthood* The National Children's Bureau, 1980

Times Educational Supplement, 2 May, 9 May, 1980. Monday's Children, (a child's eye view of the curriculum—extracts chosen from some 3,000 entries to the competition for pupils aged 5-11).

3 The middle years of education
The evolution of the middle school (9-13)

The middle school bridges the gap between primary and high school education. The middle years of schooling illustrate the greatest change in education during this century. Indeed one could argue that its evolution is almost a post-war phenomenon. My own father left school in 1895 at the age of eleven years. His subsequent education was acquired through his own interest and effort after working hours and continued until his death in his mid-eighties. Today eleven years marks the half way point of a pupil's sojourn in the middle school. It is still five years away from the statutory school leaving age and seven years from entry into higher education. Since the Second World War the statutory school leaving age has risen twice, first from fourteen to fifteen years and then in the early seventies to sixteen years.

It is basically due to this extension of the number of years of compulsory schooling to eleven that has created the middle school. The present day pupil can therefore view the period of time spent within the middle school, not as his grandfather and father did, as a preparation for entering the world to earn a living, but as a further period of investigation, consolidation, discovery and enjoyment. Furthermore there are no final examination constraints upon either pupil or teacher. One finds, therefore, particularly in the first two years, fewer similarities between schools and more attempts by teachers to develop individual, personal, and local interests.

Size of school

Middle schools are generally larger in size than first schools with the number of pupils ranging from four hundred to nine hundred. These pupils may be drawn from a number of first schools over a wide geographical area. This may represent a wide range of socio-economic family backgrounds. In large cities this may also result in the school drawing children from as many as thirty different nationalities.

Administrative grouping

The school population may be divided chronologically into four year groups. Each group is administered by a leader who is directly responsible to the head teacher. This leader is called the *year head* and organises the curriculum, staffing and timetabling for that particular year group.

Subject leaders

Within the school there will be specialist subject leaders. They are responsible for developing that subject through the four years of the school's curriculum. In small schools there may only be four such people who may also correspond to the year leaders. It follows therefore that some subjects will be seen to be essential and therefore more prestigious, eg science, mathematics, English, modern languages. Other subjects may be seen as important or desirable. Recognition for status for subject leadership may well depend upon the size of the school. Indeed in smaller schools specialists in some subjects may be very scarce. Subjects falling into these categories may be home economics, dress, crafts, art, music and PE.

The class teacher

It has been noted earlier that in the primary school children remain for the most part in one classroom or home base and are taught mainly by one teacher. In the middle school pupils are still, particularly in the earlier years, in the main the responsibility of one class teacher. They may however be exposed to some specialist teaching particularly in the third and fourth years. This may be in subjects such as mathematics, science, English, modern languages, physical education, home economics, art, craft or music.

Ideally teachers in a middle school need a good level of general education which has enabled them to acquire a significant level of knowledge. This will provide a background to their work in teaching language skills, human studies, science studies and expressive arts. In order that each may contribute to the specialist teaching within the school a wider, deeper knowledge is needed in one subject area. This might be in home economics, art and craft, mathematics, science, English, history, music, etc.

Teaching methods

The general organisation of middle schools lends itself to co-operative teaching and co-operative learning. All subjects are usually studied by both boys and girls. Pupils who until now have been taught in mixed ability groups may find that 'setting' is taking place. This means that pupils sharing a particular common need are grouped together for more specialised tuition. This applies to those children who, for example, find difficulty in reading or mathematics. When difficulty is diagnosed, such pupils can be withdrawn from their class and grouped together for additional help. Similarly children who are particularly gifted who may feel frustrated working at the general speed of their class may be withdrawn. They can then have the opportunity of working with specialists in particular fields, eg French, mathematics, English, etc, to develop their talents.

Administratively this is not difficult to arrange when a school is divided into year groups if all the classes in that year are studying the same subject at the same time.

Whole year grouping also permits all the pupils and staff engaged on a particular piece of work to meet together. This may result in a teacher (or teachers co-operating) giving an introductory or key lesson to launch a particular section of work. Films or tape slide programmes may be viewed or recordings heard by the whole group at once. Groups are able then to return to their classrooms to pursue assignments with their individual class teachers. This may involve like or differing aspects of a theme. At the close of the session whether it be morning, weekly or term, the whole year group can be reassembled. They can then hear reports of work carried out and look at visual presentations if appropriate. In this way the efforts of the whole group can be evaluated by both pupils and staff. To conclude the assignment a member of staff may round off the topic.

Year groups both in terms of staff and pupils become closely united in their shared activities. These may relate to academic pursuits, drama, music, physical education, field studies and even trips abroad. Professionally, the situation helps the young and inexperienced teacher. From the start he or she is involved within a team headed by an experienced teacher. The novice participates in the planning and execution of the work. Opportunity is afforded to watch experienced staff in action. Contributions by the probationer are given to a group of pupils without discipline worries since the staff team is in control.

Methods of keeping order, awarding praise, blame and the imposition of sanctions, all can be observed by the novice in this situation. Team teaching is supportive to the inexperienced and enables him to grow both in skill and confidence. For the year leader his own experience is excellent from a professional standpoint. He is responsible for the curriculum, timetabling and pastoral care of one quarter of the school's population. The staff who teach those pupils are also in his care. Such a post forms a natural bridge to a first headship.

The pupils and the curriculum

The curriculum in the middle school is designed to build upon the knowledge, skills and experience gained by pupils in the primary school. Close liaison is maintained between the staff (particularly the head teachers) of middle schools and their 'feeder' primary schools. This enables a smooth transition from the curriculum studied in the primary school to that studied in the middle school. It is usual now for the head teacher of the middle school to visit a primary school to meet briefly with his prospective pupils on their home ground. This enables children to witness a meeting as between friends, of their own staff whom they know and feel secure with and the as yet unknown figure, who is to be their new head teacher at the 'big' school.

This preliminary meeting is followed in the final term at primary school by a visit with their class teacher to the middle school. On this occasion they will meet their prospective head teacher on his home ground. He shows them round the school and introduces them to their prospective teacher. After this visit many children look forward to the impending transfer to the middle school not with fear and apprehension but with visible pleasure.

Personal development

During the four years spent in the middle school considerable personal development is evident in all pupils.

Language development

In language skills significant progress is made in both English and mathematics. From the close, common roots and association in the early years, seen in the previous section, these subjects diversify and separate. Each subject is studied in its own right and each diversifies in a manner which will be easily recognised and familiar. Self-expression in both spoken and written language leads to an increased social competence. Through an increased use of language (read, spoken and written), knowledge, understanding and a sense of values will be discovered. This experience will bring with it great pleasure. As pupils develop they find that many problems can be solved by working them out with words. This strengthens and intensifies the power to reason. In some schools a modern language may be introduced, eg French or Spanish.

In mathematics pupils continue to develop the ability to read, think and reason using symbolic language. Gradually they begin to progress from problems which involve consideration of concrete actuality to abstract forms of thought. This transition usually occurs around the second or third year. Opportunity is given to construct and use apparatus. Appropriate standard procedures and processes within the field of mathematics are learned and tested for personal confirmation. Simple hypotheses arrived at by reasoning may be tested by applying them to concrete situations. Wherever possible such studies are linked to their everyday application.

Human studies

In this area of study pupils are extending their knowledge about man in his home and family, community, country and world setting. Studies begin in the integrated form seen in social education in the primary school. Gradually from this the independent subjects of history, geography, religious instruction, home economics, or social studies may emerge. Many ideas and interests overlap within these subject areas. Man is studied in the context of the past, present and future.

It is hoped that an increased knowledge will enable individuals to understand the viewpoint of others within a diverse religious, ethnic, cultural and racial community. Active involvement through responsible practice can help in the development of acceptable moral values and attitudes among pupils. An acceptance of and respect for other individuals and groups is the first step in enabling man to live in peace with his neighbour. It is essential however to remember that attitude change is very difficult to achieve and can never be arrived at without constant practice of the behavioural pattern it is hoped to attain.

Science

Techniques used continue to be investigatory and follow the basic principles of scientific method. Practical experiments test facts and assumptions about materials, substances, phenomena, and both animal and human behaviour. Experience is given to pupils in observation and recording using both familiar and new pieces of apparatus. Appropriate standard processes and techniques in science are introduced and familiarised. It is hoped that by the end of the fourth year some understanding of the relationship of man to his environment and the effects and consequences of his influence upon it can be achieved. Pupils will also witness the gradual emergence of those elements which form the basis of studies in chemistry, physics and biology.

Aesthetics

Appreciation in aesthetics is developed through studies in art, craft, drama, music, movement, home economics, etc. Pupils have regular opportunities to look, listen, experience and experiment in a variety of situations and media. Since there are no constraints imposed by external examinations both teachers and pupils are free to develop or discover individual aptitudes and talents. Schools may therefore become known for an especial interest and expertise in drama, art, music, choral speaking, etc. In such schools resources and reserves of talent seem to abound. Given the appropriate climate within the school and the requisite member(s) of staff to unfold that talent successful fruition is assured.

Physical education

This is an extension of the music and movement, large apparatus work, swimming and games which began in the primary school. There is a greater emphasis upon team games, netball, football, rounders, etc. These provide a useful means of inter-school competition and opportunity for individual social contact.

Home economics and health education

There may be a home economics specialist teacher on the staff but it is unlikely that she will devote more than half her time to the teaching of the subject. The remainder of her timetable may be devoted to teaching health education and/or general subjects. The specialist teaching area in newer schools is likely to be small and may accommodate some twelve pupils. In older schools where an existing specialist kitchen is used it is likely that a whole class of up to thirty boys and girls will be accommodated at one time. The facilities which exist, the number of children and the time available largely determine what is taught. In brief, in both home economics and health education pupils are made aware of physical, mental and emotional developments as they affect themselves. Topics covered relate to diet, sleep, exercise, clothing, personal cleanliness, safety and control of infection. These will be dealt with more fully later.

The transition to high school

This brief look at the middle school shows an emergence of pupils' potential in those elements which will prove the key to their ultimate success. So although outside constraints upon the curriculum are few, planning does need to include a consideration of the expectations of the high schools, which will admit pupils to the third stage of their formal education at thirteen years. Some high schools draw from as many as sixteen middle schools. The wider the limits of parental choice, relative to high schooling offered by local education authorities, the greater the number of middle schools from which individual high schools will draw. Conversely, where a strict zoning system is employed and only a selected number of middle schools relate to a selected number of high schools, the number of 'feeder' schools is greatly reduced.

The transition of pupils from middle to high school is greatly facilitated if middle and high schools plan together to ensure that the key subjects in the curriculum continue in an ordered sequence. This is more difficult to arrange if many 'feeder' schools are involved. Staff can do a great deal to help each other and the pupils in their care by consultation and co-operation between the different stages in education. For example, syllabuses and schemes of work followed in the middle school indicating content, processes and techniques in mathematics, science, home economics, needlecrafts, etc, are invaluable to subject leaders in the secondary school. Incoming pupils in the high schools can then be grouped according to what they already know. This makes for a more economic use of both teachers' and pupils' time. It also helps to foster motivation and a continuing interest by the pupil.

Middle and high schools can also collaborate to their mutual advantage in their choice of certain specialist pursuits. For example, it is very unsatisfactory for pupils and annoying to parents if a middle school offers a modern language, eg Spanish, and the subsequent high school offers only French or German. By collaboration schools can ensure a reasonable continuity in pupils' learning. Many high schools open their doors to prospective September middle school entrants during the preceding summer term. This serves to make the transition from childhood to 'teens' on the part of the pupil a less painful and a more exciting prospect.

Summary

1 The years in the middle school represent the third important stage in a child's learning. It will be remembered that the first and second stages are usually spent in the home and primary school respectively.

2 The curriculum builds upon the broad areas of study begun in the primary school.

3 Learning starts in a secure class teacher directed situation.

4 'Setting' may occur as specialist subject teaching is introduced.

5 Pupils are grouped in chronologically determined year groups under the direction of a year leader.

6 Year leaders function as a 'mini' head teacher in their responsibilities.

7 The curriculum begins to divide from broadly based areas of study into the familiar school subjects.

8 Syllabuses and schemes of work in each subject are prepared under the direction of a subject leader who is usually a specialist. He/she is responsible for the content teaching in that subject throughout the school.

9 Both year leaders and subject leaders work under the direction of the head teacher.

10 The head teacher's duties are broadly those outlined in chapter 1.

11 It is essential to the continuity of pupils' learning, for close liaison between staff in middle and high schools to be established and maintained.

The following section focuses attention upon the final stage of pupils' statutory education.

Selected references and further reading

Department of Education and Science, Towards the middle school, Educational pamphlet, No. 57, HMSO, 1970

Lovell, K *Educational Psychology and Children* University of London Press 1967

Lovell, K *An Introduction to Human Development* Macmillan 1968

Schools Council Curriculum Bulletin, 4, Home economics teaching Evans/Methuen Educational, 1971

Schools Council, Curriculum for the middle years, Working Paper No. 55 Evans/Methuen Educational, 1977

Schools Council Home Economics Team, Home and Family 8-13, Forbes, 1979

See also publications listed at the end of sections 2 and 4 of Part 1.

4 The later years of education
The high school (13-18)

One of the most significant changes in post-war education has been the introduction of the comprehensive secondary school. This has been a century of accelerated and unprecedented technological change. It has brought with it a need for a more highly educated work force. The introduction of comprehensive schools was a response to this need which developed alongside the egalitarian ideal that a good secondary education should be freely available to all who could profit from it. At the present time more than eighty five per cent of pupils of secondary school age are being educated in comprehensive schools. These pupils represent a complete cross-section of the full ability range within the whole school population.

Transition from the middle school

Entry to the high school at thirteen years, allows only one full year before pupils, who are able, begin their chosen examination courses. Many teachers are still uneasy about the task of preparing pupils within the initial year adequately to enable them to embark with confidence upon their chosen course options in the next year. Some teachers look back wistfully to a time when secondary transfer took place at eleven years. This enabled staff to plan three year foundation courses which they felt were a necessary pre-cursor to the examination syllabus. Now the high school teachers have no direct control over the syllabus content of the pupils aged eleven to thirteen years since they (the pupils) are still in the middle schools. As has been said in the last section some middle schools work closely with their linked high schools but others do not. Some high schools receive pupils from as many as sixteen 'feeder' middle schools. The problems facing high schools are many.

The new entrants

Pupils may enter high school with widely differing ranges of knowledge, skills and experience within any subject area. Some may already have studied a modern language whilst others have not. A recent survey indicated that some pupils had covered a comprehensive three year course in home economics. Other pupils had received only a total of thirty hours over the same period.

A time for diagnosis and prescription

The first year in the high school is therefore for both pupils and teachers a time for diagnosis and prescription. It is important to note here that a recent survey by HM Inspectors of Schools (resulting in the report Aspects of Secondary Education in England) noted that eighty per cent of all sixteen year olds in secondary schools were entered for public examinations. Prescription therefore in practical terms may mean a hasty attempt to remedy what needs to be done prior to embarking upon the General Certificate of Education, Ordinary level, or the Certificate of Secondary Education. As a result some pupils feel that they are repeating what they have done previously. Others feel disadvantaged since they are rushed through telescoped courses which other pupils have already completed in a more detailed and leisurely fashion. Some high schools view the first year in school as a purely introductory one where art, craft, needlecraft and home economics are concerned. These schools do not view the year as a preparatory one to public examination courses. Their aim is merely to introduce subjects briefly to the pupil to illustrate the future range of course options. In many schools at the time of writing the choice of subjects which can be studied is wide and the larger the school the wider the choice.

Size of school

Schools vary in size from seven hundred and fifty pupils (a small school) to two thousand (or more) pupils. When the transition to a comprehensive system of secondary education began large schools were envisaged from the outset. At that time the examination system in the General Certificate of Education and Certificate of Secondary Education was already based upon a single subject certificate. This enabled pupils to choose in the second year those subjects which were of interest or those which they felt they could conquer. The traditional subjects of mathematics, the sciences, English, history, geography, art, domestic science, etc, continued to be offered. At the same time many new variations of traditional subjects appeared. Subjects and subject variations which could be studied, mushroomed. Although some careers advice was available in schools the final choice of subjects often ultimately rested with the pupils and their parents. This system of choice so like supermarket shopping, flourished. The larger the school the bigger the choice of wares.

Trouble however loomed. Firstly because the many expected larger numbers of pupils did not stay on after the statutory school leaving age (of sixteen years) as forecast. Secondly because a dramatic fall in the birthrate over a period of years was felt in the secondary and high schools. Sliding school populations have caused many educationalists to think or rethink about a future viable size for secondary and high schools. It was one thing to administer a grammar school of moderate size where all pupils were expected to be able to select from the normal range of General Certificate of Education courses. A different problem is posed in a comprehensive school of a like size where only twenty per cent of the school population is expected to enter for the General Certificate of Education. Immediately questions are raised about the number of courses it is possible to offer, with the number of staff and staff competencies available in such a school.

In a comprehensive school it is necessary to arrange for General Certificate of Education courses for the top twenty per cent of the pupil ability range. Certificate of Secondary Education courses are designed and offered to the next forty per cent. Alternative non-examination courses should be designed and offered to the remaining forty per cent of the pupils. Thus taking a coldly realistic view, a comprehensive school in order to function effectively must offer courses at three different levels and in a wider range of subjects than either a grammar or secondary modern school if it is to provide for the full ability range of its pupils. This demands a generous staffing of teachers with a wide range of academic and technical competencies and particular experience and skills. It is not possible for a moderate or small sized comprehensive school to do this.

What are the administrative options?

Firstly, to reduce the number of secondary schools to enable fewer, larger schools to be established. This would have the effect of reducing choice of school and could mean that pupils would have further to travel which would prove more costly and time consuming for them. It is also argued that larger schools can aggravate or increase disciplinary problems and make an atmosphere conducive to learning difficult to achieve.

Secondly, the number of schools can be held at a level which permits the functioning of moderately sized institutions. It can be argued that such establishments permit a more readily achieved level of good working conditions for both staff and pupils. Such schools, however, would be too small to allow adequate staffing of advanced level courses for the more able pupils. Where schools were situated in cities this could be overcome by schools agreeing to provide a limited number only of advanced courses. Subjects could be shared beween schools to establish specialist centres, eg mathematics, sciences, home economics, etc. This would mean a more economic use of both specialist staff and specialist resources in terms of rooms, equipment and books.

Thirdly, post-sixteen work could be concentrated in sixth form colleges. This would enable a very wide range of subjects to be offered with a highly qualified staff complement. From the pupil point of view, study would be in an adult community, encouraging a more mature attitude both to work and to life. Such institutions may attract a proportion of mature students. Sixth form colleges (if generally accepted) might well provide a half way house between school and college, polytechnic or university. For those who left at eighteen to enter a job or profession it would prove a valuable experience as a forerunner to working in an adult community.

Such a system would mean a lower level 'feeder' high school with a thirteen to sixteen year intake. It could be argued that these schools would lack academic vigour since the most highly qualified staff are concentrated in the sixth form college. On the other hand pupils would all leave the institution at sixteen years. This would allow the non-academic school leaver to assume more responsibility within the democratic government of the school. The possibility of doing so was lost to these pupils with the demise of the secondary modern school.

Of the options discussed all are in operation somewhere at the present time within the country. Where local education authorities have not completed reorganisation, it is possible that they will decide in differing ways to solve the pressing problem of falling school rolls, which is now aggravated by acute economic problems. It is perhaps pertinent to note here that pupils do have the option open to them at sixteen years, if they wish, to leave school and to pursue Advanced level General Certificate of Education courses at a college of further education. Traditionally these colleges have provided further education in technical and business subjects for young people of sixteen to eighteen years and part time education for mature students.

The structure of high schools

With the increase in size of high schools came changes in their government. This was inevitable. In small schools head teachers knew both staff and pupils very well. As schools grew in size a situation was reached where only a small proportion of pupils were personally known by the head. Staff too became remote figures to the head as they reached and sometimes passed the one and two hundred mark in number.

Clearly schools needed a different form of management if both pupils and staff were to feel that they were a significant part of the whole structure. Schools can be very frightening places for individual staff and pupils alike. The sheer size of a school complex of buildings and the spatial remoteness of one's colleagues can be daunting. The writer, as a visiting tutor, found the greatest difficulty in finding the appointed room even with a map in some schools. Students on teaching practice have reported that they could not find the appropriate staff-room or a particular teacher.

The hierarchy

The head teacher still assumes overall responsibility for the academic, administrative and pastoral management of the school. In practice, however, he may function principally as the chairman of a highly organised administrative structure within the school itself and as a spokesman and link between it and outside bodies at local, regional and national levels. He may be supported by two and sometimes three deputy heads. Delegation of duties to these three may be as follows:

First deputy

This post is the most senior of the three. This staff member may be charged with responsibility for curriculum innovation, development and organisation. Overall responsibility for the maintenance of standards within the school will be his. This includes assessment of qualities of existing staff, their career development and any additional staff required. Closely linked with this is the task of liaising with colleges, polytechnics and universities. He will advise senior pupils on careers and entrance requirements to institutions of higher education. Whenever the necessity arises the first deputy head assumes the role of head teacher.

Second deputy

This teacher is responsible for implementing the curriculum needs by relating these to the resources of buildings, rooms, time, staff and pupils. In short, this deputy masterminds the timetable. This is done on a yearly basis with termly variations according to need. A daily morning review of staff absentees is necessary to provide a continuous staff coverage of each individual class. Closely linked with this is the responsibility for the general discipline within the school. This staff member may have overall responsibility for the general welfare of either boys or girls.

The third deputy

Assumes responsibility for the care and maintenance of buildings and resources. This staff member will have responsibility for the general welfare of girls or boys. The pastoral care of pupils of both sexes is shared by the second and third deputies. The third deputy may also be responsible for careers advice to early leavers. He may also liaise with the careers officer, local colleges of further education and employers. Finally he may deal directly with the various social agencies, eg the police, probation officers, welfare officers, social workers and local medical and dental officers.

The posts of deputy head carry with them areas of great responsibility. The exact arrangement of duties may differ in individual schools but the responsibilities outlined have to be shared and covered. In addition to this such staff usually teach for approximately half a normal teaching timetable in their own particular expertise.

Heads of school

The head teacher and his deputies are assisted by a head of lower school (with responsibility for years one to three) and a head of upper school (with responsibility for years four and five). In very large schools or ones where two schools have amalgamated the upper and lower schools may occupy different buildings or even different sites a distance apart. Each school 'head' is responsible for the general academic, administrative and pastoral management of that school.

Year heads

Within each school are year heads. Their responsibility is directed to their head of school. Each year head oversees staff, pupils and the curriculum for his particular year. The year head holds a key position and function within the hierarchy of the school. He receives and holds records and reports from tutors and group tutors relating to every child within his particular year. It is his responsibility to know and be known by each child personally. He must be aware of each child's background and cognisant of any physical, mental, emotional or social problems which may impede a pupil's actual or projected progress. Where problems do arise relative to a pupil either inside or outside the school it is the year head's task to attempt to resolve matters. This includes the pupil, his parents and any other relevant body or bodies. It may relate outside the school to the medical officer, community welfare officer, social worker, probation officer or police. Inside the school he resolves these matters with his colleagues and the head teacher.

The year tutor has a reduced teaching timetable to allow him to carry out his many non-teaching duties. It is essential that he establishes close links with parents and can inspire and count upon their co-operation. To this end he organises parents' evenings. He may well open these by an address to all parents in which the policy of the school both academic and administrative may be given. This is particularly valuable for example as a means of explaining to parents the outcomes of choices which are made when differing subjects are studied or 'dropped' as the case may be. General information relative to uniform, sanctions or future organised school trips may be given. In this way, links with parents are established and they in their turn view the year leader in much the same role as a head master in a small school.

Within school the year leader finds that discipline among staff and pupils is a matter of constant concern and attention. In addition he has responsibility for the vocational guidance of pupils and also for the career development of staff. Extra curricular activities have become more varied and complex as schools have grown larger. These are organised and co-ordinated by the year tutors. Such activities may take place during the lunch break, after school or during vacations. They may include physical education practices or matches, drama, music rehearsals or concerts, or the many facets associated with the Duke of Edinburgh award scheme. Clubs are many and varied and may include chess, bridge, dance, drama, railway, canoe, wild life, climbing, etc. School visits, journeys, residential holidays and courses are organised.

It is important to note here the significance for intending teachers to develop their own interests in leisure time pursuits. Future employers of intending teachers will look for evidence of ability, aptitude and willingness to contribute to these important areas in school. Both attitude and prowess are seen as a measure of a candidate's ability to contribute to the full life of the school as a whole.

Group tutors

Each year has group tutors accountable to the year head. These staff are in charge of a group of teachers each of whom in turn is responsible for the pastoral care of a number of individual pupils.

Individual tutors

These are responsible to a group tutor and comprise all members of staff not previously accounted for apart from the subject 'heads'.

Subject heads

These staff have departmental status. They are usually highly qualified academically. It is their function to determine the parameters of the school's subject needs and to organise the implementation of these through school year groups. This demands a high level of expertise in curriculum planning in order to implement courses at each and every age and ability level. At a practical level the subject head pleads his case at the financial resources committee. According to his own strength as a counsel and the prestigious level of the subject so will he be awarded a share of the school's yearly financial resources.

Subject heads are entrusted to decide, in consultation with staff, not only content of syllabuses and schemes of work but also the teaching methods to be employed. The latter is not always important but in many subjects it is. For example, in mathematics some methods may be decided in conjunction with both primary and middle schools so that pupils follow a common mode of linear progression.

In home economics it is helpful for staff and less confusing for pupils if common methods of food preparation and garment construction are used within the high school. This enables a flexible movement of staff and pupils within the system without problems arising. For the subject head too, the problem of non-specialist teachers is a constant concern. This problem arises in almost every subject. In this situation the subject head functions as an in-service tutor and advisor. It is essential that this is done to ensure that pupils do not suffer and that the smooth running of the department is not impaired.

The assistant teacher

The assistant teachers form the bulk of the staff membership. In large schools there may be in excess of a hundred. Each assistant teacher has many commitments. He will be a member of a year team under the guidance of a year head. As a team member he will attend meetings every two or three weeks. He will also be a member of a subject department. This department will also meet regularly under the chairmanship of the subject head. Thirdly he will be a tutor to a small group of pupils of varying ages for whose pastoral care he is responsible. This will entail regular meetings with his pupil group (usually at a set time on the timetable). It also entails regular meetings every two or three weeks (in company with a small group of other tutors) with the group tutor.

Apart from these duties the assistant teacher will have responsibility for a form or class. He deals with daily routine matters of registration and weekly registers. Absences are recorded. Within the administrative framework of the school the form teacher is responsible for the discipline of his class. Whilst teaching he is also responsible for the discipline of the class within his care and deals on the spot with any minor difficulties. As form teacher he gets to know each pupil and informs himself of matters within a child's background which may be of concern to the school. Information from school to child or school to parent passes through the form teacher. Similarly communications from parent to school pass via him to the appropriate member of staff. He receives the reports of each individual member of his form from the subject teachers. These are discussed with pupils before dispatch to parents. Careful records of progress are kept. Vigilance by the form teacher is essential so that appropriate action can be taken when any personal difficulties arise affecting pupils either inside or outside school. Finally each assistant teacher is appointed to carry out a specific academic function within his own subject(s) specialism.

Non teaching staff

The academic staff are supported by laboratory and workshop technicians, secretarial and clerical staff. Large schools may have a bursar and a resident school matron or nurse. Domestic matters are dealt with by catering and cleaning staff. The school caretaker on a large campus has a wide ranging responsibility and may be supported by several assistants. Together they will be responsible for the cleanliness and heating of the buildings and the care of gardens, sports pitches, etc.

Buildings and facilities

These vary widely in age, geographical layout, facilities and equipment. Reorganisation of secondary education often brought with it the amalgamation of two schools on different sites sometimes a mile or so apart. The administrative structure outlined earlier allows for a satisfactory government to emerge even in these circumstances. Normally school buildings will comprise an assembly hall with a stage for dramatic productions. A library, teaching rooms, science laboratories, workshops, technical drawing studio, art and craft rooms, home economics suite, dress and textile rooms, gymnasium, business studies' room, dining hall and kitchen. There are usually playing fields and sometimes a swimming bath. Some schools accommodate older pupils in a separate sixth form block.

The curriculum

Many schools do (and others are being encouraged to) appraise parents fully of the work of the school by means of a school prospectus, news letters and an annual report. High school prospectuses may be sent to the parents of pupils still in their middle schools. This may help parents to decide upon a particular school as a first choice for their son or daughter.

During the first year in the high school pupils usually study a broad curriculum. This may comprise English, mathematics, science, history, geography, religious education, drama, a modern language and physical education. During the year pupils are offered 'sampling' courses in home economics, handicrafts, art and woodwork. At this stage it is usual for both boys and girls to participate in a common curriculum. It is possible that 'setting' may take place in English, mathematics, science and modern languages. During this first year parents will be invited into school and the year leader will explain the procedure for pupil choice in the curriculum during the following second and third years. Parents are given appropriate literature to help them and their sons and daughters in their choices. Final choices are made during the summer term in conjunction with class teachers, personal tutors, subject heads and year leaders. These choices are important since they will involve the level of course to be studied, ie non-examination, Certificate of Secondary Education or General Certificate of Education.

The number and balance of courses will also affect the breadth of the pupils total education. One might argue that it is at this stage that the individual's future place in society is determined and his future economic viability. From the beginning of the second year pupils will be 'setted' according to the level of the course. This will also tend to stratify the social mixing of pupils for their friends will be among those who study alongside them. Work experience courses may be introduced into the third year for those pupils planning to leave at sixteen years of age. For those pupils planning to stay on at school for a fourth and fifth year, counselling helps them to make wise choice of General Certificate of Education, Advanced level courses, relative to possible entry into higher education and a future career.

This very brief and general picture of current educational practice is intended to set the scene for the intending home economics teacher as she begins her professional training. It is hoped that it gives a clear indication of:

1 The continuity of learning as the individual pupil grows to adulthood.

2 The school as an environment which promotes, encourages and cultivates this development.

3 Teaching as a varied, exacting but worthwhile career for a well-educated able person.

4 A professional career structure with a wide range of opportunity for entrants with differing skills.

Selected references and further reading

Department of Education and Science, Ten good schools, HMSO, 1977

Department of Education and Science, Local Authority arrangements for the school curriculum (a review of the report on circular 14/77), HMSO, 1979

Department of Education and Science, A view of the curriculum (in its fullest sense), Matters for Discussion HMI Series No. 11, HMSO, 1980

Department of Education and Science, Falling Rolls in Secondary Schools, HMSO, 1980

Lovell, K, *Educational Psychology and Children* University of London Press, 1967

Lovell, K, *An Introduction to Human Development*, Macmillan, 1968

See also publications listed at the end of sections 2 and 3 of Part 1, and Sections 1-5 of Part 6.

Part 2

Teachers

1 A teacher's role

In Part 1 a brief sketch has been drawn of what the intending teacher may expect to find in primary, middle or high schools at the present time. This section examines in greater detail the framework for the teacher's role. The Shorter Oxford English Dictionary gives the following definitions of 'teacher'.

'A teacher is one from whom one learns'
'One who instructs'

An individual's first teacher

It has already been noted in Part 1 that when an individual enters school and formal education at the age of five years, he is already very knowledgeable. He walks and runs with ease and can talk fluently. Already he holds both real and imaginary conversations. Communications both verbal and with bodily gestures are within his experience, knowledge and expertise. Certain muscular skills have been mastered including control of his immediate bodily functions. He can feed himself and can recognise when both hunger and thirst have been assuaged. Often dressing and undressing are within his grasp. How then has he acquired this knowledge? Probably up to the time of entry into school the biggest single influence in his life has been his mother.

Much of what he has learned has been from her. She has from the moment of his birth supervised both his waking and his sleeping hours. It is to her that he reached when hungry, for rest when sleepy, warmth when cold and solace when distressed. She has smiled and encouraged him to take his first steps and praised each milestone reached, however tiny. He has listened to and imitated the words she uttered. When from time to time he has rebelled she has chastised him. Through love and firm direction a mother lays the foundations not only of language, but also physical and emotional behaviour. She teaches moral values of right and wrong, of selfishness and unselfishness and friendliness and unfriendliness. Early knowledge and habits of diet, health and hygiene all are rooted in her teaching.

Individuals learn in their pre-school years to a much lesser degree from father, other adults and brothers and sisters. Usually the constraints of attending work or school mean that less time is spent by them with the pre-school child. Child studies and research have for some years suggested that the most significant years of development of the individual are from birth to seven years. Five of those years are spent principally in the care and company of the mother. It could therefore be argued that she is the most significant of all his teachers. If the mother is an able one then there is no better teacher.

The class teacher

Many mothers are not able or even willing teachers and perhaps their offspring would progress more effectively in the care and company of a nursery school teacher in the immediate pre-school years. For all children when school begins, their class teacher is a most influential figure in their lives. In their later years it may be a specialist teacher for whom they feel a particular affinity. This may be because the pupil has a particular liking for, or ability in a subject. Or it may simply be rooted in a liking for the teacher as a person.

It is important for intending teachers to know and understand the characteristics which pupils expect to find in teachers. An absence of such characteristics may evoke an unwelcome response from a class. One of the best ways for students to confirm this is through observation. Most professional courses provide opportunity early on for students to visit schools armed with a check list. The latter will have been compiled by tutors from their experience, from the researches of others and not least from what pupils have written themselves about their expectations of their teachers. Let us now examine some of these expectations.

Mutual liking and respect

Perhaps the best starting point for understanding this is a return to the mother child relationship. Why do mothers have a special relationship with their children? It is often spoken of as mother love. A mother seemingly gives her child all her love and affection. Yet when another child arrives she appears to be able from some insatiable source to lavish upon the second child just as much as she did upon the first. Nevertheless she is still able to give to her husband and the first child all the love which they originally felt to be their due. The origin of this love is as indefinable as that infinite source of energy locked within the confines of a tiny seed or drop of water. All are inexplicable wonders which cannot be explained. It is due to this special relationship between mother and child that the mother is able to exercise such an influence upon his development within the early years.

Teacher and pupil

The teacher pupil relationship is not as strong as the bond between mother and child. Nevertheless a successful teacher does like his pupils and he respects them both *en masse* and as individuals. In their turn if pupils like and respect their teacher they will wish to please him and make every effort to fulfil his wishes. Since his wish is that they apply themselves to learning then they do learn. Sometimes if all sanctions have failed and pupils can see no reason for learning the only plea that a teacher can use is for the task to be done for him because it will please him. It is at moments like this that both teacher and pupils really witness the strength or weakness of the pupil teacher relationship.

Liking the unlikeable

Every teacher meets individual pupils whom he finds so unattractive either in person, personality or behaviour that he just does not like them. It is then that the teacher throws on the cloak of the actor and pretends. This will not be the only occasion upon which he assumes this guise. It may be used to feign anger, indignation, coldness, warmth, enthusiasm, encouragement and a host of other emotions. This can be used to make, consolidate or reinforce a point or condition. Yet underneath an assumed exterior there must be a willingness and ability to like and wish to get to know individual pupils despite their faults, ignorance, shallowness and inexperience. It is sometimes necessary to accept people as they are even if they are not as one would wish them to be.

At ease with the group

As teachers it is necessary to feel equally at ease with individuals, small groups and large groups. For some it appears effortless to fit into this role without apparently having to learn it. What about those who view the prospect with unease, fear and sometimes even terror? How does one approach the task coldly, objectively and in a manner whereby the role is learned, practised and perfected until the performance can be portrayed over and over again with imagination, skill and expertise? Take comfort—it can be learned and with practice can ultimately be enjoyed.

Firstly one needs to study children. This involves looking at, listening to, talking to and mixing with class members. Then to wonder at and reflect upon that which has been seen, heard and experienced. Children are not like adults either in their thinking or their behaviour. Each individual child will have his own peculiar patterns of thought and behaviour. Studying pupils is like experiencing a course in human development in action. A teacher develops patterns for remembering identity, ie faces, names, voices. Familiarity with these patterns enables the teacher to sense, even when he cannot see, who is responsible for a word or action.

We have all experienced the sensation of someone committing an offence whilst the teacher with back to the class is writing on the board. Without pausing, looking or obvious concern the offender is checked by name. The teacher has no superhuman powers he is simply in tune with or familiar with the voices, gestures and expected behaviour patterns of his pupils. Often such control evokes an amused response from the class. Humour in a teacher is appreciated by a class and is an invaluable personal asset. It links him to his pupils through enjoyment. A shared task; a common appreciation of humanity; at moments like these he ceases to be separated from his pupils by individuality, age or authority.

Likenesses and differences

A teacher looks for both likenesses and differences among his pupils. He learns to look for and to recognise types and sub-types among his class. There are rebels, those who do not wish to conform for one reason or another. Some pupils are diligent and others lazy. Others are amiable and happy go lucky whilst some are miserable and born pessimists. Sometimes there is an eccentric. The gifted child often sits uneasily among his fellows. He presents the strange phenomenon of an apparently adult mind in a child's body. However young one meets him he doesn't seem ordinary or even young. For him there seems to be no intermediate position between the cradle and middle age. He sometimes has a mind which can with ease outstrip the teacher in certain fields of reasoning. This means that he often sits uneasily in both the company of his teacher and his fellow pupils. Yet emotionally and physically he is chronologically the equal of his classmates.

Group control

Within any class one has the basics of an explosive mixture. Thus the teacher must be able to control before he can teach. No one can teach a group in which each is free to talk, move freely and even fight whether mentally or physically. Initially a teacher must be able to establish and then maintain control. It has already been said that there must be a mutual liking and respect between pupils and teacher for him to be accepted as a symbol of authority.

Knowledge and communication

The two cornerstones of teaching are knowledge and communication. It is upon these two that effective teaching is based. It is generally accepted that teaching is the transmission of knowledge from one person to another. Thus any teacher must have a sound fund of knowledge on which to base his teaching. Secondly, this knowledge cannot be used effectively without the ability to communicate.

Knowing one's subject

A good teacher knows his subject. This does not just mean knowing sufficient to teach that lesson or that syllabus but the absorption of knowledge on a continual basis. It can be argued that no one fully understands the rudiments of a subject without knowing and experiencing it at a significantly high level. Teaching and learning are inseparable and the skilful teacher constantly feels the need to learn and extend his knowledge within his subject area. His pupils must be able to witness his enjoyment of the subject. Unless he believes in the value of that subject he will never be able to teach with sincerity and persuade others of its validity.

The limitless capacity of the human mind

An effective teacher believes in the limitless capacity of the human mind. However much one absorbs there is always room for more. Pupils (particularly adolescents) tend to believe that adults have fixed and limited minds. A teacher strives to dispel this belief by his daily example. He will never know how much a child can absorb if only the minimum is presented.

Interest

If less than the minimum is presented then interest flags and eventually dies. It should be remembered that interest may be natural or acquired. Interest will lead the way to increased knowledge. Conversely increased knowledge will open up a new and lasting interest. After all the purpose in teaching a subject is not confined to satisfying the school requirement, but to open up an interest in it, and bring to the recipient hours of enjoyment and satisfaction which will be lifelong. For those who teach home economics this is particularly pertinent, for everyone from the cradle to the grave needs knowledge and expertise in this area. It is the task of teachers to inspire, encourage and teach, so that involvement in what may at first sight seem mundane, can be seen to have infinite goals of creativity, for those who are willing to explore.

Strengthening the ability to discern

Concomitant with an increase in knowledge comes a strengthening of the ability to discern and formulate judgments. This is true of both pupil and teacher. Thus a pupil needs to feel that a teacher knows his subject before he can trust that teacher's judgment. Young people are quick to spot insincerity, and dislike it. They don't demand that a teacher knows all that is to be known or that he is always right but they do demand sincerity. Thus if one does not know the answer to a question or one makes a mistake, admit it. Find out the answer and tell the class or rectify the mistake. In either case sincerity will be respected.

The organisation of knowledge

If a first essential is knowledge then the second is surely the ability to organise and communicate it. The organisation of knowledge relates closely to an ability to plan. This planning relates to the course to be followed as a whole. A course, apart from satisfying any outside constraints such as examination requirements must be such as to give enjoyment and encouragement to the newest learner and yet at the same time, give enjoyment, stimulation and challenge to the most knowledgeable participant. Such a course is then broken down into smaller parts, the smallest of which is the individual lesson. Through the course as a whole and the lesson as an individual part of that whole should flow a readily discernible structure.

Planning like this involves writing down knowledge in developmental form. At a day to day level this involves writing notes for the actual lesson to be taught. It also involves planning a record for pupils to keep so that the knowledge given forms an intelligible developmental structure for them to follow. These plans are not prepared on a once and for all basis but in such a manner as to allow for revision and addition of new knowledge acquired from new books, journals, etc. (This will be developed further in the chapters on syllabus planning, schemes of work and lesson planning.)

The bridge between

In many ways school stands in an artificial position between home which is real and the world outside which is real. The pupil remains in this artificial position for eleven years and possibly longer. It is the teacher's task to bridge the gap between these two realities and to interpret the seeming unreality which lies between. The teacher is seen also to be a link between age and youth whether in a real or an imaginary sense. For example, although many teachers are older chronologically than a child's parents, teachers do seem to the child to be related to the ideas, interests and activities of children at a child's particular level. To many children their own parents seem to be out of touch with the pursuits dear to the hearts of youth.

Communication

Knowledge and the organisation of it is linked inextricably with communication in a teacher's work. The passing on of knowledge from one generation to the next is an essential function of civilisation and one in which the teacher plays a key role. Considered in this way it seems an awesome and even frightening responsiblity but one which does induce a feeling both of wonder and exhilaration. Let us now consider the means by which this may be done.

A captive audience

In its simplest terms a teacher can stand in front of a class and expose them to a steady flow of facts and ideas. To do this he would require a silent and receptive audience, no interruption and no discussion. Almost all pupils are exposed to this daily in their own homes through the medium of television for many hours. Schools too, are making an increasing use of television particularly for specialist programmes. Some children will experience this method of teaching too on Sunday mornings if they attend church and listen to a sermon. Perhaps the most famous example of this in the Christian world comes from the account in the New Testament of Jesus's Sermon on the Mount. This was delivered to his disciples and (we are told) to a large, completely attentive audience. Today the interpretation of this method of teaching would be said to be lecturing. It would be reserved for older learners of near or adult age. This is because we now know that the maximum length of time that children can concentrate upon a particular theme without variation in activity is about twenty minutes.

Direct teaching

Teachers do engage in direct teaching particularly with older pupils and where groups are evenly matched in ability and attainment. It can prove in these circumstances to be the most economical of time for both teacher and pupil. For example, a teacher can conduct a series of experiments in food science to a large whole class group. This then leaves a maximum amount of time for individual laboratory practice.

Secondly if a whole class is ready to make buttonholes, direct teaching is the most economic way of using time. Large scale working specimens can be used for the demonstration so that each pupil can see. These are supported by blackboard sketches, normal sized stage specimens, a finished garment and illustrated books. The blackboard sketches can be used during the demonstration. The actual scale stage specimens are passed round and then displayed in a prominent position for reference. These may be supported by the actual garment and the selected reference books.

In direct teaching one plans to deliver the knowledge interspersed with questions, answers, discussion, writing of notes, drawing of diagrams, pictorial illustration, etc. New or difficult words, dates, formulae or diagrams can be written up on the board. The teacher frequently pauses, summarises, introduces key words or phrases. Perhaps as in the case of the buttonhole there is a demonstration which will precede class practice. Note that the teacher does not expect pupils to remember everything but, on the other hand, self-help is to be encouraged. This is the purpose of the back-up materials, ie the specimens, blackboard diagrams, actual garment and reference books. Only if pupil reference to these prove unsuccessful, does the teacher demonstrate the process to an individual a second time. The degree of retention by pupils depends a great deal upon the teacher's skill in persuading pupils to look, listen, think and act along certain carefully planned and prescribed lines.

The use of the voice

A teacher's voice is one of his most precious assets both in delivering knowledge and in class control. He can use it to express pleasure or displeasure, anger, joy, impatience, encouragement, chastisement and a wealth of other emotions. The voice can be used to stir, stimulate, quieten, hurry or arrest the attention or activity of the class. By using variations in force and speed or by pausing at appropriate moments a teacher can add colour, emphasis and effect to his theme.

Facial expression and bodily gestures

Often oral technique is reinforced or supplemented by facial or bodily gestures. Eyes and/or eyebrows can be used to question, demonstrate displeasure, amusement, to tease or to encourage. A hand may be used to point to a pupil signifying that an answer to a question is expected. It may be used to direct attention to an illustration or to the blackboard. Clapped sharply together, hands indicate a wish for the class to be quiet and attend to the teacher. Pupils learn to read a teacher's face and gestures and to respond as readily to them as to the spoken word. Many pupils say that they can read a teacher's mood and his intentions from the way in which he enters a room.

Dress

One's mode of dress is also read as an indication of intent. A recent survey among teachers indicated that they wished all student teachers to be instructed in appropriate dress before they, the students, entered school to teach. Teachers intimated that they felt that suitable dress had a measurable desirable influence upon discipline and class control. It also reflected, they said, expected attitudes to work among the pupils. Research indicates that both pupils and teachers expect student teachers to dress neatly and tidily. They are expected to be smart but not excessively so and to look as if prepared for work. This view is clearly expressed in 'Teacher Education—the teacher's point of view,' which gives a collective view of teachers' opinions.

'Children on the whole will not, and do not have respect for the "couldn't care less" appearance and attitude of some students. Too many appear to be ready for a hike rather to face a class. This dishevelled appearance does not help discipline problems.' Obviously this refers not only to matters of dress but also to hair, shoes and general grooming. Clearly both teachers and children believe that a neat appearance is a precursor to an ordered mind and orderly teaching the pre-requisite of an ordered and comfortable classroom.

Investigation based teaching and learning

Much teaching in schools now at primary, middle and secondary levels is rooted in the setting of tasks which as they are accomplished enable pupils to establish the truths underlying specific concepts for themselves. The teacher adopts a practice of asking questions either oral or written. The pupil responds with an oral or written answer. The knowledge revealed in this exercise is likely to stay in the pupil's mind longer than if it was delivered by direct teaching. This is because the pupil has arrived at the solution by himself and will be able (if called upon to do so) to recall the path he followed in order to arrive at the desired conclusion. This method usually involves experimentation and practical work. It is a most valuable mode of teaching since class may be divided so that tasks are individual. Or alternatively the class can be split into groups. This means that tasks may be set by the teacher which allow for differences in ability, attainment and speed in working among the pupils.

Tutorial based teaching

This method is usually used with older pupils. The pupil prepares a set piece of work which is read by the teacher. Pupil and teacher than meet and the preparation is discussed in detail. The teacher by using carefully planned, constructive questioning sets out to examine, criticise and guide the pupil towards a deeper insight and understanding. Sometimes this exercise is carried out by a small group of class members in a seminar situation. In this instance the teacher has adopted a further role, ie as a guide to learning in what is largely a self-directing self-help situation.

Summary
An effective teacher will:

1 have a thorough knowledge of the subject to be taught;

2 be able to organise that knowledge according to the needs of the institution in which he teaches;

3 plan courses suitable to the ability and maturity of his pupils in the light of any outside constraints, eg examinations;

4 be able to break down courses into manageable parts, ie terms, weeks, individual lessons;

5 appreciate and demonstrate the value of the subject taught both for its own sake and the part which it plays within the general school curriculum;

6 demonstrate in his own life that his subject forms a part of a wider field of intellectual interest thus illustrating that learning is a continual process;

7 appear well groomed, neatly and smartly dressed;

8 cultivate a clear, well modulated voice;

9 have the will to teach pupils to concentrate; to enjoy work and reach the goals which together they set themselves;

10 be firm and fair and treat people the same;

11 temper discipline with kindness and good humour;

12 develop a good memory

Conclusion

Much of a teacher's work is routine in that it follows a cycle of preparation, communication and evaluation. Yet it is at the same time spacious in that research and reading during leisure time give an opportunity to widen and deepen knowledge. The fruits of these labours are many. A teacher is an artist. He takes an unformed, developing mind and shapes and moulds it as surely as a craftsman whittles wood or a sculptor fashions clay. A teacher experiences the same joy in creation in introducing ideas and ideals into a mind which grows from unawareness and incomprehension through knowledge, understanding and skills to reasoned action and creativity.

Selected references and further reading

Leeds University Institute of Education, Teacher Education (The teacher's point of view), NFER Publishing Company, 1974

Taylor, P H, Children's evaluations of the characteristics of the good teacher, British Journal of Educational Psychology 32, 1962, 258 to 266.

2 Those who teach

Parents

Chance introduces us to our parents. No one is able to exercise choice in this matter. Nor is it practical for us to choose our teachers. Both parents and teachers exert a powerful influence over the young and both are instrumental in teaching. Parents consciously or unconsciously base their teaching upon their own early family experience. This is modified to some extent by their own education and the current social influences of the time.

When advice is needed many young mothers turn to their own mothers for help and counsel. Where family groups are close knit and the social environment encourages the close proximity of family homes, grandmothers may play a very dominant part in the upbringing of their grandchildren. It may well be that a grandparent 'baby sits' whilst the young parents go out in the evening or even on holiday. Later 'granny' may take the infant to nursery/primary school, collect him from school and look after him until his mother returns home from work. In families such as this the thinking of two generations will fashion the early teaching of the child.

The professionals

But what of the teachers, the professionals whose task it is to educate in a formal sense the younger generation? Today the preparation for teaching is a serious business. Well-educated young people seek a specialised professional training which will give them, on its successful conclusion, the authorisation to embark upon a teaching career. It will be interesting first, however, to ponder upon some influences and signposts in man's history which brought us to this stage in time.

Ancient Greece

Perhaps the most familiar and influential of early teachings and teachers were centred in ancient Greece. If one pauses to consider some of the language used today one finds that it has its origins in those early days. Within the school itself such words as arithmetic, anthology, aesthetics, biology, geography, gymnasium, phonetics, all have their roots in the Greek language. So also do words like diet, barometer and lamp. It is interesting to read in the daily press of a renewed interest at the present time in this ancient language across the Atlantic Ocean in America. One reads that Greek is being taught to 'minority' groups of children who find difficulty in learning English. It is said that the teaching of the source or root of a word enables that word to be more readily recalled. Early evaluation of this work is said to be promising.

Early Greek teachers

The influences of the early teachers can be seen daily in many facets of the world in the realms of government, education, administration, religion and social beliefs. The most important of these early teachers were Socrates, Plato and Aristotle.

Socrates 470-399 BC

Socrates lived in Athens from about 470 to 399 BC. He left no written works but convincing testimony to his character, life, and philosophical teachings abound. Much is to be found in the written works of his pupil, Plato, and in the writings of Aristotle, the historian Xenophon and the playwright Aristophanes. It is said that Socrates possessed a magnetic personality. His greatest passion in life was to acquire knowledge. He sought diligently after truth and tried to persuade men to pursue what he felt to be the highest ideals. To further this aim he talked to people in simple terms about everyday experiences and problems. He employed a technique of subtle questioning which encouraged those whom he encountered to look deeply into their mind and indeed into their very souls. Socrates was an idealist for whom truth was not to be found through mere sensory perception but through the examination of the soul and the cultivation of reason.

You will note that the mode of teaching described here closely accords with the tutorial method (section 1).

Plato 429-347 BC

Plato was a pupil of Socrates. The quality of his writings and the esteem with which he is still held may be judged by the survival of those writings and the respect accorded to them to this day. Unlike Socrates, Plato was a wealthy man from an aristocratic family. Like Socrates he had started his adult life as a soldier. Plato forsook army life early to study under Socrates. He devoted the remainder of his life to learning and later, to teaching. Plato founded the first university near the ancient shrine of Academos. This first school became known as the Academy. To this day Academy is used to signify a place of learning and often an institution of high repute, eg The Royal Academy of Art, The Royal Academy of Music.

Plato's most famous work, *The Republic,* contains the elements of what he taught his pupils in ethics, politics, psychology and metaphysics. Plato was said to be an artistic man who found a supreme delight in the skilful use of words. He developed the thinking of Socrates further, teaching that sensory perception can never give man a true appreciation of reality. Beyond mere sensory perception lay, he believed, an intuitive truth which no man can define. This truth or divinity was centred both in man and in the universe and could not be explained by logic or reason.

Aristotle 384-322 BC

For many years Aristotle was Plato's pupil. He did not disagree with the central teaching of his master but took the view that introspection was not sufficient for him. He felt that his answers to reality and truth were to be found in observation and experiment. When the time came for Aristotle to teach he taught his pupils that truth was to be found by examination, experiment and the application of the knowledge thus gained to further problems.

With his pupils he set about a systematic classification of plants and animals of the then known world. This formed the foundation of the study of physical science as we know it today. From that time onwards wherever man studied, he looked not only to the philosophers (whom Plato had immortalised in his writings) but also (thanks to Aristotle) to the development of scientific observation and methods. You will note that the investigation based teaching and learning described in the previous section has its roots in the early methods developed by Aristotle.

Early European teachers
Marcus Quintilian AD 35-95

Quintilian was born in Spain of Roman parentage about the time of the Crucifixion of Jesus in Jersualem. Marcus Quintilian is remembered for his views on teaching methods. These were committed to a book in which his thoughts and practice have been preserved. He believed that pupils should be placed in an environment which would promote a desire to learn. Quintilian was totally opposed to harshness and coercion. One of the principal aims of education, he felt, was to teach men to be honourable and just. He believed that a teacher could not know too much. All knowledge could be stored against a time when it could be used. The power of the spoken word was supreme both as a means of imparting knowledge and as an agent in bringing about controlled changed with order. It is perhaps for his view, that oratory and the skilful use of words are central to effective teaching, that he is best remembered.

The birth of the Holy Roman Empire

More than six hundred years have elapsed since the death of Marcus Quintilian. During this period the Roman Empire declined and with it the interest in learning which it had valued and encouraged. Christianity grew steadily. The eighth century witnessed the rise of a great surge of Moorish fanaticism which originated in the East and threatened the whole of Europe. Indeed Christianity could have been destroyed and replaced by a ruthless Mohammedism but for Charles Martell. He was the Frankish King of France and Germany. In AD 732 he decisively defeated the Moors at Tours in France and drove them out. This great battle decided not only the future religion of Europe but also the future character of western civilisation.

Charles had two sons. Between them he divided his kingdom. One son retired to a monastery leaving his inheritance to his brother. The latter was crowned in AD 751 uniting France and Germany. His son was Charles the Great or Charlemagne. He was the most powerful ruler for four centuries, since the supremacy of the Roman Empire. Charlemagne was crowned Emperor by Pope Leo in AD 800 thus becoming the first Christian Emperor and the founder of the Holy Roman Empire. But Charlemagne was more than a powerful war lord. He encouraged both learning and music. His court at Aix-la-Chapelle became the cultural centre of Europe and the focal point for the scholars of the day. To this centre he invited the best known scholar and headmaster of the day.

Alcuin of York AD 735-804

Alcuin had been a pupil at and was at this time head master of the cathedral school at York. Alcuin was charged by Charlemagne with the task of establishing schools and libraries throughout his realm. Alcuin wrote at this time to Charlemagne in the following terms:

'In obedience to your exhortation and wise desire I apply myself in serving out to some of my pupils in this house of St Martin the honey of the holy writings; I try to intoxicate others with the wine of the antique studies; one class I nourish with the fruits of

grammatical science; in the eyes of another I display the order of the stars. I have schools of singers many of whom are already sufficiently instructed to be able to teach others. I have also done in this church what lay in my power in the copying of old books.'

This letter illustrates much about the Emperor Charlemagne and also much about Alcuin. It shows that which the Emperor valued and wished others to know and enjoy. He spoke Latin and understood Greek. It is said that he had a good knowledge of grammar, logic and astronomy and enjoyed music. Of Alcuin it shows a desire to please his patron and also to promote those values which he carried from the Cathedral School in York to the most influential centre of the then known world. One feels his love and enthusiasm for what he is doing as he speaks of:

'the honey of the holy writings'
'nourish with the fruits of grammatical science'
'intoxicate others with the wine of antique studies'

Then there is the reference to his training others to carry on his teaching:

'many . . . . are sufficiently instructed to be able to teach others'

There is also reference to the need for books when he refers to:

'the copying of old books'

Alcuin searched unceasingly for books. He left behind a good deal of helpful material for teaching including some two hundred and thirty two letters giving a useful commentary on the life of the times.

'The voice of the people is the voice of God'
(Letter to Charlemagne from Alcuin, AD 800)

Bishop Alcuin and Emperor Charlemagne together, played a very important part in the development of education in the western world. Charlemagne set the seal of Christianity upon Europe and Alcuin set the seal of the Church upon education. The latter was to dominate education for a thousand years.

Erasmus 1466-1536

Erasmus was born in Rotterdam, Holland in 1466. He was a scholarly boy who later entered the priesthood. At twenty eight he became secretary to a bishop. This enabled him to move freely in the world and he was allowed to study in Paris. An invitation to England marked the beginning of a close friendship with Sir John Colet and Sir Thomas More. For the next fifteen years Erasmus travelled Europe gathering a scholarly reputation and esteem. During this time he taught and wrote books. He settled finally in Basle where he edited classical books. It is said that he was able to study calmly and without passion and comment upon matters which invoked passion and violence without incurring the wrath and retribution which could have ended in martyrdom, the hazard of the time. His great friend, scholar and theologian, John Colet, was a wealthy man.

John Colet 1466-1519

Colet studied at Oxford University and travelled extensively abroad. As Dean of St Pauls Cathedral, London, he drew large congregations because of his skill as a preacher. John Colet used his wealth in founding and endowing a school for boys in St Pauls Cathedral churchyard. He superintended the production of books suitable for use in school. His school was placed firmly in secular hands in the care of the Company of Mercers. He stipulated that all School governors must be married. This ensured that the School would for posterity not be dominated by the Church but would be kept closely in touch with commerce and family life.

When Colet died in 1519 he left his school firmly established with a high reputation throughout Europe. He believed that a principal aim of education was to mould men of character. His school still exists today, a monument to the past and evidence that that which is built upon a firm foundation lasts. It also illustrates that institutions can and do change and in so changing take that which is good from the past and combining it with the best from the present look forward with confidence to the future.

The next three educators under consideration are important, not only because their influence lives on today in schools which bear their name, but also because each sought to develop guidelines of practice for future generations of teachers to follow. They are John Amos Komesky, the Moravian pastor known as Comenius, the Swiss, John Henry Pestalozzi, and the German, Frederich Froebel.

Comenius 1592-1670

Comenius, a Protestant, lived from 1592 to 1670. He was educated in Germany and travelled extensively in both Holland and England. Comenius was able to view education through the eyes of a child. At this time learning was still concerned principally with the use of words with little or no association with that which the words represented. Comenius felt that the two should merge in order that learning became enjoyable and more readily understandable to children. He devised language books in which pictures were used for the first time. Accompanying the picture were sentences in the language of the child's mother tongue at the child's level of language usage. These were accompanied by related sentences in the language to be learned. Thus from the beginning words were seen not in lists of vocabulary but as they would be used in normal conversation.

He wrote a book entitled The Gate of Tongues Unlocked in which he described this method of teaching. His school books were so enthusiastically received that they were translated into fifteen languages. The reader will recognise the roots of modern language teaching in Comenius' theory. Comenius became a Bishop of the Moravian Church and as such is revered by Moravian communities today. Educators respect him for his educational theories. He sought to enliven both teaching and learning by using natural resources from the environment. These were used with arts and crafts to stimulate interest and demonstrate the relevance of learning to a child's personal experience of daily living.

John Henry Pestalozzi (1746-1827)

Pestalozzi was born in Zurich a century later in 1746. Like Comenius, Pestalozzi thought carefully about educational principles and demonstrated them himself with originality and success. His methods of teaching attracted much interest at the time and may still be studied with reward. He lives on today in the international villages which bear his name. Pestalozzi started life as a farmer. At twenty nine years of age he turned his farmhouse into a school for twenty poor children. He fed and clothed them, taught them and they in their turn worked for him on the farm.

This was in fact an early industrial school. As an experiment it attracted a great deal of attention but it failed through a lack of funding. In 1798 the French invaded Switzerland and as a result many children became orphaned. Pestalozzi tried again and established a school for some of them at Stanz. Again it attracted much attention and this time it was successful. In 1801 Pestalozzi committed his theories to a book which he called *How Gertrude teaches her children*. He believed that all a child's faculties could be developed through the exercise of its senses.

Centres for his work were opened all over Switzerland. Educators from all over Europe visited these to study his methods. He is remembered as one who tried in a practical way to improve the lot of the poor and in particular orphaned children. His success lay in focussing attention upon the need for universal education and in persuading others of its importance and urgency. Pestalozzi believed that education alone provided the route to freedom for each individual. His influence was international and one of the young men whom he inspired was Frederich Froebel.

Frederich Froebel 1782-1852

Froebel is now known as the founder of the kindergarten system. He was born in the Thuringian Forest lands of Germany. The son of a minister his mother died whilst he was in his infancy. As a child he was lonely and neglected. Perhaps these early experiences led to the formation of Froebel's theory that the earliest years of life should be passed in activities which give pleasure. These activities should, however, be so guided that, although appearing to the child to be play, are structured to a pre-conceived pattern of learning experiences. After studying at Jena University Froebel became tutor to three boys. He took the boys to Yverdun to Pestalozzi's school in order to study his teaching methods. Froebel was immensely impressed but felt that the system needed clarification and refinement.

War with the French intervened and Froebel entered the army. During military service he met with and enthused two other young men. When peace was declared they joined him in his work. From his experiments he evolved a system of teaching now known as the kindergarten. This took its name from the school which he founded in the Thuringian Forest. Froebel called it the Garden of Children. Like plants, in it children were 'cultivated according to the laws of their own being, of God, and of Nature'. With patient thought and great care, Froebel devised a series of activities which would on the one hand please the child since it could readily recognise and be proud of its achievement, and at the same time show the development of definable educational concepts and skills.

Frederich Froebel's system modified since by generations of teachers throughout the world forms the basis of nursery and primary school education today in this and many other countries. It is our loss that Froebel did not realise his dream of formulating a system of education covering the whole period of education from infancy to adulthood. Nevertheless he did lay firmly the foundations of developmental education through enjoyment for the young. What is perhaps even more valuable, the methods which he used were carefully documented and therefore readily available for less gifted originators but nevertheless sincere practitioners to follow.

This concludes the very brief overview of the lives and work of Comenius, Pestalozzi and Froebel. Each tried to define and establish principles upon which education could be founded. Each tested his hypothesis over a long period of time. Each enthused and inspired others who followed. Generations of teachers have since modified, extended and developed, both theories and practice.

Britain in the early nineteenth century
Lancaster (1778-1838) and Andrew Bell (1753-1832)

Both are remembered and often adversely criticised for the method of teaching which they pioneered. Each developed the system independently of the other. It was perhaps a response to a pressing need, and was for the time being the only way to open the door to education for significant numbers of people. It should be remembered that at this time there was no government sponsored system of universal education.

The monitorial system of teaching was based upon the principle of teaching a small group of older pupils who would then teach a further group of younger children. This was a very economic use of teaching staff. It meant that one teacher could teach ten monitors. If each monitor then taught ten other children then one teacher could supervise one hundred pupils and ten monitors at one sitting. Monitors or pupil teachers could in due course if successful become teachers. Pictures of the day show large numbers of pupils sitting in neat rows in what appear to be very big rooms. Lessons were very formal with the curriculum very narrowly based upon the three Rs.

Joseph Lancaster, the son of a Chelsea pensioner, began his work in south London at the age of sixteen. He opened his first school in his father's house. Lancaster proved to be a gifted teacher. The demand for education was so great that he soon had a large school taught by himself and older pupils in the Borough Road, Southwark. Lancaster was a member of the Society of Friends. In 1808 influential, wealthy fellow members of the Society established a body which they called the British and Foreign School Society in order to found similar schools all over the country. In order to staff the schools a training college for teachers was opened. These schools were sometimes called Lancaster Schools and sometimes British Schools. These schools remained in existence until the country took over full responsibility for education.

Andrew Bell began the monitorial system in India where he served as an army chaplain. He had observed the way in which Indian children in open air schools taught each other. Bell was in charge of the military orphan school in Madras. He taught an older group of pupils in the mornings. They then taught what they had learned to other children in the afternoon. On his return to England Dr Bell prospered in Clerical Office. He died in 1832 as Prebendary of Westminster. He lies buried in Westminster Abbey. A very wealthy man, he left his fortune for the development of education. The National Society for promoting the Education of the Poor in the Principles of the Established Church had been founded in 1811. This followed Dr Bell's monitorial system.

In 1870 the Elementary Education Act divided the country into school districts each with its own School Board responsible for providing elementary education within its own borders. Thus the Lancaster and Bell schools handed over their functions to the 'Board Schools'. These became known subsequently as Council Schools. Lancaster and Bell proved very influential in the development of education in this country through the work of the great societies founded to carry on their work according to the systems which they had devised. The methods of teaching for which they are remembered have passed away and one would not mourn their going. Nevertheless, Lancaster and Bell were men who recognised the scale of the demand for education at the time and they devised a practical means of satisfying it with a maximum return with a minimum use of space, teachers and resources.

Summary

1 *Before Christ*

The early Greek influences remain powerful today. These are seen in language, literature, government and education. The teachings of Socrates, Plato and Aristotle reveal the basics of a curriculum not so far removed from what is recommended for young people today. Emphasis in education was placed upon the development of the mind and that elusive, intransigent quality, the spirit. This was achieved by the use of words to reason, question and debate. Aristotle added the dimension of developing scientific method.

2 *AD 35-95*

In Europe Marcus Quintilian saw education as a principal agent for bringing about controlled change with order. His goal was to produce just and honourable men.

3 *Circa 800*

The Emperor Charlemagne founded the Holy Roman Empire and secured for Europe a Christian heritage. Alcuin of York founded schools and libraries throughout this empire setting the seal of the church firmly upon education. The curriculum consisted of languages (spoken and written), science, history and music. The content of the few available books was preserved by manual copying.

4 *The sixteenth century*

Books played a more dominant part in education. Erasmus wrote, taught and edited books. John Colet founded St Paul's School in London. Although a respected theologian himself he established his school firmly in secular hands. He placed its government in the hands of those who were both business men and head of a family. This demonstrated his view that education paved the way to earning one's living and a successful family life. John Colet supervised the production of books for use in his school, recognising the need for special books for educating young people.

5 *Seventeenth century*

Comenius, the Protestant Moravian bishop, recognising the need for enjoyment in learning for children, used the natural resources of art and craft to stimulate interest. He developed illustrated books for language teaching with matching texts in the mother tongue and the language to be learned. These were translated into fifteen languages and our modern language teaching is rooted in these methods.

6 *Eighteenth century*

Pestalozzi devoted his life to working with the orphaned and destitute in Switzerland. He believed that a child's faculties could be developed through the exercise of its senses. He worked for universality in education believing that only through the medium of education could an individual become completely free.

Frederich Froebel founded the kindergarten system. This provided a structured series of experiences embodying defined educational concepts. Through this children learned with enjoyment. This forms the basis of nursery and primary school education today.

7 *Nineteenth century*

Lancaster and Bell introduced the monitorial system to this country. Through it and the two powerful societies which they founded the three Rs reached large numbers of the population. The schools which they had founded provided a network for universal elementary education when the country accepted responsibility for this in 1870.

Conclusion

We have looked briefly at some of the paths trodden by those who became notable teachers; founding schools and establishing that which they felt to be of importance for posterity; each one preparing men to follow them to carry on and extend their work. As men the early teachers emerge with few common characteristics. Some were of humble origin where education was unknown, whilst others came from the intellectual elite. What was certain was that they all possessed enthusiasm, drive, persistence and a relentless pursuit of knowledge. Perhaps the latter could be said to be particularly common characteristics of the early teachers Socrates, Plato, Aristotle, Quintilian, Alcuin, Erasmus and Colet, they all concentrated it is felt upon the development of the mind and character of man.

The later teachers Comenius, Pestalozzi and Froebel seemed to accept that men were firstly children who developed gradually along certain paths, which could be prescribed and governed, before they became men. One felt that it was of importance what children experienced as they grew to maturity since this would affect the type of man which resulted. One may also wonder if Froebel would have developed his system of learning for children, had he not experienced an unhappy childhood, since his desire to ensure that children enjoyed childhood, arose from his own memories of neglect and loneliness.

Pestalozzi stressed the need to educate the poor. He saw education as the avenue of escape, from the bonds which held the poor in hardship, misery and poverty. In England Lancaster and Bell sought to teach large numbers of the poor the elements of education through the three Rs and a monitorial system. Then came the establishment of some training colleges for teachers in response to a growing demand for education.

The nineteenth century witnessed the acceptance by central government of the responsibility for educating all children and also for training increasing numbers of teachers to implement this. These teachers did not (as did the early teachers) pursue knowledge for its own sake. They aimed to dispense some knowledge to the greatest possible number of people. Education had become a social agency.

Selected references and further reading
Rusk, R R *The Doctrines of the Great Educators,* Macmillan, 1954

Part 3

Professional education

1 Educating the teachers

As the training colleges expanded in number, they provided teaching staff for the elementary schools now attended by the bulk of the school population. Universities continued to provide most of the teachers for the grammar schools which offered education on a fee paying or 'scholarship' basis. This practice continued into the twentieth century.

The college teacher training courses (apart from giving a professional training) had a twofold aim. Firstly to extend the individual's personal education and secondly to equip that person to teach in a generalist sense. It was accepted that teachers in elementary schools and later secondary modern schools (after World War Two) would be non-specialist class teachers. This implied that such teaching responsibilities covered a range of subjects, usually referred to as general subjects. Often one subject was studied to a greater depth giving a semi-specialist status.

There were exceptions to this. 'Practical' subjects like art, craft, home economics, woodwork and metalwork, physical education, were studied as specialist subjects. Since universities did not offer courses at degree level in these disciplines teachers worked in elementary or secondary modern schools as well as in grammar schools.

Length of training

The first courses in domestic subjects for teachers in the nineteenth century lasted for six months only. These were validated by a private body, The Northern Union of Schools of Cookery, now known as the National Council for Home Economics Education. When the government accepted responsibility for training teachers towards the end of the century, courses were then validated by the Board of Education. During this century, prior to 1962, courses for teachers of general subjects were two years in length. Courses for teachers of domestic subjects were, however, three years in duration. Teachers' courses included primarily the subjects which were to be taught, plus psychology, philosophy and methods of teaching. The institutions which offered these courses were known as teacher training colleges. Universities were responsible for validating teacher training courses and the Ministry of Education conferred qualified teacher status.

After 1962 the length of courses for all non-graduate teachers increased to three years. By now the term 'home economics' had become more widespread. Courses for home economics teachers remained three years in duration. Training colleges became known as colleges of education and course content broadened. The emphasis still lay on the personal development of a student's education. In most cases this was still done through a study in depth of a main subject. Liberalising elements of art, drama, music and literature were added. The professional element of education became known first, as the Principles and Practice of Education and later as Educational Studies. Since the study of the main subject ran parallel to the professional studies these training programmes were known as concurrent courses. In the 1960s colleges went through an unprecedented period of expansion.

Entry qualifications

Until 1951 most colleges accepted candidates offering the School Certificate with matriculation. After 1951 a minimum of five Ordinary Level General Certificates of Education plus evidence of sixth form study became the norm. The level of qualifications offered by candidates rose steadily reaching its peak probably at the end of the 'sixties. The writer recalls that at that time it was not unusual to meet entrants with four Advanced Level General Certificates of Education. This did not mean that all candidates at that time were well qualified. It should be remembered that this was a period of rapid expansion in higher education. It was freely available to all, with the requisite qualifications for entry. This resulted in a great variability in standard of student. The early 'seventies saw a widening of opportunity for women to enter universities and professions which had hitherto not been freely open to them. This began a gradual decline in the numbers of good calibre students entering concurrent courses of teacher education.

Awards

The three year concurrent course culminated in the award of a Certificate in Education. The early 'eighties will see the phasing out of this award as an all graduate teaching profession is introduced. The later 'sixties saw the introduction of a Bachelor of Education degree. This allowed those students who had entered the Certificate course with Advanced Level General Certificates of Education, and who had, at the end of that course, achieved a minimum standard of a B grade in their main subject and Education, and a Pass grade in Practical Teaching, to proceed to a fourth year's study. The successful culmination of the fourth year led to the award of a Bachelor of Education degree.

The status of this award varied from institution to institution (Bachelor of Education degree, general, classified honours or unclassified). Serving teachers were admitted to these fourth year studies on an in-service basis. For them this has proved a very satisfactory way to graduate, thereby increasing their status, salary and career prospects. The fourth year did not, however, prove popular with concurrent course students and only a minority stayed on.

Graduate teachers—the consecutive route

Graduates have always followed an alternative path into teaching. University entrance requirements lay down that students must be matriculated on entry. Degree courses have therefore a higher academic starting level than Certificate courses. Graduates have therefore a deeper specialist knowledge of their subject than non-graduates. Prior to 1974 graduates were able to enter schools to teach without a professional training. Even so many did enter a post graduate professional training course at university prior to entering school.

Since 1974 all graduates except those in shortage subjects (for the time being) have to complete satisfactorily, a one year course of professional training. Since this professional training follows graduation this mode of entry into teaching is termed the *consecutive route*. Professional training courses contain studies in psychology, philosophy, sociology and methods of teaching. Experience with and observation of children in primary, middle and secondary schools is usually included. This is supported by a contextual study of the educational system in this country. Students spend a minimum of sixty days in schools on teaching practice. On the successful conclusion of the course a Graduate Certificate in Education is awarded. Most graduates are still trained in University Departments of Education.

It should be noted that all students whether they follow a concurrent or a consecutive course of professional training are required to complete satisfactorily the present minimum of sixty days teaching practice in schools. A recommendation that Qualified Teacher Status be confirmed is passed by the employing Local Education Authority to the Department of Education and Science at the conclusion of a satisfactory probationary year spent teaching in a maintained school.

The early eighties and beyond

All teachers entering schools will have either a B Ed degree or a degree plus a Graduate Certificate in Education.

The Bachelor of Education degree

This will still be a concurrent course but it will differ from the Bachelor of Education degree which was preceded by a Certificate in Education. All students taking concurrent courses in the eighties will be matriculated (ie will offer two General Certificate of Education Advanced level subjects on entry). The starting level of the course will therefore be post A level. Students may either follow a three or a four year course. The three year course will have qualified teacher status built in. The award is a degree at ordinary level only. Students may proceed to a fourth year in order to qualify for a classified honours degree.

Recruitment

The mid-seventies saw a sharp reversal of the teacher training expansion programme begun in the mid 'sixties. The effects on the school population following a dramatic fall in the birth rate resulted in teacher training programmes being cut by four-fifths. Over production of teachers in the mid-'seventies together with large numbers of excess staff in colleges led to unemployment. Towards the end of the 'seventies this was aggravated by a further fall in numbers of children in schools. These problems were not confined to this country but seemed common to all Western nations. Constant adverse publicity from all aspects of the media which highlighted falling school rolls and unemployment has resulted in a sharp fall in numbers of good quality students presenting themselves for training as teachers.

This has affected entry to concurrent courses in particular. Now that matriculation is necessary for entry to the concurrent B Ed degree courses recruitment to them is likely to fall even lower. The three year B Ed ordinary degree is likely to be less attractive to employers than the four year B Ed honours degree. It is possible that the candidate who will seem most attractive to employers will be the graduate with the three year specialist degree plus a Graduate Certificate in Education.

From the student's point of view it means that a decision to teach need not be made until nearing graduation. It also means that he has a more marketable product from an employment standpoint if he has a specialist degree as opposed to a B Ed degree. If his ultimate choice is a career in education then a degree plus a postgraduate professional certificate offers better prospects of promotion than a B Ed degree. There is little doubt that the B Ed degree which experienced a difficult birth and a sickly childhood is unlikely to make 'old bones'.

Where to study
The institutions

Although the number of institutions offering teacher education has drastically declined, with the closure of colleges brought about by cuts in initial training, this may be counterbalanced by the greater variety of courses in those institutions which remain. Prior to 1970 (which saw the birth of the polytechnics) there were two main sources of teachers. Firstly the colleges of education and secondly the universities. Since 1970 the polytechnics have absorbed a wide variety of colleges of education. Other colleges of education have joined together to form colleges of higher education. These amalgamations have brought about the implementation of a proposal in The James Report 1972 (Teacher Education and Training) that institutions training teachers should have no fewer than seven hundred and fifty students engaged in initial courses in higher education.

Home economics courses
Universities

Only two universities in the British Isles offer degree courses in Home Economics; Surrey and the University of Wales. Both courses began within the last ten years.

Polytechnics

These offer degrees in Home Economics and Bachelor of Education (Home Economics) degrees. Where courses are based in polytechnics there are obvious advantages for course planning. These institutions contain constituent schools which offer degrees and post graduate studies in a wide range of professional specialisms. This means that there is a bank of highly qualified staff on which to draw for specialist knowledge. For example, nutritionalists, dietitians, food technologists, interior designers, textile designers, architects, town planners, lawyers, economists, etc. Their associated specialist facilities are available for use by home economics students which would not be possible in a college or small complex offering limited specialisms. Also, the libraries are usually much larger than in a college.

Geographically, polytechnics are normally sited at the centre of large concentrations of population, which makes them easily accessible for both staff and students. Often a university is in close proximity, with its libraries an added source of staff expertise.

Colleges of higher education

These were formed by amalgamating two or more colleges of education. Whereas a polytechnic may embrace from four to nine thousand students a college of higher education may not exceed greatly the minimum of seven hundred and fifty students recommended by The James Report. They are therefore smaller, more intimate communities. The latter may be accentuated if the college is sited in a rural area of great beauty such as Ilkley, Yorkshire, or in a small city, like Bath, with its priceless architectural heritage. These colleges offer degrees in Home Economics and Bachelor of Education (Home Economics) degrees.

It is important for intending students to make an objective assessment of their abilities, skills and present and possible future attainment when considering which type of institution to enter. This should be studied in conjunction with one's known ability to survive emotionally. Large institutions demand a personal ability to be more self sufficient than a smaller more intimate college. It is advisable to visit several institutions if possible and to ask to meet students currently studying on the course which interests one. They will give a frank opinion of the course, staff and students. Try to establish, how various institutions and the courses they offer, are viewed by your future professional colleagues. Having gathered as much data as one can, then make up your mind.

Perhaps the next section will help a prospective student with this since it deals with the student teacher.

Selected references and further reading

Department of Education and Science, Teacher Education and Training (The James Report) HMSO, 1972

Central Office of Information, Britain 1980, An official handbook, HMSO, London, 1980

Employment and registration as a teacher in Scotland (Form RR1 issued by the Scottish Education Department)

Boehm, K and Wellings, N (edited by), *The Student Book 1981* (where to study), Papermac (Macmillan Press), 1980.

2 The student teacher

From what has already been said it is clear that no one enters the classroom totally unprepared. All student teachers have experienced some eighteen to twenty one years of learning and will already have engaged in some aspect of informal teaching. Nevertheless the real test comes when one faces a class for the first time. Every student wonders, 'will I be able to cope, can I control a class of youngsters?' 'What will I do, if?' Realising such natural fears, most Education Departments aim to place students in a school setting as quickly as possible. Some students will be asked to spend a period of time either in school or working with children before formal training begins. In any event they will be asked to go into school very early in the course, perhaps even during the first or second week. Let us examine the reasoning behind this.

Guided school experience

Firstly students need to see schools in action. This does not just mean only the age group they are planning to teach. It is essential to view the teaching and learning process on a progressive basis throughout the whole period covered by compulsory education. Even during a one year postgraduate course there is time to spend at least a few days in nursery and primary schools prior to actual practice in teaching in middle and high schools. Such visits are undertaken on a carefully directed investigatory basis. Students on their return to base will report upon the aims of the school and how these are achieved. They will be asked to note staffing, resources, administration, the attendance of children, their backgrounds, ability, response to staff and each other as far as time allowed. A brief outline of the curriculum offered would also be noted. In brief, this exercise is one of looking at child development in action and how the school responds to pupils' emotional, mental, physical and social maturation. If the exercise is done effectively, teaching and learning relative to older age groups can be seen in the context of an eleven year curriculum.

Most students enjoy this brief encounter with younger pupils. They fit easily into the informal atmosphere of the nursery and primary school. Teachers in the latter are usually by nature outgoing, friendly and enthusiastic. They create the atmosphere in school of optimism, action and hope for the future, referred to in an earlier chapter. Students are readily enfolded into this community. They read stories to the children, help with those learning to read and listen to those who can read. The delights of early number are explored and some of the possibilities of hand, mind and body, in writing, art, music and movement. Many students have forgotten their own early school days, remembering only a more formal approach to life in the classroom. The re-discovery of the less inhibited approach to the exploration of the world and its wonders, rarely fails to inspire even the most controlled person.

Back at the Department such visits form a basis for discussion in psychological studies. Sometimes head teachers, and teachers from the schools visited, also participate. Already it can be seen that teacher education includes the schools, the teachers, Department of Education staff and the students themselves. The students will engage in reading, attend specialist lectures and study both teachers and children in action.

Patterns of teaching practice

To the early school experience, others will be added. During a three year course, nursery and primary school visits may be followed by experience with middle school pupils on a day, or part-day basis, during the year. Alternatively, a block of several weeks may follow later in the year. Teaching practice itself may be taken in blocks of several weeks in the second and third years. For those following a one year postgraduate course teaching practice may principally fall in the second and third terms. This allows a teaching practice in both middle and high schools. Alternatively a short middle school practice can be taken immediately after half term in the first term followed by a twelve week practice in a high school in the second term. I have experienced both policies, and have found that the latter works best in practice for intending high school teachers.

Schools are relatively undisturbed during the autumn and spring terms and give an unbroken period of teaching practice. The student really has a better chance to show what can be done particularly in the twelve weeks of the spring term. Mock examinations for the General Certificate of Education and the Certificate of Secondary Education take place during this period. These give a student an opportunity to learn the rudiments of examination practice and evaluation. Final teaching practice held in a summer term, must always prove somewhat unsatisfactory. In a term broken by examinations, sports days, swimming galas, school camps and visits at home and abroad, it is difficult for a student to show an advantageous, continuous programme of work.

From the standpoint of Department of Education planning, the summer term is best left free of teaching practice, to enable curriculum planning projects to be done. These projects can be attempted in a more intelligent and realistic manner, after students have had a significant length of experience in teaching. Projects can then be more accurately directed towards pupils of a chosen age and ability. Students can, therefore, direct their efforts toward preparation of materials to be used in their initial teaching post.

Preparation for teaching

Opportunity is afforded during experience in school for working alongside children and for noting their reactions to one's self, the student, the teacher and each other. The actual act of teaching is perhaps the easiest to learn. Forecasting the effects upon individuals and groups of individuals is far more difficult to achieve. This is dependent upon so many contributory factors, eg the age and ability of pupil(s), their maturity, their motivation to learn, their willingness to co-exist with companions, the teacher and other groups, their attentiveness, interest, and the ethos of the school. Teachers vary in age, experience, ability and style. Some are very successful, a joy to watch and contrive to make teaching appear deceptively simple. They are skilled performers, and pupils seem to respond with pleasurable anticipation and success. Other teachers appear relatively successful, but not all the time. Yet other teachers seem way out of their depth, and at times submerged beneath waves of pupil response. Students entering school are given a check list of particular management and teaching skills to note. Let us now consider some of these.

Management in the classroom

How do pupils enter the room? Do they wait at the door, and enter when invited? Do they rush in madly, in a group? Are they quiet or noisy? Most teachers do not permit a noisy rush to tables or desks. Usually pupils are expected to behave in a manner conducive to the activity they are about to pursue, ie work. Thus most teachers introduce a routine which promotes this, ie pupils enter, put on aprons, put bags or satchels away and sit down ready to begin. A call to order signifying that the lesson is to commence should bring silence. If it doesn't, repeat it and wait until it does. Class routine is a matter of conditioning pupils to respond in a particular manner at a given time, on a regular basis. Thus, when the teacher is ready to begin, he says so, greets the class and proceeds. Where a teacher doesn't follow a regular procedure, time is lost, for pupils do not automatically respond to a given cue. An unruly class must be brought to order before any work can be done.

Cued responses

Although routine may seem, to the new teacher, pernickety, noncreative and boring, it does establish order in a minimum of time without friction. To the pupil it gives a feeling of comfort and security within which to work. An immediate response to cues is an important aid to management and class control. It should be used in school right from the beginning, even in the nursery class. Indeed the following indicates that its use may, in an emergency, save lives. In nursery schools, the playing of a well known tune on the piano, is often used as a cue to bring all children from diverse activities, back to home base to listen to a story, or to engage in a group activity. Recently, a teacher in charge of a nursery school was alerted that fire had broken out in the building. Immediately, teachers and children were cued back to base by the piano. The response was immediate, and teachers and children marching to a well loved tune, left the home base for safety outside the building. Within minutes, fire gutted the timber construction. There was no panic, and all the children and staff were outside before realising what had happened.

This illustrates the need for certain cues to be known and understood. What other cued responses may one expect to use? Already the cue for opening a lesson has been given and it may be used to close one. At the given cue at the end of a day, books and equipment may be collected and put away, the chalk board cleaned, chairs put on tables, windows closed, gas and electrical appliances checked, etc. During the day cues may indicate registration, the lunch time break, etc. Teachers may have different procedures, it does not matter, since children quickly adapt to any routine. Every new teacher encounters the words, Mrs Brown always did . . . . This may relate to the looking after of stock, books, pencils, marking work, rewards and punishments, etc.

Routine practice in a home economics room

For the student who will only be in school for a short time, it is wise to ask Mrs Jones (the teacher) what routines she follows, so that these may be continued without interruption or disruption. In the home economics room these may relate to costing of dishes, shopping, food, orders, bringing, sharing and giving out ingredients, washing up, laundering of aprons, dishcloths, teatowels, checking unit cupboards, sinks, stoves, store cupboards, emptying waste bins, checking that appliances are switched off, sweeping the floor . . . . In needlecraft lessons, these routines may relate to giving out and collecting of small equipment like needles, pins, thimbles, threads, scissors, tape measures. At the beginning of a lesson ironing boards will be set up and pressing cloths given out. Sewing machines will be made ready. At the close of the lesson pressing equipment and sewing machines will be made ready for storage. Work boxes will be put away and the wardrobe tidied. The floor, tables, chalk board, chairs, windows, all may need attention before the class leaves the room.

Social education

Not only are these routines necessary to ensure an economic use of time, and to promote orderly class work, but also for social reasons. They illustrate a need for a personal and a collective responsibility, not only for one's own property, but also for the property of others. It also demonstrates a practice of good housekeeping in the economic use of time, money and resources. Finally it illustrates the division of labour within the school, in the sharing of duties for learning and teaching, between the teacher and class as a whole and between individuals. At a time when vandalism is rife, attention to these aspects within school cannot be stressed too firmly. If individuals participate physically, in the care of something, they are less likely to damage it. Care for personal and public property can become part of a daily routine, an automatic response, without fuss.

Teacher behaviour

Teacher, pupil attitudes vary. Observation will reveal the effects that these have upon pupils. The authoritarian approach, maintains order and gives pupils the security necessary for them to work in comfort. This results in an efficient output. However, it does tend to produce individuals who may rely upon the teacher for decision making, thus inhibiting the development of self determination and responsibility. Look for the friendly, but firm teacher who allows the pupils (when appropriate) to take the initiative and grasps this opportunity to direct learning.

There are many 'shades' of teacher in between these two examples. The most effective teacher is one who accepts the authority vested in him by the school. This is apparent in his behaviour for he uses this authority in such a manner as to promote a calm, peaceful, secure atmosphere in which many kinds of learning can take place. Pupils expect teachers to keep order and to organise time so that a variety of activities can take place. They expect to be protected from aggressive behaviour by other pupils directed against either their person or their property. Pupils expect lessons to be planned, prepared and delivered in an interesting manner. They expect the teacher to be interested in them, the subject under discussion and to know it well.

Observation will indicate that where a teacher shows himself to be unable or unwilling in any of these respects then pupils tend either individually or collectively to rebel. Continued observation will indicate positive and negative pupil response to teacher behaviour. It will also show the repetitive nature of such responses. Research into pupil attitudes toward teacher behaviour illustrates that pupils prefer a firm teacher. This firmness can extend to being hard so long as the management is impartial, fair and seen to be just. A sense of humour is appreciated. Interestingly, human beings like to be managed and feel uneasy when they are not. Perhaps this explains why as a nation we meekly queue at every possible opportunity, whether it be at the cinema, football match, supermarket check out, restaurant or bus stop.

For the student teacher such knowledge is at one and the same time, comforting and threatening. Children expect certain clearly defined behaviour from their teachers. Knowing this, if a student does not comply, then life will be very uncomfortable, as pupils seek to force him to accept his role.

This highlights the importance to a teacher of prior knowledge, preparation, planning and organisation, if a lesson is to be successful. Thus observation can be illuminating as a pre-cursor to teaching in focussing upon teacher behaviour and response, pupil response and behaviour, as a guide to future classroom action by the student.

Selecting and using language

Apart from this, what does early experience in school offer? It gives opportunity to talk to pupils and for the student to adjudge his own ability to select and use vocabulary which is understandable and interesting to pupils. It gives practice in using the voice on a continuous basis, in enunciation, in selecting volume and pitch. Opportunity is afforded to students for listening to and understanding local, national and international dialects. This may be a two-way experience for student and pupils. For example, Scottish students working in Yorkshire schools discovered that they used the word basin to describe what the English usually call a bowl. Pupils were interested to learn this and also that the reverse was true, ie that the English basin was a Scottish bowl! Differences in language usage are interesting and can add variety and colour to teaching as long as understanding is reached by all participants. More difficulty can be experienced when the teacher, or pupils, or both, are of overseas origin and the mother tongue is not English. Problems also arise when the spoken English is heavily dialectic as with West Indian pupils. Student teachers will find immense gain in their school experience in extending their knowledge of verbal communication and understanding.

The ethos of the school

Some visitors to schools claim that they can 'feel' the atmosphere and ethos of the establishment within a short time of entry to a building. What they are really saying is that there are clues which indicate certain inherent factors. For example, the entrance or foyer may indicate a pride in the building and the pupils. There may be flowers and a range of pupils' work tastefully displayed. This may be apparent also as one walks along corridors to parts of the building. Where there is nothing, this may indicate a lack of interest, a lack of pupils' work at a reasonable standard or a feeling that anything displayed may be quickly vandalised or taken. Similarly a litter-strewn play area, kicked paintwork, vandalised walls, broken tennis nets, missing railings, indicate a lack of care of both private and public property.

Arrival in such a school as 'break' is due may result in being almost trodden under foot, as pupils pour recklessly from classroom into corridor. By contrast one can find oneself lost in another school and discovered by a pupil, who asks courteously, 'Can I help you?' and quickly proceeds to do so.

As one walks through a school one may often observe class after class engaged in quiet, purposeful activity. In another establishment throbbing temples indicate that the noise level is such as to curtail and possibly prohibit thought and reasoning. These two situations represent an expression of quality in social education and in learning and teaching.

Leisure activities

A school also expresses its interest in its pupils' present and future leisure activities. This is not shown only in the range of sporting activities but in the development of hobbies and interests, which add meaning and purpose to life long after one's youth has gone. The following examples illustrate schools where this aspect of education was taken very seriously. I had occasion to visit a school in a small town tucked away in rural central Wales. Having an early morning appointment, I arrived midway through the previous summer evening. Journeying by taxi through the town to the place where I was to spend the night, I commented to the driver upon the completely deserted appearance of the streets. Almost everyone (young and old) in that town had, he told me, gone to the evening performance of one of Shakespeare's plays at Stratford-upon-Avon. That community had a love of dramatics which spilled over from home to school and school to home. Similar instances are brought to mind of choral speaking groups, choirs and orchestras which developed on a shared school and community basis.

Another example relates to a secondary school in a Yorkshire mining village. It was a typical 1930 quadrangled design, in single storey red brick. Classrooms were windowed on two sides and one side looked through a windowed corridor onto the quadrangle. Every corridor was luxuriant with foliage and blooms. I commented one day to the headmaster on the beauty of the scene and what pleasure it gave to my visits. The head reminded me that most of his boys would spend the bulk of their working lives under ground in the dark ugliness of the pits. *'Was it not'*, he asked, *'the purpose of education to bring beauty, enjoyment and life to the individual? After a shift spent underground a man need go no further than his back yard or garden to enjoy the beauty of propagated plants and flowers.'*

This headmaster had two principal educational aims. Firstly, pupils were encouraged to read and enjoy books, since through them they would in later years be able to escape from the utilitarian dullness of their working lives. Secondly, pupils were taught how to create from tiny seeds and cuttings the beauty of the universe in flowers and plants. A man could then find contentment in life even if he did spend his working life trapped and incarcerated in the bowels of the earth.

There are lessons to be learned from the philosophy underlying education in these two schools. As technological advances are made, fewer people will be able to enjoy the luxury of job satisfaction. Many may find that there is no possibility of a job at all and have time in plenty, but little money, for expensive pleasures. Leisure pursuits with lasting appeal will be more and more necessary to fill the abyss in people's lives. From an educationalist's point of view, where are these interests to be initiated, engendered, nurtured and developed, but within school? Home economists should be reviewing with great seriousness the extent of the problem and the contribution which they could and can make in the content of courses in school both now and in the future.

Learning to teach

This begins in the Education Department with simulated exercises. Sometimes these involve teaching in front of one's fellows or microteaching practice with a group of children. Teaching fellow students can be a nerve-racking experience. It does, however, give the necessary practice in selecting, compiling and delivering a specified presentation of knowledge, activity or skill. This may entail a lecturette on energy conservation directed at first year student level, or analysing the skill of grating cheese for a group of eleven year old pupils. In these situations Education Department staff assume the role of guide, adviser and critic. If there are no children present when required, then students have to try to imagine themselves in the relevant role of a pupil. This is not ideal but the presenter does get practice in planning, preparing teaching and learning aids, delivery, selecting and asking questions, and in timing the component activities without the additional strain of controlling an actual class and all that it implies.

If children are present, a more natural response can be evoked. In both situations video-taping adds to the value of the exercise. With instruction, students can operate the relevant equipment, and with it a record is available for group discussion after a teaching session is concluded. The 'teacher' can then be confronted with evidence of his performance. Appropriate praise and encouragement can be given and suggestions made for improvement. From the standpoint of time this kind of exercise is expensive. It involves preparation by staff with students prior to the presentation, the actual delivery, clearing time, re-running and discussion time. Nevertheless it does provide the most accurate means of recording what actually took place, the teacher's performance and the response of the class, etc. It also offers the fairest platform for criticism. Ideally, a second performance by the presenter should be given to a parallel group of children, incorporating suggestions made during discussion as the aim.

This may not be possible, particularly on a one year course if every student is to participate individually. If students are given a checklist of points to look for in a performance, they readily learn to assess constructively not only each other but also themselves. Assessment will relate to choice of objectives, content, presentation, conclusion, evaluation, teaching and learning materials. Furthermore a number of 'heads' are better than one and individual students benefit from seeing the approach taken by their fellows and learn from the concerted view of the group. The student group benefits from the advice, leadership and counselling of staff. The latter have usually seen a number of students and teachers attempting to solve similar problems before. This knowledge is often re-inforced if, as was stressed earlier, staff are successful and experienced teachers. Mini-teaching or micro-teaching exercises are really sessions for putting forward and sharing ideas in action. This is very much what teaching is all about.

The teaching process

It is not difficult to get to know what to teach for instance in Home Economics. There are syllabuses in plenty published by the regional examining boards of the Certificate of Secondary Education and the independent boards of the General Certificate of Education. Heads of department and assistant teachers in school will have their own schemes of work which they have planned for use in their own particular classes. Some local authority advisers have collaborated with teachers in their area to prepare a guide booklet outlining the knowledge, skills and areas of concern relating to each age group within the three tier system. From these sources the new teacher can establish a clear picture of what needs to be done. What is much more difficult is to decide how to apply this information.

The continuity of learning

Much of what is taught in home economics is developmental. This means that it is presented at different times and at different levels during a pupil's school career. Thus the pupil may learn about 'digestion' in primary, middle and high school. What is taught in each school has its roots in the same process. But the actual content and the manner of its presentation will be very different. As the subject is explored in greater depth at each stage, the language used will be extended and the amount of detail will increase. In the case of digestion this not only involves the actual process, but leads on from the implications for the health of the individual, through specialist categories of individual diets, to the wider aspects of community health.

In the very early stages, pupils' learning will take place primarily through sensory experiences. Thus teachers concentrate upon and accentuate the work covered, where appropriate, in terms of seeing, hearing, tasting, feeling and smelling. Within the middle school, teachers move gradually to use more abstract means of illustration and experience. At high school in GCE classes at 0 and A level, teachers rely more on pupils' understanding in the abstract. When explanation is required, this is usually done by the written or spoken word or diagrammatic representation.

It is important to remember that some pupils at high school do not reach the stage of thinking in the abstract (or do so much later). They need, therefore, to be taught in a more sensorially, stimulating manner. It could be argued that teachers at primary and middle school level have to be more imaginative and inventive in seeking for creative ways in which to express their teaching content. All intending teachers would do well to study the methods employed by advertisers in selling their wares. They concentrate heavily upon the sensorial appeal of their presentation. Some of the procedures followed can be adapted for use in teaching.

Teaching content

The study of teachers in action, the participation in simulated teaching exercises and micro teaching, will all have contributed to the student's basic understanding of the teaching process and to a growing awareness of the underlying principles of lesson planning. In teaching home economics, individual lessons form a part of a carefully thought out pre-determined programme. This plan may be examined at three levels: the syllabus, the scheme of work and the individual lesson.

The syllabus

Firstly, the overall design which embraces the full extent of the pupil's course, and may vary in length extending over a few weeks, a term, a year or even two years as in the case of a CSE or GCE course. These overall plans for action are called syllabuses. The Shorter Oxford English Dictionary defines 'syllabus' as follows: 'A concise statement or table of the heads of a discourse, the contents of a treatise, the subjects of a series of lectures, etc.' The content of a syllabus, therefore, is expressed only in headings or the briefest of terminology. For example 'household management', cleaning techniques, laundry processes, home laundry appliances, care labelling, home dyeing, etc.

The above gives little (if any) indication of the level of the course. Indeed all the headings chosen could relate to a variety of courses which could be studied at middle school to graduate level. It is not until the syllabus is extended that a full appreciation of its content in scope, depth, difficulty and manageability within the institution for which it is intended, is arrived at. The appropriateness for the age, ability and aptitude of the participants can then be determined. Content can be matched against staff qualities and qualifications for teaching it. Resources in terms of money, rooms, time, support staff, can be compared with those necessary for its implementation. All these considerations apply to all syllabuses at whatever level they are looked at.

Syllabuses are always preceded by their aims. Couched as they are in stark written terms, these sometimes appear to the reader vague, abstract, often unattainable and sometimes pretentious. For example 'to develop aesthetic awareness and appreciation', 'to prepare pupils for life', 'to prepare pupils for the world of work', 'to give a knowledge of scientific method'. From the wording used it is clear that these aims are long term. They are difficult and at times impossible to evaluate in terms of the degree of success of a course. Nevertheless this is no reason for setting only those aims which can be evaluated within the pupils' life time at school.

Scheme of work

From the syllabus is planned the scheme of work. In writing a scheme of work one is determining the extent of the content of the syllabus relative to the level of the course and fitting it into the time allowed in school for it to be implemented. School terms vary in length, but can be based roughly on a twelve week norm. Thus schemes of work may be related to courses within a year, in blocks of time of six weeks, twelve weeks, twenty four weeks or thirty six weeks. Weekly allowances of time per class may be 40 minutes, 60 minutes, 80 minutes or longer periods. Where examination work is undertaken a recommended amount of time is usually specified. This may be allocated at one or more sessions during a week. With these constraints in mind, a teacher sets out to plan the break down of the syllabus into weekly portions and finally into individual lessons. Only by so doing can he determine how much time can be apportioned to each part of the syllabus.

For a teacher following an examination syllabus, planning is relatively straightforward. The teacher called upon to plan a six week session of home economics which will form the only subject experience for a particular group in a single academic year has a very different and difficult task. It requires much thought and heart searching to choose six lessons which will, as a group, stand alone forming a complete course to be remembered for its own sake rather than as a part of a continuous whole.

The individual lesson

This will vary according to the subject being taught and the age and ability of the pupils. The efficacy of a lesson can be evaluated by the student, the pupils, the class teacher and sometimes a visiting tutor. The purpose of a lesson should be clear both to teacher and taught. In lesson preparation this intent should be defined specifically. The various aspects of this purpose are called objectives. Unlike the aims (discussed earlier relative to the syllabus) which cannot readily be measured, except in the long term, the objectives of a lesson can be evaluated after each session is concluded. Objectives may relate to cognitive, social or sensori-motor skills. The study of home economics gives opportunity for the development of all three, lesson by lesson. Initially, it is

Structuring a lesson

1 Planning	**Objectives**
	Review of pupils' previous knowledge
	Selection of content
	Methods of teaching
	Methods of learning
	Selection of resources for: viewing listening investigation consolidation
2 Performance	**Opening the Lesson**
	Call to order
	Greeting
	Objectives
	Arousal of interest
	Manner of Presentation
Skill as a communicator	Appearance
	Bearing (manner)
	Choice of language
	Voice
	Rapport with pupils
	Management skill
Skill in content selection for communication	**Introduction**
	Development
	Quality depth of knowledge
	Quantity
	Relevance
	Pace
	Timing
	Appropriate use of materials for viewing, listening, investigation, consolidation
3 Evaluation	**Conclusion**
	Procedures
	Use of information gained.

advisable to choose objectives carefully and sparingly. It is better to be economic in early selection so that success can be readily evaluated.

Plan for success

Remember that a teacher's own achievement accords with that of his pupils and that success breeds success. Plan for pupil success and teacher success follows. The beginner should, therefore, set a few carefully chosen goals and work to achieve them. Set a standard by aiming to achieve some development in pupils each lesson in cognitive, social and motor skills.

1 Planning

It could be argued that eighty per cent of the success of a lesson depends upon the efficiency with which it has been planned. How then can this be achieved? Shown on the previous page are the three crucial aspects of teaching; planning, performance and evaluation. Let us consider each in turn.

Objectives

The objectives for the lesson are first selected. As stated elsewhere, choose sparingly and try to include one from each of the cognitive, social and sensori-motor domains (Part 6, section 3). Spend time in thinking, writing and re-writing these until their import and purport are absolutely clear. Try to check that they are appropriate for the age, maturity and previous knowledge of the group. Select and simplify those which are appropriate to be stated to the class at the beginning of the lesson.

Selection of content

This includes knowledge, intellectual, manual and social skills (Part 6, section 2). Ponder upon the knowledge. Is it appropriate for the age, ability and experience of the group? Is it right for the particular course being undertaken? How can it be presented? It this is not obvious, consider the alternatives: direct teaching, demonstration followed by class practice/group assignments/individual assignments, reading/comprehension, etc. It is possible that the method deemed most suitable is not practicable because of the constraints of time, money, equipment, space, the room, or size of class. Lack of adequate facilities for practical work may preclude other than a demonstration. Try to relate the method chosen to the expected length of concentration span of the group. Remember that this varies according to the age and ability of the group.

Teaching and learning activities

The activities chosen, therefore, will vary between a variety of combinations of the following: looking, listening, thinking and doing. With large groups of pupils, practical work for everyone is bound to be restricted. This means that alternative programmes of work must be chosen which place less reliance upon the existence of practical facilities. For example, food studies can be approached via experimental work on raw materials. This can be done by demonstration with pupil involvement brought in with exercises in sensory perception. Food appreciation panel testing also requires only a single person cooking at any one time. Good nutritional practice can be taught by an examination of the eating patterns of individual families. The breadth of knowledge of pupils is increased if these are sometimes looked at in a religious, historical or geographical context. Even if space and lack of facilities determine that your class remains captive in its seats, there are innumerable ways of presenting the material to be learned, if one thinks about it.

Selection of language

Having chosen the content and the method of presentation the choice of language is important. Speech is simply the means by which thoughts are put into action, so that they can be communicated to others. In teaching, thoughts based upon knowledge and experience are shared with those with less knowledge and less experience. In preparing what is going to be said during a lesson, the teacher engages in an intellectual exercise, the quality of which will rest upon his own knowledge and understanding of the meaning and the use of words. Each teacher is responsible for ensuring that pupils are introduced to the means by which intellectual development, through the understanding and use of words, takes place. This is done principally through two agents: the teacher and books.

Some home economics departments are curiously lacking in the range, number and quality of their books. They rely too heavily upon the teacher's spoken word and too little upon the stimulus, variety and breadth of the written word.

The teacher's choice of words is, therefore, very important. Student teachers would be well advised to work with a dictionary or thesaurus at hand both in preparation at home and at school. I have found the checking of the actual meanings of words and their spelling quite addictive. In school I realised that pupils from the age of seven years, derive great enjoyment from using a dictionary, finding alternative words with the same meaning, searching for hidden words, doing crosswords, finding missing words, etc.

Earlier it was said that pupils comprehend language at different levels. You will recall that infants understand spoken language long before they can read, and read before they can write their own composition. Thus vocabulary of greater difficulty can be used by the teacher than would be found in the books being read by the class. The level of written language produced by pupils will be lower than that which they are capable of reading. This means that a teacher constantly reviews goals in listening, reading and writing, to be achieved by a group.

Organisation and supervision
Organisation

Whether a class remains captive in its seats or mobile in a kitchen or laboratory it requires both organisation and supervision. Organisation enables a lesson to proceed smoothly with all the planned work being completed by teacher and pupils in the pre-determined period of time. It should plan for the safety of both persons and property.

Safety

The safety of persons relates to the correct use of tools and the observance of safe practice in the use of gas, water and electricity. Plotting traffic flow for practical class exercises ensures that pupils travel along recognised paths, do not run, do not carry hot irons, pans, food, etc, indiscriminately about the room. Pan handles are not allowed to project over the sides of a stove. Kettle spouts face the back of a stove.

Safe practice is necessary, too, in storage. Food is kept at all times well away from detergent packets, cleaning materials, bleaches and other harmful agents. Discarded food or drink containers are never used for the storage of detergents, bleaches, cleaning agents or other corrosive or poisonous agents. Remember that what you teach may save the life of an infant or toddler, realising that only a brief period of time separates school days from motherhood. Child development classes raise other aspects of safe conduct including the importance of cleanliness in personal and family hygiene and the control of infections and communicable diseases.

The Times newspaper (10 April 1980) carried the headline 'Bottle feeding on slides to save immigrant babies'. The article referred to the high mortality rate in this country, particularly among Asian babies. A tape slide programme to be shown in ante-natal and post-natal clinics to combat this was prepared by pupil midwives. The commentary, whilst encouraging mothers to breast feed, explained to those who cannot, or do not want to breast feed, how to sterilise bottles and mix powdered milk. It showed the results of incorrect feeding, in particular the dangers of giving babies too rich a mixture. The programme is marketed in Urdu, Bengali, Gujerati, Hindi, Punjabi, Turkish, Arabic, Armenian, Greek, Spanish, Dutch, Italian and French. This illustrates the enormity of the problem viewed from the outside, not by home economics teachers, but by those engaged in community health. Both share responsibility for education in this field, as the mothers referred to by the newspaper may currently, or in the future, be parents of pupils in school.

Activity time

Other areas of concern requiring organisation relate to the talking and/or activity time for teacher and pupils. Activities may include demonstration, class practical work, writing, reading, question time, etc. The timing for all these is important. Where possible, time a pre-run of a demonstration, time the activities of others, teachers, staff in the department, and other students. Extend this to the timing of certain manual skills, eg peeling a potato or apple, grating 100 g of cheese, rubbing 50 g fat into 100 g of flour, covering a pie dish, etc. This will help in planning your own demonstrations and in planning pupils' practical work. Double the time it takes you to complete the activity when estimating pupils' performance. It is necessary to remember, however, that individuals differ in speed. The latter will depend upon age, ability, experience, quality of mental and muscular co-ordination, and not least, the degree of motivation. Poorly motivated pupils can slow a lesson to a standstill, particularly when engaged in plebian tasks like washing up.

Pacing

It is appropriate here, to note the importance of pacing in lessons. Pupils need to be taught to respect and value time. Thus, the amount of time thought to be necessary for the completion of a task, should be adhered to where possible. Pupils who strive to do this should be praised and allowed to use any additional time gained in tasks of interest of their own choosing. Sometimes one observes in practice that these pupils are given additional cleaning or tidying jobs which had been allocated to their sometimes more wily and indolent fellows. Pupils need the challenge of pacing themselves in both mental and physical activities. Neither you nor they will know what they can achieve unless this is done. Sometimes, when faced by the unwilling, less able, or those lacking confidence, the teacher faces his most severe testing. It is at times like this, that the quality of personal rapport between teacher and pupil may be critical to optimum progress being made.

Group cooking times

Planning the length of group cooking times is also complicated. This will depend upon the number, portions and variety of dishes being cooked, the number of oven shelf spaces and/or hob positions. The length of lesson may not allow a shift system to be operated if all dishes cannot be cooked at once. It may, therefore, be necessary to chance the programme of work or the method of teaching/class practice. The ability to organise the latter efficiently depends upon having a clear view of the quantity and range of equipment available. Practical work involves a wide range of equipment. Some items like sinks, washing machines, stoves, tables, cupboards, are fixed in position. Pupils have, therefore, to be matched to equipment rather than the other way round. Teachers plan exactly the number and identity of pupils it is safe and efficient to use at each station. The use of small equipment like cutlery, utensils, baking trays, cake tins, is planned to ensure that the work proposed is possible within the constraints of available items. This includes relating the number of items in stock to the number of pupils, the order of use, the time when needed, the length of time in use and the method of using, for efficiency and safety.

Fabric care

When fabric care is undertaken, planning is necessary. Time is allocated to use the space in sinks, washing machines and drying cabinets. Time is estimated for drying, ironing, pressing and airing. On completion of work, all equipment is left ready for use by the next class. This is not regarded as a chore but as positive social education and good housekeeping.

Care of room and equipment

Pupils are trained in the procedural use and aftercare of all the equipment in a room. This makes for smooth organisation and supervision and reduces the time required to restore a room to rights at the end of a lesson. A check list is prepared of items to be scrutinised at the close of each session. Areas of common concern are laundering equipment (dish cloths and tea towels), refrigerator, ingredient table, waste bin, stoves and floor. These are dealt with best on a weekly rota system within each class, to ensure fairness.

Supervision

Supervision is a constant process whether pupils are sitting at their desks or moving freely about the room. Good organisation is a first step towards efficient supervision. Planning what is to happen, the time, the place, enables a forecast to be made of the supervision which is required. Nevertheless it is one thing to prepare and quite another to carry a plan into action. At first a student finds the sheer physical strain overwhelming: being on one's feet all day and using one's voice continually. It soon becomes clear, that in order to conserve strength, alternative action is necessary. Study the room where practical work is to be supervised. Select a position from which it is possible to survey the whole room. Try to use this as a station from which to supervise, not only the general operation, but much of the specific activity.

In practice a pan may boil over, there is a smell of pastry overcooking in the oven, someone is rolling pastry with too much flour on the board, another is dicing vegetables with peelings still on the table, water has been spilled on the floor and not wiped up. All such activities which need checking can be put to rights with a sentence from the teacher. The voice as stated before is such an asset. All that is needed is clarity and sufficient volume. Students are frequently very self-conscious initially about the sound of their own voice. Do use it, it will save your legs and ensure that you feel less tired. If you can see what is going on whilst sitting down, don't be afraid to do so. A tired teacher is not an efficient one, so take the necessary steps to conserve energy.

Supervision also relates to careful practice in the use of utensils, equipment, furniture, furnishings and the classroom environment. Attention to this by pupils is central to their social development. Some schools show evidence of little wear and tear after many years of use whilst others illustrate a careless and sometimes vicious abuse of both contents and environment. Responsibility and self-discipline by pupils is evident where books are neat, pages in them conserved and not disfigured. The same applies to the walls, the furniture and school generally not being vandalised.

Within the home economics room, equipment is fully represented and in good order. The finished dishes of fellow pupils are not picked at or abused. In needlecraft rooms, sewing machines and their covers are in good repair and working order. Supervision is one of the most exacting tasks in teaching a practical subject. Many hours will be spent by students thinking out organisation and supervision, and in trying to anticipate unexpected difficulties which may arise. All this routine planning is necessary. When once learned and mastered it will become almost automatic.

Resources for listening and viewing

There is a great temptation when selecting resources for listening and viewing, to do so with a lack of discrimination. Whatever is chosen for a lesson must be selective. It should illustrate, extend or re-inforce a particular point or theme. If at the end of the lesson no constructive use has been made of the supportive resource, consider, could it have been used or was it simply superfluous? There is a skill in choosing and using, such aids to learning and teaching. Most professional training courses recognise the importance of this by including highly specialised instruction for students in modern methods of communication. Many students achieve a very high standard of performance in this area of study. This is most rewarding for them and the pupils they teach. Self-made aids can be designed to lay emphasis on the precise knowledge which the teacher aims to communicate.

2 Performance
Opening the lesson

The beginning of a lesson is of supreme importance. It commences with the teacher calling for silence, and waiting for each pupil's full attention. To begin without full attention is fruitless. A first request may need re-inforcement. With ill-disciplined classes this can be an initial skirmish which it is well worthwhile pursuing and winning, since the success of what follows is likely to hinge on this. Class silence is followed by an appropriate greeting. Good morning 2B/boys and girls/everyone.

A statement of intent for the lesson follows this. Whilst this may include the essence of the written objectives of the lesson, it will not necessarily include them all, or in the manner in which they are written in the lesson plan. These introductory sentences are designed to inform the class what both teacher and class are going to do during the lesson. The introduction should be couched in terms which will arouse expectation, curiosity, anticipation and interest. The teacher's skill as a communicator at this stage may well decide the level of motivation of the individuals or class.

Skill as a communicator

Manner of presentation   The assessment of communication skills is largely subjective. Nevertheless, observers, ie teachers, pupils, tutors, do have a significant measure of agreement in stating those qualities which characterise good communication. Firstly, appearance should be smart, in a professional sense, ie workmanlike for the job to be done. This means neat, tidy, pleasing to the eye without being outlandish in appearance. In bearing the person should be business-like and friendly without being familiar. The voice should be clear, well-modulated and loud enough to be heard by all pupils. Dialects are unimportant so long as enunciation is clear and fully understood.

Choice of register is important with opportunity given for pupil progression in knowledge and understanding. New or unfamiliar words can be written on the board. This enables a visual image of the whole word to be captured. With younger pupils one can pretend that the eye is a camera. It is then fun to find out which cameras are functioning! Try also to get pupils to work out ways in which the spelling can be remembered, eg ba/na/na, to/ma/to, po/ta/to; in/gred/i/ents, re/frig/er/a/tor, de/lic/i/ous, temp/er/a/ture. As a variation present this sometimes as a new problem to you, the teacher. Pupils love to find the answer for you.

Aim to develop a rapport with each pupil group. This may prove difficult at first, particularly for those students who have had little to do with those younger than themselves. Note the teaching approaches which appear to evoke and sustain regular positive pupil responses, leading to levels of good motivation. Repeat and develop practice which is successful and discard that which is not. Try to use pupil response and incorporate it into the development of the lesson. Praise efforts to respond even if these are unexpected, incorrect or misguided as long as they are sincere. Encourage verbal communication between yourself and the class. Regular interchange of this nature will enable your own managerial skills to develop. Remember that the self-imposed discipline of waiting to be invited to answer a question is part of an individual's social education.

With older pupils, opportunity can be given for pupils to simulate the views of others through role play. This provides practice in damping down emotions or transferring aggression when dealing with controversial issues. It enables each individual to stand back and consider the problem before taking what could be violent action. During the period of consideration, a cooling off may take place and excessive emotional response evaporate. Dramatisation allows those with strong or pent up feelings to release them in a legitimate manner. Supervision of this kind of dramatic exercise is difficult for the inexperienced teacher. Such a lesson requires very thorough preparation by the teacher so that expected paths can be explored and the response by pupils anticipated. This enables appropriate teacher action to be planned.

Before dramatisation, both actors and audience must be made aware of exactly what behaviour is expected from them. Then if they do not comply during the performance, stop and return to other class work. It may be that the actors do not attend seriously to their roles or that the audience does not listen. One can use the strength of the peer group to stiffen the resolve of those pupils with less motivation. If neither actors or audience show a constructive interest, change the plan and do something else. There will always be another day to try again.

The management of time, money, equipment and other resources is difficult, but all of these pall into insignificance when one considers the most complex form of management, ie people. Many both inside and outside school, learn the principles underlying management techniques, but few exercise the art with conspicuous success, whilst at the same time exhibiting integrity, humanity and skill. Classroom interaction between pupils and teacher and pupils and their peers has been the subject of much research. Pupils look to the teacher to direct classroom activities in such a manner as to bring order and interest to the lesson and those engaged in it. Positive class management inspires a spontaneous, sustained interest towards a common goal. This brings out the best in people by promoting a higher level of motivation and a more positive performance.

In simple terms, interaction involves a making of choices. When a teacher manages his class, he is putting behavioural choices before the pupils and by subtle skill and design manoeuvring them along his path. Observation will indicate some of the choices which pupils make for themselves. For instance, they choose consciously or unconsciously, those with whom they feel at ease, or have most in common, to sit beside. Thus within a class small groups emerge which give substance to the expression, 'Birds of a feather flock together'. This grouping may have its roots in a common enjoyment in sport, or a particular hobby like dancing, cycling, model making, chess, etc. Or such affinities may derive from commonly held social or religious values which are rooted in the home, eg Christian, Jewish, Moslem. Sometimes it may simply be linked to a particular district or origin. Pupils who attended the same primary school continue these friendships through middle and high schools.

There are also personal differences which may seem to account for the company of one individual being more readily preferred to anothers. Given a free choice more people will wish to sit next to X than next to Y. It is interesting to ask children within a class to rank from one to three those they would choose for their companions. If these choices are then plotted on a sheet the resulting diagram is a sociogram. Careful observation and action by the teacher based upon patterns of preferred association within a class can be a powerful aid to discipline and harmony. This was illustrated in some schools which received large numbers of pupils from the West Indian Islands during a peak period of immigration. It was found that more harmonious groups could be formed in the home economics classes if pupils were placed initially with others originating from the same island.

Development of the lesson

This relates to the staging of the content and activity within the lesson from its commencement to its successful conclusion. It is concerned with the stage management of many of the aspects already discussed in the planning of the lesson. This includes the introduction, the selection and presentation of content relative to the quality, quantity and relevance of the chosen knowledge. Additional aspects are the timing of the lesson and the use during its execution of both teaching and learning aids. The mode of lesson presentation is likely to be left to the student to decide but the class teacher will offer advice on most of the aspects already discussed. Teachers expect students to bring into school up to date thinking and practice in education, research, the use of new food products, equipment and textiles. Some teachers regard an ongoing contact with students and their institute of higher education, on a par with participation in inservice education. School practice is a two-way experience. The student learns from an experienced practitioner and, in turn, hands on knowledge. This is done through the lessons which the student gives to the pupils.

Conclusion

The way in which a lesson is concluded will depend upon the type of lesson. It may require a summing up or recapitulation of the salient points. With experimental work there may be a discussion of results and from which conclusions may be drawn. Where dishes have been prepared, a comparison of them with comments on appearance, texture, taste, accompaniments, number of servings, cost and nutritive value may be made. Reasons for success or failure can be elucidated and consolidated so that in the future, success can be achieved or repeated.

3 Evaluation

Apart from those aspects above, a teacher may measure the extent of pupils' learning by oral or written questions. These may be given at the end of a lesson or for homework. A quick revision by questioning at the beginning of a subsequent lesson will indicate how much knowledge has been retained and the quality of that learning.

Summary of the general principles for course planning

Course content is considered at three levels:

1 The syllabus

(i) This is set out to fulfil long term aims

(ii) An examination syllabus is published by the appropriate examination board

(iii) It covers a set period of time

(iv) Course content is expressed briefly—often in headings only

(v) Large numbers of pupils in many schools follow the same syllabus

(vi) Non-examination syllabuses are planned by individual teachers.

2 The scheme of work

(i) This is a plan for action prepared from the syllabus by an individual teacher

(ii) It extends the brief outline of the syllabus identifying breadth of content and its appropriate level

(iii) It divides the content into yearly, termly, weekly and individual lesson portions.

3 The individual lesson

(See also Part 6, The curriculum).

Selected references and further reading

Department of Education and Science, Making induction work (pilot scheme, Liverpool and Northumberland), HMSO, 1978

Hall, O A and Paolucci, B *Teaching Home Economics,* John Wiley, Second edition, 1970

Part 4

Home economics teachers

1 The professional needs of home economics teachers

These may be determined by a careful study of home economics teachers working in a variety of situations. The list which follows was compiled for the University of Leeds Institute of Education investigation into the objectives of teacher training. It can be found in:

'The Objectives of Teacher Education', Leeds University Institute of Education, NFER, 1973, (pages 46-48)

The professional needs of the teacher

Knowledge of the content of the subject and of home economics as a science as well as an art;

Skill in selecting work in home economics to suit given groups of pupils and in preparing suitable schemes of work;

Knowledge of the needs of individuals and families;

Knowledge of the backgrounds and traditions of communities;

Skill in using this knowledge in teaching home economics;

Knowledge of the ways in which people live, and particularly of the home backgrounds from which the pupils come;

Skill in relating one's knowledge of pupils' home backgrounds to the teaching of home economics;

Knowledge of recent developments in home economics;

Skill in devising schemes of work, syllabuses and lesson plans in home economics;

Knowledge of pupils' previous work in home economics, and of their likely future work;

Knowledge of the curriculum in the home economics department as a whole;

Knowledge of pupils' work in other areas of the school curriculum;

Knowledge of themes and links within home economics and between home economics and other subjects;

Skill in relating work in home economics to pupils' work in other subjects;

Skill in the use of written and spoken English;

Skill in speaking to individuals, small groups, large groups;

Knowledge of methods appropriate to the teaching of home economics, and their advantages and limitations;

Skill in organising a class for individual and group work, and particularly for practical work;

Skill in organising and arranging material for a lesson;

Skill in demonstrating practical skills to individuals and groups;

Skill in presenting work in home economics at a level appropriate to a given class;

Skill in coping with a class of mixed ability in home economics;

Skill in handling in the context of the subject, pupils who are regarded as difficult in terms of their behaviour and motivation;

Skill in recognising, encouraging and guiding backward pupils;

Skill in organising and conducting visits outside the school;

Skill in promoting and maintaining discipline in the context of home economics;

Skill in devising and setting homework, and in marking and interpreting the work done;

Skill in writing, printing and drawing on the blackboard, etc;

Skill in making and displaying materials in the home economics room;

Skill in maintaining the home economics room and its equipment;

Skill in using aids such as a film projector, slide projector, tape recorder;

Knowledge of the materials used in association with these aids (eg film, slides, tape, felt pens) and skill in preparing materials for teaching purposes;

Knowledge of other resources available to aid the teaching of home economics (eg books, pamphlets, journals, apparatus) and where they can be obtained;

Skill in using the resources of the library in teaching home economics;

Knowledge of the techniques available for questioning and testing groups of pupils and individual pupils;

Skill in questioning groups and individuals;

Skill in constructing, setting and marking tests and examinations in home economics;

Skill in interpreting the results of tests and examinations in home economics;

Skill in initiating, maintaining and using personal and school records of pupils' work and progress, and other relevant information;

Knowledge of the system of external examinations and of the procedure to be adopted when entering pupils for external examinations;

Knowledge of elementary first aid;

Knowledge of the responsibilities of the head of a home economics department;

Knowledge of the procedures to be adopted in ordering and arranging the maintenance of equipment used in teaching home economics;

Knowledge of factors (including those of a legal nature) to be taken into account when taking pupils away from school for visits;

Knowledge of relevant courses in further education and of the opportunities in employment for pupils who have a particular interest in home economics.'

Selected references and further reading

Leeds University Institute of Education, The Objectives of Teacher Education, NFER Publishing Company, 1973

Hall, O A and Paolucci, B *Teaching Home Economics,* John Wiley, Second edition, 1970.

2 Implementation

Having identified the professional needs of home economics teachers it is the task of course directors in establishments offering professional training to translate those needs into the context of their own courses. This applies equally to concurrent and consecutive courses. The means by which the needs are satisfied in the courses will be different. Concurrent courses since they extend over a period of three years allow for a more gradual development by the student. On the other hand postgraduate students have the advantage of being able to draw upon the knowledge acquired during their specialist three year degree studies, which are already successfully behind them. They also bring an added maturity to their task. Even so, graduate entrants will be wise to learn as much as they can about their future tasks (in the post-graduate year) and their future role as home economics teachers by pre-course reading.

Let us now consider in more detail the reasons behind the selection of these particular course needs.

Knowledge of the subject

This is placed first on the list as the principal priority. The question which may be asked is, 'how much knowledge does a teacher need?' The logical answer is, 'far more than a pupil can readily absorb'. A practical means of seeing this measurement in action is to look at the career structure within secondary schools. It can be seen that departmental subject heads who are responsible for Advanced Level General Certificate of Education courses, ie university entrance work are honours graduates usually with a higher degree at Masters level or above. Ordinary level General Certificate of Education teaching is usually in the hands of graduate teachers. Certificate of Secondary Education and non-examination courses may be taught by non-graduate staff. There are, of course, exceptions to this, but this is the developing pattern in larger schools. One sees in schools, therefore, the recognition of an increasing need for a deeper and more specialised knowledge directly proportional to the level of ultimate attainment of the pupil being taught. An appreciation of this at the outset may greatly influence the choice of the initial Home Economics course undertaken by a prospective teacher. Perhaps it would be fair to argue that the greater the depth of study in a subject, the greater the knowledge of its underlying principles.

Knowledge of individual, family and community needs

If one accepts that education is concerned with the development of the 'whole' person then a teacher is involved in a far more complex task than one which is encompassed by subject boundaries alone. This was seen earlier to be the philosophy of Comenius, Pestalozzi and Froebel. Comenius introduced arts and crafts into children's education. He recognised the importance of developing a critical awareness of beauty and the means by which individuals can seek to achieve this.

By awakening a child to the joy of personal creativity an invaluable civilising force was being introduced, since it can be argued that those who create, do not then destroy. Pestalozzi and Froebel also subscribed to this view. Froebel was perhaps the most explicit when he described his pupils as flourishing like plants and developing the whole of their gifts. This implies a flowering of practical creativity as well as intellectual gifts. It is of equal importance that teacher education provides opportunity for a student to broaden, extend and cultivate, those aspects of his interests which derive from his cultural heritage. He may then in his turn and in his generation pass this on to others within the school.

The success attending the passing on of knowledge is dependent upon an understanding of the ways in which individuals learn and therefore can be taught. This entails a study of human development and behaviour. A knowledge of man's physical, mental, emotional and social developmental potential, enables methods of teaching and content appropriate to a pupil's age, ability and maturity to be structured. Piaget has perhaps had the greatest influence upon teachers and their teaching methods in recent times. Bruner, Eysenck and many others have contributed significantly by their researches and theories to the discussion, debate and practice of our age.

The 1960s saw an upsurge of interest in the study of man within his social setting by those who believed that environmental influences played an important role in man's development and subsequent behaviour. This included the influence of the immediate condition of the family and the wider environment of the community. Educational researches confirmed these theories and as a result, sociological studies now form an important part of all professional training courses for teachers. Home economics at all levels, in school, colleges, and university, reflects the importance of a knowledge of human development and sociological studies within the content of present courses.

Devising syllabuses, schemes of work and lesson plans

Each teacher plays only a contributory part in a pupil's total education. Similarly he plays but a small part in the teaching of a subject. If subject matter is to be taught in a relevant, understandable continuum then it must be organised. The preparation of syllabuses, schemes of work and lesson plans represent the organisation of subject matter in practice. Student teachers are introduced to the principles and practice of doing this. They engage within the Education Department, in simulation exercises against the time when this is done in practice, in school under the direction of a teacher. Simulation exercises may be video-taped by fellow students and played back to enable staff and students, to make a constructive appraisal of teaching performance. This is often referred to as micro-teaching.

The opportunity to plan groups of lessons is afforded by continuous teaching practice in schools, when students meet the same children, week by week and are then themselves, able to appraise their own developing skill as teachers, by assessing the performance of the pupils. The translation of syllabuses into schemes of work with a weekly breakdown into constituent lessons, also enables teachers to substitute for one another, at different times during a course or in case of staff absence. A specimen syllabus and scheme of work is usually prepared in the latter part of a student's training and if possible after experience of final teaching practice.

Curriculum links with other subjects

This can be viewed in two different ways. Firstly, there is obvious overlap in course content between a number of subjects. Secondly, general problems or issues of interest or importance may be viewed with advantage by other disciplines. Teachers are aware of both views. Some schools respond with co-operative teaching programmes. This has already been referred to in the overview of school practice in the middle years (Part 1, section 3). A whole year group may engage in thematic work when staff and pupils join in a common topic for investigation, eg How did they live—in Elizabethan times? Such a topic would include the historical context of the time. Pupils would explore the features of the country as it then was and its position within the then known world.

They would look at the government of the day and at an individual's constitutional expectations. Studies would include provision for education and services if any. Individual groups of pupils would examine likely occupations of the people and matters of health, safety, law and order, and family living. The latter would include the design and construction of houses and include the likely decor and furnishing. The management of the home would include a study of food, clothing, equipment and cleaning materials and methods for their use. Money and other means of exchange, would be examined. Pupils might well engage in role playing to identify the expectations of the age, for boys and girls, men and women.

As a team teaching exercise the parameters of the proposed activities would be set and agreed by the staff. The likely contributions of teachers according to their particular subject expertise would be explored. So the proposed contributions of staff and pupils would be decided. These contributions might be individual or group, in the guise of talk, models, tableaux, play, costume, sketches, poetry or prose. Modern technology would play its part in linking past and present with films, television, tape slide programme, radio or books. Community sources include local historians, museums, art galleries, costume collections, historic houses and their gardens. Such a teaching experience demonstrates not only the links between the subjects in the school curriculum but their common purpose in the whole canvas of education.

Links of another kind between subjects arise when content spills over into another subject area. This illustrates the common ground between subjects. For example, a science department teaches many scientific principles which are applied in the home economics room. For example, heat is applied during the preparation of a jelly. The use of hot water enables the jelly to melt and liquefy. This is a physical change. We know this because when the jelly cools it sets. The operation can therefore be reversed. However, when toast is made, the heat from the grill converts the starch within the bread to dextrin. This is a chemical change which cannot be reversed. Professor Tessa Blackstone argued recently that much work in science would be more readily learned, particularly by girls, if the materials used in experimental work were familiar, eg food.

Even closer links are visible in biology, health education and home economics. An examination of syllabuses in biology and home economics at General Certificate of Education Ordinary Level reveal that both require some identical knowledge. For example, a knowledge of the human digestive system, its functioning and the contribution of major nutrients to bodily health is required learning in both biology and home economics syllabuses. From the examples given one may begin to see that home economics is an excellent vehicle for education. For physical science, biology and health education may teach theoretical knowledge, but only home economics can teach the theory and follow this up by the practice in daily living.

Using written and spoken English

This is very closely linked with class management and control and involves talking to individuals and both large and small groups. It involves situations within the classroom and during various school day pursuits both about the school, in the yard or on the playing field. It includes such plebian tasks as class registration, collecting dinner money, doing 'yard' duty, first aid, and supervising classes travelling to and from assembly. Other activities include invigilating examinations, helping with the school play, Christmas parties, carol concerts and supervising detention. These are all aspects of teaching nevertheless and they all require skills which can only be learned by practice on the job.

What a gift a versatile voice is to a teacher. There are so many different 'voices' needed. These vary from the quiet word to an individual, quietening an unruly class, calling pupils to order in the hall or outside in the yard. Practice is needed in volume control, modulation and confident use of language suitable for a variety of situations. Sometimes facial expressions or a bodily gesture can be used instead of words. For example, the sharp clapping of hands to bring a group to attention, raising the eyebrows, beckoning, nodding and shaking the head. All these may be used to give tone and colour to your performance and are essential in developing management and control.

One of the most valuable aspects of early contacts with pupils lies simply in learning the art of mixing easily with children of differing ages. This does not come readily to all adults who have left their childhood behind and during their subsequent education, have been urged to adopt adult attitudes in behaviour, modes of speech and in both written and spoken expression. In the classroom one is at one and same time seeking to adopt attitudes of behaviour which are acceptable both in the adult sense of being an adult, appearing adult and yet being in sympathy with and readily understood by children, at the varying ages and stages of their development.

The same is true of the language one uses. A teacher has a tremendous responsibility in ensuring that the example which he puts before his pupils is one from which they can consistently learn. You will read elsewhere in your sociological studies, of the registers of language and in particular those registers which relate to one's social origins. Education can provide the greatest avenue for social mobility and language may be the biggest single factor in the practical expression of this. Language and being able to use it with confidence is perhaps the most valuable asset a child has both in school and in later life.

The teacher who adopts a stereotype, identifying with the popular usage of the media, the popular press or light entertainment, does nothing to help the pupils in his charge. The use of slang, OK, sure, current catch phrases and monosyllabic replies should be avoided. A teacher should encourage pupils to use sentences and to explore alternative ways of expressing the same view or information. If children use a wide range of language in written and spoken exchange it gives them assurance and a degree of social competence which they would otherwise lack.

This is a particularly important factor in education where pupils come from homes where a varied language is not used with confidence. Perhaps this derives from ignorance, lack of education, social constraints, or because the mother tongue at home is not English. For many children, the example in the development of the spoken word comes not from the home but only from the classroom. What misfortune befalls them, therefore, if the teachers speak only in the slang and current catch phrases of the day. It follows also that a teacher must wean away children already addicted to this practice and guide them into more profitable fields.

Talking with children plays a major role in the daily life of a teacher. It is good to study those who do it well and to seek accomplishment in this art. There are several aspects of this including talking, listening, responding and questioning. The latter is invaluable as a means of assessing knowledge and understanding, of that which has been taught. Questioning can arrest a pupil's wandering attention, enliven a lesson by stimulation and probe for knowledge already within the pupil's experience.

The written word

Allied to the spoken word is its written counterpart. It is an invaluable asset and may be used on question papers, handouts and on the chalk board. Pupils get used to their teacher's handwriting and complain bitterly when a different mode is presented to them, eg by a new teacher or a student. Clarity of form and expression is essential. Opportunity is given during professional training to learn the principles of writing and drawing on a chalk board. It is an art which can only be mastered by practice. Writing and drawing on the board can be a daunting prospect for a student who is at the same time concerned with controlling a class.

It is wise to plan the board so that parts are prepared beforehand with excerpts left to be filled in. The chalk board can be used with great profit to note down a build up of points (carefully thought out beforehand) during a lesson. Confident usage should be the aim. A dampened chalk stick will quickly dry to a bolder outline than a dry one will give. Coloured chalks can provide a contrast in diagrams to pick out different things, eg blue can be consistently used to indicate a tacking thread and yellow to show finished permanent stitching. In this way certain recognised lines of thinking can be engendered.

In the postwar years blackboards fell into disfavour and were replaced by green boards. These were said to be more restful to the eyes. Many postwar schools were not built with a fixed board at all, or if they were, these were white boards. These are not chalk boards but are used with a type of felt tipped pen. Writing can be removed with a cloth. Teachers do not seem to use these white boards with the same freedom and panache. This may be because they are a little more difficult to clean and present a rather smudgy appearance if alterations are required.

Boards in general are not used to the same degree as they were. This is due to changes in teaching methods and school design. The concept of open areas in many schools, embracing a number of small groups, has led to a decline in direct teaching. None the less all teachers should seek to develop skill in writing, printing and drawing on the board.

Knowledge and skills for effective teaching

As already stated and as your own experience will show, teaching demands personal qualities, knowledge and skill beyond the subject to be taught. Efficient class management and discipline, the right appearance, attitude and voice, the promotion of interest and learning via personality, the use of supportive aids and materials should be the concern of all teachers. For this reason Education Departments are now teaching intending teachers with different subject specialisms together, in the general principles of teaching practice.

The principles of teaching a specialist subject are usually taught by staff with a knowledge of the specialist discipline, backed preferably by a succesful and significant period of school teaching in that field. The James Report, 1972, specifically recommended that such experience, if not continuous should be revitalised at regular intervals. Teachers have to keep in touch with the current changes and influences in society and its schools. They have to come to terms with things as they are and the only way to speak about these with authority is to be a part of them.

Economic progress

Having witnessed some of these changes in a northern city over some thirty years, I have found that in physical terms children today have never been more robust. It is extremely rare to see a thin, under nourished child and pupils are on the whole extremely well dressed. In the same schools I vividly recall past children: those who stood up in the only clothes they had and those who could not come to school because they had no shoes. Today, pupils accept a modern flush lavatory as the norm in school, and in their modern homes nearby. In the same Victorian schools, the modernisation programme brought a thrill and excitement as the first individually flushed lavatories were installed. For some time these were more exciting than the classrooms, since most children did not have this facility at home.

On the same sites today, primary school children bring to school daily 10p to 20p to spend at the tuck shop. Whilst such schools are still thought of as being in educational priority areas, this relatively modern term would not mean the same today as thirty years ago. The average wages have risen to a level where people can provide for a family. The State welfare benefits buffer the unfit and unemployed. The City Fathers have provided, over the years, new schools and new housing for which they have reason to be proud. Why then are the same school sites educational priority areas? What is meant when head teachers speak of deprivation?

Home conditions affecting learning

Many pupils suffer from an unsettled family life, not a lack of money or material things. Some children are not talked to and lack needed parental companionship. Others are members of single-parent families. These may be 'latch key' children. Many homes are not harmonious places in which to live for a variety of reasons. Some pupils experience difficulty in school, because they are learning in a language foreign to their parents. This places stress not only on them, but on class teachers and fellow pupils as well. With older children there may be problems of glue sniffing, drugs, alcohol, smoking or whatever happens to be the current eccentricity of peer groups. It is fair to say that teachers in many schools face the same problems, to a greater or lesser degree, in a society which has experienced a period of widespread affluence.

Responding to this need

Professional training courses must come to terms with current teaching problems. The lecturing staff must be involved in schools, in order to guide student teachers to solutions or to achieve a compromise strategy for survival. For instance, teachers at middle and high school need to understand how to teach the rudiments of reading. Specialists, such as home economists, must be able to use their subject as a vehicle for teaching language.

Selecting teaching experiences

The need in general terms to be able to plan a syllabus and organise this into a workable scheme of work and individual lesson units has already been discussed. In practice this is a highly complex task since planning must relate to a wide range of pupils and to their age, ability, experience and expectation of the course. Early teaching programmes whether simulated or actual, can only be prepared successfully under experienced teacher guidance. However, a student can apply his own knowledge of social, economic, ethnic and cultural backgrounds to his planning according to a known school population mix.

For instance, a knowledge of foods and patterns of eating associated with Jews, Mid-Europeans, West Indians, Chinese, Indians, Pakistanis and the vagaries of the British indigenous population, is necessary now when teaching food studies and nutrition. Some schools have as many as thirty diferent nationalities among their pupils. Not only is a sound knowledge of food and nutrition necessary but an ability by a teacher to be able to translate this into a practice with which individual pupils from diverse homes can freely identify. The problem of individual identification does not relate only to food. It relates to clothing, furniture, laundry and cleaning practice, male and female roles, personal hygiene, child rearing and indeed almost every aspect of home economics teaching. Some of these individual differences are referred to later.

Apart from planning for these individual racial, social and economic considerations there are constraints relating to sex, age and ability. If an individual's interest and progress is to be maintained, regard must be given to experiental knowledge and skills. These may derive from the home or from school. Current teaching should reflect that which has gone before and be undertaken also in the light of that which is to follow. This relates not only to courses undertaken in home economics, but also to those followed by pupils in the rest of the curriculum.

As indicated before, schools vary in the degree of discussion and co-operation, which takes place between staff teaching different subjects. On the one hand staff may group together as a team and undertake a topic common to them all, or staff may simply as individuals agree to collaborate. For instance Mr Brown (science) may agree to carry out work in chemistry on mixtures and compounds before Miss Smith (home economics) illustrates this in the preparation of french dressing and mayonnaise. A teacher's knowledge of the work covered in other subject areas can be most profitable. Often a friendly interest in a colleague's work can be the pre-cursor to active collaboration. When this does exist, in either team teaching or personal contact, it gives added support to the inexperienced teacher.

Teaching methods used in home economics

In home economics, teaching is addressed to individuals, small groups and large groups, by direct teaching (including practical demonstration), indirect teaching (through investigatory exercises) or to older students at a seminar/tutorial session. All methods have their strengths and weaknesses depending on the situation, the teacher and the pupils. The aim is to select and use the appropriate method of teaching for the task in hand. Successful teaching is measured by this.

Class organisation

Implicit in a correct choice of teaching method is a knowledge of class organisation. This may take the form of organising a whole class (direct teaching), group work or individual investigatory work. Often pupils' practical work is involved. The latter seems at first to pose almost insuperable problems for the student teacher. There seems to be so much to know, plan, prepare, organise, supervise and evaluate. Only by a disciplined evaluation of each lesson, followed by amendment in subsequent lessons in the light of experience can pupils' learning and a teacher's teaching be improved. This involves an appraisal and re-appraisal of the substance of lessons, modes of organisation, and the presentation of teaching at a level appropriate for the class(es) concerned. The latter presents great difficulty in home economics since many classes (particularly in middle school and the early forms of high school) contain pupils with a wide range of ability.

There is a great temptation to pitch a lesson mid-way between the optimum possible performances of the pupils of the highest and lowest abilities. If this is done, disciplinary problems usually follow. The least able finding the work too difficult may opt out and apply themselves to other less desirable activities. The most able on the other hand, finding the work too easy, finish early and may also put their spare time to undesirable disruptive purposes. The lesson has, therefore, to be structured to give individuals or groups of individuals, work commensurate with their ability. This demands skill and ingenuity and taxes even the most experienced practitioner. Students who are introduced early to the structuring of lessons for mixed ability classes by enthusiastic college tutors and teachers in school, seem to master this method of teaching remarkably well.

The reluctant learner

It has been said earlier, that failure to organise a class effectively can result in disciplinary problems. This may arise with pupils who for one reason or another do not have the will, wish or intention of conforming to a learning situation. An awareness of the possible or probable reasons for this, whilst not providing a panacea or simple answer, can help to suggest a range of teacher responses to try. Such information may be found in your studies in human development and psychology, arising from the research and experience of others. Further insight may be derived from the class or home economics teacher, or from your own experience as this grows. For example, some pupils regularly do not bring money, ingredients, dishes, aprons, etc, so that they cannot participate fully in the work of the group. If there are no apparent family reasons for this, but the reluctance to learn appears to derive from an unwillingness to co-operate, then alternative theoretical work may be given.

It may be pertinent to note here, that practical lessons can be rejected by whole classes, if recipes are unbalanced resulting regularly in a poor finished product. Similarly, if teacher organisation of oven management allows overcrowding or insufficient time for cooking, the resulting imperfect products whether burned or semi-cooked, will not bring approbation at home and may result in parental non-co-operation. This is important since all practical classes in home economics, whether they be food or clothing, are dependent upon parental financial support. Parental co-operation and goodwill is therefore to be sought after and recognised with appreciation.

Pupils who are persistently non-co-operative may as a last resort have to be excluded from a class. Handling difficult pupils is a skill which develops with practice and experience. Older colleagues (head of department, head of year or head of school) will help in this respect. Really difficult pupils are known by all staff throughout a school and a policy for dealing with such pupils is usually well established. It is profitable to study the methods employed by individual staff members in coping with such problem pupils.

Learning on the job

Students and young teachers working in a team teaching context are ideally placed to study and evaluate organisational and disciplinary methods employed by their older colleagues. They learn which methods to ignore and which to emulate. Aspects of organisation relating to the use of money, time, equipment, resources, space, the demands of safety, good health and hygienic practice are all important. Study too, the differing performance of pupils in the same class. Note those who appear to be slow and fall behind. Does this happen regularly? Why does it happen? Are these pupils physically handicapped in some way through a weakness in sight, hearing or other disability? For instance, does a pupil walk with the aid of a caliper or is he considered delicate, by virtue of a weak heart or some other physical cause? Is a poor or indifferent attendance the problem? If so, is this due to illness or to truancy. If the latter, is the truancy general, or does it apply only to your lessons? Perhaps the pupil suffers from a mental handicap which renders him less able than his fellows? Whatever the cause seek to identify it, consider all possible options for dealing with it and then act. Skill is essential in this field so that the appropriate encouragement and guidance can be given.

Skill in selecting work for able pupils

Where the learning of motor skills is concerned sometimes the intellectually able appear awkward, uneasy and lacking in confidence. These children need added encouragement and patience in helping them to enjoy practical activities whether these involve craft skills, athletics, games or other physical activities. Gifted pupils enjoy the challenge of using words. Tasks involving crosswords, finding hidden words, creating verse, looking up the meanings of words, suggesting alternative words, all give immense satisfaction. Assignments which involve interpretation, investigation, extrapolation or calculation may kindle the spirit of exploration in the able, not only sustaining interest but opening up new frontiers to be won. By devising suitable tasks for pupils, commensurate with a known ability, a teacher enables those pupils to use both mind and fingers fully. This enables pupils to feel the joy of achievement through progression. Where such children are denied intellectual satisfaction they may appear sullen, unco-operative, or downright disruptive. I have found that some pupils enjoy the spirit of conquest in the ways suggested as early as six and seven years of age. By the age of eight years some pupils show keenly developed skills. Such evidence leads one to conclude that often too little is expected of pupils in the middle and later years in school.

Homework

Intending teachers also need to develop skill in devising tasks, to be set and carried out by pupils at home. Schools vary in their attitude to homework. Some do not give any, others encourage it. Observe on visits to the primary school, that even children in the reception class go home clutching a first reader. This encourages parents to help with early first steps in their child's reading. In a home in which English is not the mother tongue an infant and his mother may even learn the first steps in the language together. At this early stage 'homework' may consist of two or three words written on a sheet of paper by the teacher, which are to be found in the reader and which are to be learned. It is from such a humble beginning that a 'word bank' is gradually built up. The teacher-pupil-parent relationship is critical at this stage. It can shape the whole future attitude of a child to reading and so, to education. For if a child cannot read and does not have a positive attitude to learning, what possible future is there for his progression along the educational road? Would it be too emotive to say, that at this stage a child's life chances are decided?

Perhaps this is not a usual view of 'homework' but nevertheless, it is 'homework' relative to a pupil at this particular age and stage in his development. Teachers of pupils at any age may decide (unless it is against the policy of the school) to set homework. It may be seen to serve a useful purpose in consolidating that which has been learned during the day at school. From a teacher's point of view it serves as a guide in indicating whether or not a pupil has understood what he has learned. Skill in marking and interpreting the work done is shown by the teacher's consequent action in deciding whether further explanation or consolidation is necessary before proceeding to the next stage in the programme. Results of homework indicate whether problems arising relate only to individuals or to a whole group. Thus, it provides a valuable means of assessing the understanding and progress of both the individual and the group. It therefore acts as an early warning system, which enables a teacher to pick out those pupils who are struggling.

Over recent years homework has become less popular as evening television programmes have become more and more seductive in engaging pupils' interest. Many schools do not set it for the school population as a whole. These schools tend to confine its use to those classes entering pupils for external examinations only. Indeed there are those who would advocate its total abolition. I feel that surely there must be a middle road which can be followed. Total abolition seems to infer that there is something distasteful in the studies undertaken. If this is so then surely as teachers we have failed? Then again, if the studies followed at school are enjoyable then it is reasonable to suppose that to pursue them further will give additional proficiency which will in turn bring an extra satisfaction.

Evaluation in home economics

Closely associated with developing skill in selecting and interpreting homework is the ability to construct, set and mark tests with understanding.

Formal practice is already established in this field in both written and practical examinations. This has evolved over a long period of time. It follows the same general principles as those used in other disciplines and students will learn about these during their professional training. The construction, setting and marking of practical tests is very complex. The criteria by which practical work is marked is difficult to define accurately. When analysed and applied, a consensus of opinion on individual component marks is often difficult to agree. I and others have observed, however, that experienced teachers do not generally disagree over a final aggregate mark. It is just that they arrive at the same destination having followed different paths. Nevertheless, the marking of practical work whether it be in food, clothing, art or craft, will always remain to a certain degree, subjective.

Students working alongside teachers in schools in the spring and summer terms, will have the opportunity to observe the marking of practical examinations set by the validating boards, for the Certificate of Secondary Education (16+), the Certificate of Extended Education (17+), and the General Certificate of Education Ordinary Level (16+) and Advanced Level (18+). Teachers are very willing to explain the various systems to students and often allow them to mark in tandem, comparing results at the end of a session. This provides the necessary guide lines and confidence for carrying out similar tasks in school during an appointee's probationary year.

Interpreting written and practical results

What then can be derived from the results of practical and written tests? Examinations or tests are given to establish a pupil's knowledge and understanding of the course which he has undertaken. In school this will test the quality of the information recalled and the ability to use this knowledge in a variety of situations to solve the problems set. Appropriately constructed tests will reveal not only the ability of a pupil but enables the teacher to place him in rank order with his contemporaries. This knowledge is required by a teacher in order to plan work commensurate with an individual's ability and attainment.

The performance of a group as a whole, will give a teacher a measure of the value of the course taken. In the light of this performance, courses can be modified or improved if different outcomes are desired. When national examinations are undertaken which are marked or moderated externally this enables a teacher to assess his pupils' performance relative to that of pupils in other schools. In the case of the Certificate of Secondary Education this give a local comparison of pupils within a region. With the General Certificate of Education the comparison is nationwide.

Written profiles of pupils

Part one discussed briefly the records which are kept relative to a pupil during the whole of his career. Class teachers are usually responsible for collating each pupil's marks in primary and middle schools. In high schools this is usually the task of a personal tutor. The year tutor in middle and high schools holds a complete profile (including performance) of each pupil in the year for which he is responsible. In primary schools the written profile of all pupils is held by the head teacher. Individual teachers have, therefore, to develop an organised means of recording the attainment and progress of each pupil in his care in each area of the curriculum. This profile will include attitudes to fellow pupils, staff, study, honesty and any distinct behavioural traits. Any physical disabilities are recorded. For example, 'A' must not indulge in strenuous physical exercise because he has a weak heart.

From time to time the public gaze focuses upon the keeping of pupils' personal written profiles in school. There are those who argue that all records should be freely accessible to parents. Others reason that certain matters are better kept confidential to the school. This information may relate to factors which are known to influence a child's performance which derive from the home. Such knowledge is invaluable to a subsequent school when a pupil moves. It avoids the time wasting and often damaging exercise of rediscovering particular problems. If school records were all freely available to parents, then knowledge relating to home circumstances could not be included and a pupil's progress might be impeded.

Maintenance of a home economics room

A thorough grounding in the choice, performance and care of equipment forms part of all home economics courses. In a technological age this knowledge must be soundly based upon scientific principles and practice. In school several hundred pupils may use the appliances in a room each week. For the protection of the pupils and the economic use of equipment, rules for use are essential. These relate to the safe usage, care, cleaning and maintenance of equipment. First establish those rules which are necessary. Try to make these as few as possible. Make sure that they are clearly understood and practised by each and every pupil. Similarly rules will apply to the use of services such as gas, electricity and water. Other rules relate to the use and storage of dangerous chemicals, for example, detergents, bleaches and other cleaning agents. Simple rules for the hygienic use and care of dishcloths, floor cloths, tea towels, bowls, buckets and sinks are necessary. The safe use of knives, scissors and other potentially dangerous equipment both small and large is taught and practised.

Responsibility for the practice of these guide lines lies in the hands of both pupils and teacher. Full confident, working independence will only be experienced by pupils when they know and understand this. Potential dangers such as frayed flexes, loose plugs, leaking electric kettles or washing machines need expert attention. In the meantime, label the defective equipment and take it out of circulation. Civilised behaviour in the room at all times lessens the incidence of breakage, or damage to equipment. This is a valuable social training for pupils, since the room and its contents belong neither to the pupils, nor teacher. Jointly they are the custodians during their stay in school. The general appearance of a home economics room and its contents and the degree to which its equipment is functional, can sometimes be a measure of the exercise of social responsibility, by both pupils and teacher. The exercise of constraint, restraint and informed use of appliances and equipment is critical. The safety and even lives of the pupils may depend upon it. Today this practice may be concerned with school and home only. Tomorrow it will extend into the place of work whether it be factory, office, restaurant or food store.

The law and the teacher

The Health and Safety at work, etc Act 1974, introduced a new awareness of the responsibilities of employers to employees and *vice versa*. Teachers at their place of work in school, are protected in the same manner as other exployees under the Act. In their turn, teachers have a responsibility for the pupils in their care. Teachers working in kitchens, laboratories, workshops, etc, have far more potential danger spots to supervise than the teacher working in a classroom. The law requires that a teacher exercises the same care in the supervision of the pupils as would a careful parent. This relates not only to the supervisory aspect of the work but also to a reasonable choice of activity in the first place.

Thus if an accident does occur both factors will be carefully examined. Let us suppose that a pupil suffers burns as a result of working at a gas cooker where curtains at a nearby open window have blown over a lighted gas jet and have themselves ignited. It could be argued that the pupil acted irresponsibly in working in that situation. The siting of the gas cooker was not the initial responsibility of the teacher. However, the teacher could control the hanging of the curtains, the opening of the windows, the choice of which equipment is used, who uses it and the supervision of it.

The question is, 'Did this teacher exercise a reasonable control?' Home economics kitchens and laboratories are full of potentially dangerous equipment, substances and situations. The maximum time possible should be spent in a consideration of the safe usage of equipment, storage of dangerous substances and the planning and organisation of safe class practice. The area is too dangerous to be left to chance or intuitive practice, both for pupils and teachers.

Work out a definite policy for using irons, ovens, pans, chip pans, sewing machines, kettles, mixers, etc. Spell this out to the pupils as they need to use them and insist on compliance. Remember that spread of infection and contamination are also the concern of the Health and Safety at Work, etc Act. Good hygienic kitchen practice includes the handling and storage of food whether it be shelf food or that usually kept in a freezer or refrigerator.

The supervision of activities outside school

This poses many problems not normally met within the school. Outside activities include visits, field trips and holidays both in this country or abroad. Travel may be by foot, car, coach, train, sea or air. Pupils may look around an exhibition or visit a store to select and puchase fabrics for a dress task. In these instances pupils may be crossing busy streets, boarding public transport or passing through a crowded store. Most schools have an agreed pupil to staff ratio for such activities. Prior to leaving the school premises pupils need careful instruction on the procedure to be followed and the time to be apportioned to each activity. The teacher supervises the crossing of roads with everyone observing the usual pedestrian procedures. On public transport, the display of socially acceptable behaviour by pupils is the responsibility of their teacher(s) towards fellow travellers, the conductor and the driver. If a teacher feels unable to control pupils competently it is wiser to refrain from escorting them outside school.

In crowded stores close supervision is difficult and may prove impossible. A careful choice of pupils or painstaking oversight is essential otherwise a teacher may find himself the unknowing and unwilling accomplice in a shoplifting exercise. On trips further afield entailing longer periods, for example field trips or visits abroad, the teacher/pupil ratio is increased. This enables staff to rest and relax when not on duty. Nevertheless the criteria of 'reasonable care' is applied and pupils cannot be allowed to roam the streets by day or night in search of their own entertainment.

Accident procedure

Should an accident occur to yourself, or a pupil, either inside or out of school it should be reported immediately. Each school has an 'accident' procedure which relates to staff and to pupils. It should be followed exactly since it is designed for the protection of a teacher should things, subsequently, go wrong. It is usual during the professional training course, for the legal adviser to one of the teachers' professional bodies, to visit Education Departments, to advise student teachers on their legal responsibilities to pupils and safeguards relating to professional appointments and employment.

Aids to learning and teaching

Never in the history of teacher education, has it been more important for intending teachers to be properly skilled in the making, displaying and using of aids to learning and teaching. The learners, ie the pupils, are accustomed to being confronted by the most sophisticated visual and audio presentations on television, film, radio, advertising, newspapers and magazines. They are bombarded by the most skilful practices in persuasion that have ever been experienced. This creates a situation which is at one and the same time a blessing and a curse. It is a blessing, in that these sophisticated means of presentation have been simplified to become sufficiently economic for them to be used in school. This means, that the modern teacher must be able to design, construct and mount presentations using graphics, photography, transparencies, films, tapes, tape slide programmes, overhead projectors, etc. He must be able to handle with dexterity the relevant machines and machinery. This also includes the means of reproduction, ie photocopier and duplicator. Typing is recognised as the most efficient medium for presentation for instruction sheets, notes and question papers in school and for a student's own course work. Some home economics courses now include typing and basic office practice.

The range of resources now available for the teaching of home economics is such, that the filing, storing and lending of those resources in large establishments necessitates a more organised and business like approach to this facet of a teacher's work. A knowledge of how and where to find relevant information, within libraries, museums, industrial or research establishments, etc, both at a local and a national level is essential. The 'blessings' mentioned above are obvious since never before has there been so much knowledge or so many resources at the disposal of practising teachers, to enable them to present lessons in a stimulating and informative manner. Conversely, from a student's standpoint (particularly the student undertaking a one year professional training), there has never been so much to know, to know how to do and to prepare and store, before and during teaching practice.

For this reason alone, a one year professional training course will prove to be the busiest, fullest, but nevertheless most rewarding year of a student's life. Much can be done during pre-course preparation to ease the way by reading and acquiring some of the very necessary skills outlined above.

Home economics in the curriculum
Nineteenth century

Home economics as it is known today was preceded in the school curriculum by housecraft, domestic science, and even earlier, by the teaching of separate subjects, needlework, cookery and home management. Needlework was included within the earliest teacher training programmes at Battersea Training College which was founded by Sir James Kay-Shuttleworth in 1840. All women pupil-teachers at that time participated in the College needlework classes and were expected in each year of their course, *'to show increased skill as seamstresses, and teachers of sewing, knitting, etc.'* ('The Education of the Adolescent' (page 8) HMSO, 1964). These teachers taught principally pupils below the age of eleven years. At that time even primary schooling for everyone was not yet statutory. For the few female pupils above the age of eleven years needlework also formed a part of the curriculum.

The National School at King's Somborne in Hampshire was distinguished at the time for the breadth of its curriculum. An Inspector of Schools said of it in 1847, *'among the most interesting features of the Girls' Department was the Needlework, the elder girls are taught not only to work, but by paper patterns to cut out work for themselves, and the dresses of the First Class on the day of my examination were many of them thus cut out and all made by themselves.'* When one considers the costume of the time, the age of the girls and the limits of handstitching, that was no mean achievement. Most early records indicate, that needlework had a secure place in the curriculum of all schools with female pupils. The teaching of domestic economy was recognised in 1846 when gratuities were given to those schools providing satisfactory instruction. The teaching of laundrywork and home management did not receive grant aid until 1900.

Specialist Schools to train teachers in domestic subjects were introduced in the early 1870s. The present specialist institutions in London, Leeds, Liverpool and Bath, have their roots in these early institutions. In 1876 the Northern Union of Schools of Cookery was established. This brought together representatives from the schools of cookery, universities, education and other interested professional people. They planned, assessed and validated the earliest teacher training courses. This continued until central government introduced universal elementary education and the training of teachers became the responsibility of a Central Board. (The Northern Union of Schools of Cookery is no more, but its successor, The National Council for Home Economics Education, now validates courses for students over the age of sixteen years who are engaged in further education courses below degree level. These courses prepare students to enter a wide range of vocational positions in industry, commerce and the social services.)

From the first, schools were established in the nineteenth century, to provide education for the children of the poor. Their aims were twofold. Firstly, to give a definite training with a vocational emphasis so that the earning power of children would be greater when they left school. This was coupled with instruction in habits which would promote work and thrift. Secondly, to impart a general education.

Twentieth century

Home economics has its roots, in that education deemed to be appropriate and sufficient for the children of the poor, in the nineteenth century. Courses in school reflected elements of that philosophy, right through the early twentieth century and the lean years preceding the Second World War. During that same period the name of the subject had moved from domestic economy to domestic science to housecraft.

The boom years of housecraft in schools

The early postwar years saw a tremendous expansion in housecraft in schools. At its height pupils in the secondary modern schools (who were not then constricted by external examinations) followed a four year course during the secondary school programme which lasted from eleven to fifteen years of age. During that period the course was arranged as follows:

First year	quarter day
Second year	half a day
Third year	three quarter day
Fourth year	a whole day.

The time devoted to needlework was additional to the above and ranged from one hour in the first year to half a day in the fourth year; home economics kitchens were lavishly fitted with as many as twelve cookers for expected maximum classes or eighteen pupils. The home economics curriculum was very varied and embraced studies in food, health, hygiene, child care, home management, budgeting, craft, soft furnishing and basic interior decorating. Generally the studies were confined to the housecraft department with little active involvement either by pupils or teachers in other areas of the school curriculum.

A time for expansion

Educational building and expansion continued during the sixties and into the early seventies. The latter saw large numbers of immigrants arriving from the West Indian Islands and the Continent of India. These represented an enterprising minority of those countries who were seeking a better life for themselves and their families. They appreciated, like the early pioneers in education, that the latter would bring to their children greater social mobility and economic independence. In 1973 the expulsion of Asians from Uganda brought a further influx of immigrants. During this period, too, major changes were taking place in the educational structure of schools and the curriculum within them. These changes, have had a great influence upon the present position of home economics in schools today.

Selective schools

The 1944 Education Act (Butler) advocated educational opportunity for each individual according to his ability and need. The implementation of this Act resulted in a secondary school system which comprised grammar, technical and secondary modern schools. Selection based upon academic potential and attainment took place at the age of eleven plus. Grammar schooling was for the first time free to all. It was intended to provide a more academic education for the top twenty per cent of the school age population. Even so many Local Education Authorities exceeded this provision and the figure rose in some areas as high as twenty-eight per cent. Pupils in secondary modern schools who made rapid progress could sit another examination at thirteen years of age. If successful they could then transfer to a grammar school. 1951 marked the introduction of the General Certificate of Education. This was a single subject certificate and replaced the School Certificate (a grouped subject award).

The middle of the fifties saw secondary modern schools themselves introducing the General Certificate of Education at Ordinary Level. 'Late developers' in secondary modern schools tended then to stay in their own schools until sixteen years of age. Many pupils prospered in this climate where the pace was not so rigorous as would be found in a grammar school. Classes for examination subjects were very small and pupils sometimes had almost individual tuition. Candidates who were successful could then, if they so wished, transfer to the sixth form of a local grammar school to study Advanced Level General Certificate of Education subjects. Many then passed into Higher Education having travelled there by this alternative route. The writer has met a number of able students in Higher Education who felt very strongly that their ultimate success was due to the small class tuition and steady pace they had experienced in their secondary modern schools.

The egalitarian movement

The sixties and seventies witnessed many changes in society. Demands for a more egalitarian social structure brought with them many significant changes in education. It was argued that since monetary rewards and social prestige came more readily to those who had followed a grammar schooling then those schools were socially divisive. The remedy lay, it was maintained, in providing one school which would embrace all pupils of the same chronological age (whatever their ability). This theory satisfied those who argued that single sex schools were divisive since certain subjects, for example, home economics, woodwork and metal work were usually confined to a traditional female or male setting. It was argued that there would be the maximum opportunity for everyone, regardless of ability or sex, in a mixed all ability school in which the only means of selection was that of chronological age.

Comprehensive schools

Thence began a movement towards comprehensive education. In the early to mid-seventies, the majority of local education authorities complied with the Labour Government's directive, to 'go comprehensive'. The direct grant schools were abolished. They were given the choice of being absorbed into the maintained sector, or accepting complete financial responsibility for their own future, by entering the independent sector of education. Some chose the former path but the majority of direct grant schools opted for the latter and are now wholly independent. It would be fair to say that the majority of children in this country are educated today, in chronologically arranged mixed schools.

Consequent changes in the curriculum

The theory of equal opportunity for both male and females is illustrated in practice in Part One, where it was seen that boys and girls, usually followed a common curriculum in schools, until fourteen years of age. This marked the beginning of a choice of subjects in keeping with an individual's ability, performance and future aspirations. One might have expected that since boys and girls now engaged in home economics, that school timetables would show a greater amount of time devoted to the study of this subject, with more specialists in home economics in schools. This is not so for a number of reasons. The most significant of these, was a further outcome of the move towards equality in opportunity for all pupils.

This led to a mushrooming of subjects within the school curriculum. Some were new and others an extension of existing ones. The playing of instruments was actively encouraged in some primary schools, many middle schools and all secondary schools. This often involved individual tuition. At secondary level specialised forms of physical education made their appearance in many schools, for example skating, riding, canoeing, gymnastics, ballet, etc. The scope of games broadened from cricket, football, netball and rounders to encompass swimming, tennis, lacrosse, hockey and specialised athletics. Drama flourished and often found a special niche within the timetable in many schools.

A new examination

In 1965 a Certificate of Secondary Education examination was held for the first time. This important innovation introduced a school leaving examination for the forty per cent of pupils in an ability range, immediately below the twenty per cent for whom the General Certificate of Education was designed. With the introduction of this new examination came a further widening of the subject options. Thus under one roof, the comprehensive schools had a dual examination system, an ever widening diversity of courses and subject options within these courses. The amount of time devoted to subjects within the school curriculum, therefore, steadily diminished to a level related to the minimum amount of time required, to cover an examination syllabus. Fewer courses were studied for 'their own sake' or for pure enjoyment and more were pursued in the hope of examination success.

The dual system of examination produced staffing problems, in that staff were needed for both GCE and CSE classes. Often the numbers of pupils in each examination group was small because of the wide number of options offered. To make staffing economic GCE and CSE classes were sometimes merged. This meant that neither group actually followed the syllabus prescribed for the original target examination. Schools then began to enter some pupils for both examinations. A proposal that the two examination systems should merge, was gradually moving a step nearer. The mid-eighties should see this become a reality.

The effect of change on home economics

The consequences of the above changes upon home economics within the school curriculum may be summarised as follows. In the middle school and in the early years of the high school, a wider range of subjects within the school curriculum, has meant a smaller share of time allowed for each. Equal opportunity for the sexes has meant that the resulting time is shared between both boys and girls. In middle schools the complexion of home economics has altered as whole class participation, less specialist facilities and a differing philosophical approach to teaching in the middle years, has re-shaped the curriculum. In the high school home economics is one of very many subject options offered. Figures show that few boys choose to study it. It is a popular choice for girls in the Certificate of Secondary Education. In the General Certificate of Education at Ordinary Level a significant number of girls are entered but few go on to take the subject at Advanced Level. It can be shown, therefore, that although home economics has been treated fairly and although the time spent in its study by boys has increased in the last twenty years, the time spent by girls has decreased enormously.

What then of the future?

A dramatic drop in the school population has led Chief Education Officers to forecast a substantial narrowing of subject choice within the school curriculum. School staffing is based upon a teacher to pupil ratio regardless of subject needs. This in secondary schools at the present time is on average 1:16.9. This ratio includes the head teacher and must take account of other non-teaching commitments undertaken by other staff (see Part 1). Thus as a school population drops, so the number and diversity of subject specialists drops also. Already some middle schools' headteachers are forecasting that home economics may disappear from their schools as the curriculum narrows. It has already disappeared from some high schools. Home economics will continue to decline within the school curriculum unless teachers themselves believe in the contribution which it can make in the education of each individual. Furthermore they must be able to convince others of its value in a confident, vocal and positive way.

Vocational opportunities in home economics

The recently published report by Her Majesty's Inspectors 'Aspects of Secondary Education in England' (1980) noted that the 'lower ability bands' within schools usually had more practical and general subjects. One is reminded of the early aims for Primary Education in the nineteenth century (as reported in *Hansard*, Vol. XX, col. 159-161)

'The schools of industry would have two objects in view:
(i) The imparting of what might be termed scholarship;
(ii) The knowledge of some trade.'

Is it unfair and unkind to suggest that some practice of secondary education as quoted in the report (1980) might be interpreted in a similar fashion? There is a difference if one remembers that the nineteenth century curriculum was designed for the children of the poor. The twentieth century report relates to a curriculum designed for all children none of whom are as poor as their nineteenth century counterparts. They are of secondary school age but are within the lower ability group.

Her Majesty's Inspectors were also disturbed to find that twenty per cent of 'choices' of subjects in secondary schools were made by pupils without any specific guidance by careers teachers. Prospective home economics teachers can benefit their future pupils enormously by using wisely those two pieces of information from the recent reports. It should be noted that forty per cent of the present school population should quite properly be expected to leave school without formal school leaving certificates. There is at present no examination designed for the lowest ability group. If pupils are directed at school into courses of a practical nature then these should be designed with any specific vocational outlets in mind. Home economics courses in further education are at present under review. It is hoped that these will eventually become a part of the new national structure for examining courses within further education.

At the time of writing there are courses for students validated by the National Council for Home Economics Education with differing levels of entry. These range from no formal qualifications at sixteen, to four General Certificate of Education Ordinary Level subjects (or their equivalent) at sixteen, to one Advanced and four Ordinary Level General Certificate of Education subjects at eighteen. Courses at degree level in Home Economics (BA or BSc) are offered at a number of establishments of higher education. These require two General Certificate of Education subjects at Advanced level for entry at eighteen years. Since all validating bodies prescribe individual requirements, teachers must keep up-to-date with these. Special guidance in these matters is often the province of the careers teacher. A good knowledge in this field is an asset to a teacher when seeking promotion.

The career structure for teachers

A knowledge of this is important to an intending teacher before embarking upon an initial course at eighteen years of age. Dependent upon a person's ability, current and possible future aspirations, so will such an initial course be chosen (Part 3). Having completed a professional training then the pattern of teaching experience should where possible relate to one's future goal. An awareness of additional courses to maintain and enhance the initial education and training at the right stage in one's career, is essential. Such courses may be part-time or full-time and range from a few days to one to three years. The latter are usually courses designed to lead to a further qualification, for example diploma, degree, or higher degree. The James Report (1972) recommended that teachers be allowed one term each seven years for participation in substantial courses. In a teacher's total working life this represents some two years. Teachers may apply to their employers for a year's secondment on full salary to undertake further full-time study after five years teaching experience.

Possible future trends

Since the introduction of free tuition and grants for entry into higher education an increasing number of candidates have graduated. Many of these have taken advantage of grants and facilities for further study. This means that year by year an increasing number of graduate personnel with first and higher degrees are released onto the labour market. This pool is cumulative. Young people destined for the education service whether it be schools, colleges, polytechnics or universities would be well advised to extend their intitial education as far as they are able before entering their chosen branch of the service. As the birthrate diminishes all branches of the education service will contract. This means an increasing competition among those seeking posts. The latter, particularly senior posts, will inevitably be taken by the most highly qualified.

Most home economists are women, who in a time of shrinking employment, are particularly vulnerable. Women need to be better qualified than their male counterparts in the same employment. They are also, if married, less mobile. This may mean acceptance of work below the level for which they are qualified by education and experience. Recent legislation has enabled a woman to take leave of absence for childbirth and to return to her post if she wishes. With the arrival of children, a woman's commitment of time to her family increases. If she also works it is very unlikely that she will be able to engage in any further substantial study whilst the children are very young. As a rule a husband's career prospects take precedence and may entail several moves as he seeks promotion. It would be fair to say that a married woman's career prospects are influenced very much by chance. Young women would be well advised, therefore, to reach the highest level possible in their intitial education before they marry. This will ensure the best possible chance of success when faced with the inevitable obstacles to further study and career which will follow marriage.

Summary

Part four has identified the professional needs of home economics teachers. Student teachers have been made aware of the parameters of preparation necessary to prepare them for a professional role. Institutions offering professional courses in teacher education have a responsibility to provide the climate, context and content necessary for students to acquire proficiency in the knowledge and skills outlined. Content and practice within individual institutions in England and Wales will depend upon current requirements laid down by the Department of Education and Science. These determine entry requirements, length of course, areas of study, length of teaching practice and levels of attainment to be reached. Intending teachers who may wish to teach in Scotland must satisfy the requirements of the General Teaching Council for Scotland, before registration as a teacher is granted. This means that the course(s) (both initial and professional) undertaken must be approved by the Council. Two important differences should be noted. Firstly, the three year Bachelor of Education degree (Ordinary) is not normally accepted by the Council. Secondly, home economics teachers are usually required to give evidence of successful teaching practice in the age range 11 to 18 years, in both dress and design and food and nutrition, during their professional training course. The latter requirement is not always fulfilled in training institutions in England and Wales. Greater mobility and prospects of employment are possible for students who seek out those institutions willing to prepare teachers for posts in schools throughout the United Kingdom.

Selected references and further reading

Board of Education, *The Education of the Adolescent,* HMSO, 1926

Department of Education and Science, Safety in practical departments (handicraft, art, home economics), Safety Series 3, HMSO, 1973

Health and Safety at Work, etc, Act, HMSO, 1974

Department of Education and Science, Safety at School: General Advice. Safety Series 6, HMSO, 1980

Statistics of Education, Vol 1, Schools, HMSO, 1980

Banks, O *The Sociology of Education,* Batsford, 1968

Bone, A, *The Effect on Women's Opportunities of Teacher Training Cuts,* Equal Opportunities Commission, 1980

Part 5

Some factors influencing pupils' learning

1 Individual potential

If asked to rank their aims for pupils' education many teachers would place foremost the aim that each child within their care would reach the highest potential of which he is capable. This desire is not new and is illustrated in Part 2 by the work of the early teachers. Comenius and Froebel sought to bring about the satisfaction derived by children in achieving the full extent of their own personal development. In addition to this, Pestalozzi believed that only through education could personal liberty be attained. Since he dealt in the early days with penniless orphans, it is fair to assume that the freedom of which he spoke was social and economic.

For the student teacher, to aim at the achievement of each pupil's full potential and social and economic freedom, seems to pose an impossible task. The problem is long term, beset with a bewildering complexity of variables and one which an individual teacher may never see brought to a satisfactory solution. Indeed, perhaps because of the variables involved, absolute success can never be achieved. This should not deter either the pupils or the teachers from trying. Perhaps in truth, 'It is better to travel hopefully than to arrive'.

The focal point is the pupil. If the aim is to assist the individual to attain a full potential, then what does this mean? Potential has two meanings both of which have important implications for teachers. Firstly it means power, and secondly it is the antonym of actual. Therefore, in attempting to assist an individual to realise the optimum of which he is capable, one is helping him to achieve a maximum power over his body, mind and emotions. When that power has been realised, the second meaning of 'potential', becomes evident since, 'potential' is no longer nebulous but can be seen as the 'actual', in the reality of the individual's performance. Because of the uniqueness of the individual, the performance of each is different. Yet, the performance of each will bear similarities. Factors which influence performance are age, sex, innate ability, experience and environment.

These influences are of great importance to teachers, both in their teaching and in framing the curriculum to which pupils are exposed. That a child is the focal point of education, gives rise to the expression 'child centred education'. This education is based upon a knowledge of the needs of individuals at the different stages in human development. From this information, educational experiences are planned for individuals, taking into account their growth in knowledge, experience, physical stature and mental and emotional maturation. By looking at the known characteristics of behaviour observable in children the student teacher has a basis upon which to work.

Heredity

Human beings are derived from a single cell which is formed by the fusion of two separate cells. One of these, the ovum, originates from the mother's ovary and the other, the spermatozoon, from the father's testes. The resulting tiny cell contains all the latent qualities of the future adult. These hidden attributes comprise his ultimate potential. Particular characteristics and tendencies are determined by the species and by ancestry. These physiological qualities include the colour of eyes, hair, skin, height, etc, and intelligence. Together these potentialities form a factor known as heredity. The subsequent pre-natal development of the organism is dependent partly upon heredity and partly upon the environment in which it is nurtured. During pre-natal growth the foetus is totally dependent upon its mother for food and shelter. Nevertheless its growth is its own and self-directing. Thus from the beginning, preparation is made for independence. This is achieved some two hundred and seventy days from conception at birth. A baby enters the world, therefore, equipped with the characteristics of the species and certain inborn patterns of behaviour. He has the capacity to grow and develop physically, mentally and emotionally.

Early sensori-motor development

Soon after birth the automatic responses which are controlled by the central nervous system can be observed, for example, crying, sucking, swallowing, kicking, opening and closing the eyes and mouth. During the first month of life the infant spends most of his time feeding, sleeping and crying. At three months of age he can usually hold up his head if held in a sitting position. By seven months he can normally sit up alone in his pram or cot. This enables him to observe what is going on around him. The crawling stage follows at approximately nine months.

This is a particularly trying time for mothers from the standpoint of cleanliness, health and safety. It is often said, 'He is into everything'. He uses his new found mobility to explore everywhere and anything which he can touch, with complete non-discrimination. At ten months he is able to pull himself up and grabs anything in sight in order to achieve this. Again this is non-discriminatory and a hanging tablecloth is as welcome as the stable arm of a settee. Constant supervision is needed to prevent self-inflicted pain and hurt due to inexperience and ignorance. By his first birthday he may be able to take a few steps with help. A month later he will probably walk alone. From then on, progress is rapid. At three years he can run with ease.

Implications for the home economics curriculum

A mother needs to be aware of the stages in child development so that she can provide the appropriate response at the right time. For example, in the early months, a close physical contact, loving, talking and playing with the baby. She feeds him, comforts him and provides a secure place for him to rest. Growth is rapid and learning takes place day by day. This is a period of constant washing for a mother which is associated with feeding, lack of bladder control and defecation. Planned buying is, therefore, necessary for clothing and bedding. Clothing needs to expand or be readily enlarged. Bedding and clothing must wash and dry readily. Economic use of time between feeds is essential.

Diet is critical at this stage. From birth a baby is nourished by milk—either his mother's or a proprietary brand of dried cow's milk. Experts agree that breast-feeding is more desirable. It promotes a close physical contact between mother and child and gives a certain degree of immunity from infection. The mother's milk is less likely to cause digestive upsets. Nursing mothers require a well-balanced diet, an understanding of what this entails and to be educated to enjoy good eating habits. (It was noted earlier that this education begins in infancy and extends right through school education.)

Nevertheless, many mothers choose to bottle-feed their infants, preferring the independence afforded by packet mixes. Careful teaching is necessary to ensure that an accurate reading, interpretation and practice of directions for use is followed. Teachers and mothers, need to be aware of the unhappy consequences of careless 'feed' preparation. Knowledge of necessary additions to the diet, for example, vitamin C, weaning procedures and graduation to a mixed diet are all important. Diet is expressed in meals, which illustrate a knowledge of the qualities of food, in action.

Skilful parents teach children by example to accept and enjoy foods, which will be of maximum value to them in physiological development. Food fads are often taught by example both wittingly and unwittingly. For example, one meets an increasing number of children in school who affirm that the only vegetables eaten at home are peas, potatoes (chips) and carrots. Fads should not be confused with abstention from foods necessitated by physiological disorders, for example, diabetes and coelliac disease.

With maturation, sensori-motor skills increase. Between the ages of three and five years children discover that they can jump. They also throw balls, first with one hand and then the other. As hand and eye begin to co-ordinate with some accuracy, balls can also be caught. Research indicates that muscular accuracy in motor skills depends upon the height, weight, strength and neuro-muscular maturity of the individual. Other important factors are intelligence, motivation and socio-emotional maturity. Home economics teachers will deduce from this that those pupils in school with lower intelligence may have greater difficulty in mastering practical, manipulative skills demanding accuracy, than their more able fellows. Thus initial goals may need to be less demanding where 'finish' is required. More practice over a longer period of time, embracing more intermediate steps should be given. Imitation plays a significant part and frequent opportunity should be given for the required skill to be seen in action.

Early socio-emotional development

During the first year of a child's life he is dependent upon his mother for his biological needs, for example, food, water, warmth, and for his psychological needs, for example, love, security, freedom from fear. From thence onwards he is seemingly able to observe and understand the emotions of those around him. This enables him to establish his own social relationships. His increasing curiosity is satisfied as he toddles about exploring the home which embraces him and other family members. Doors are opened and anything moveable is moved. This can prove a hazardous period for him as a lack of experience leads to undifferentiated grasping, sucking or swallowing. Fires must be guarded, pills locked away and harmful agents, such as bleaches, detergents and cleaning fluids kept secured and out of reach.

From eighteen months to two and a half years a child passes through a wilful stage. He is aggressive and does not like to be restrained. Wearing safety harness or holding mother's hand to cross the road is found irksome. Frustration often leads to tears and tantrums. He makes his presence felt both in the family home and outside in public. Kind but firm discipline is necessary to enable him to establish self-control. By the age of three he is more obedient and amenable in his personal relationships. He learns to watch for the emotional changes in adults and to act accordingly. His relationship with other children is also changing. Until now he has played alone, but at three he shows interest in playing in the company of children of his own age. Not only does he show a more sociable image but also a much greater degree of independence. This continues and at four to five years he likes to play in small groups of children. Occasionally, however, he may be observed playing alone and talking to an imaginary companion. Fantasy and fact may become inextricably merged at this stage. He may be very talkative, sometimes 'bossy' and show little regard for other children. Tantrums may still occur but not as frequently as before.

Finally, what part does fear play in early socio-emotional development? Some researchers suggest that fear is an innate tendency whilst others believe that it arises from experience. Very young infants show fear when they hear a sudden loud noise. Yet fear of the dark does not seem to be a problem until a child is about two years of age. Other fears are instilled by parents in the interest of their child's safety. For instance the fear of fire, very hot water, bottles of pills, road traffic, etc. Perhaps it would be more correct to say that fear can be eliminated for the child, if safe patterns of behaviour are taught.

'Safe' may be defined as secure, unharmed, protected, guarded, sheltered, or shielded. Implicit within this is the important principle of parental love and concern for their child. Secondly, parents and teachers can ease the way, by providing the means by which the sequences in the stages of the child's development are reached. Thirdly, parents and teachers need to realise that restraint of the child and by the child is necessary for a safe, healthy development. Kindness coupled with firm, fair direction, is required both at home and at school.

Early language development

It is said that the two most important factors in the acquisition of speech are maturation and learning. Babies make sounds (other than crying) from a very early age. At two months they utter single syllable grunting noises. By four to five months these are repeated. Da, da, Ma, ma. It is not until a child is about a year old that he actually uses a word with meaning. By eighteen months the vocabulary has widened considerably and by the time he enters school this may have reached the remarkable level of some two thousand words. It is important to note that he is able to understand the meaning and use of far more words than he himself can actually put into practice.

This has important implications for both parents and teachers at this and later stages in education. It indicates the importance of adults using a wide range of vocabulary, if there is to be a continuance of intellectual development in the passive use of vocabulary by children, as well as the active use in their own speech, reading and writing. Two important factors in language development are the child's level of intelligence and his own cultural environment. Observers have noted that in general 'brighter' children use language earlier than their less bright contemporaries. Children from homes where books and other cultural interests are enjoyed, tend to be read to more, and spoken to more. They are, therefore, greatly advantaged since these activities greatly assist language development.

These factors should be noted by the home economics teacher who can then respond by ensuring that a good model of adult speech is used during lessons. In preparing a lesson, pay as much attention to planning good quality language usage, by both teacher and pupil, as to the content and organisation of that lesson. There should be opportunity for discussion and pupil response. Less able, reticent or unresponsive pupils should be invited to join in and make a contribution. It is valuable social education for the more ebullient class members to learn to respect others, by sometimes deferring to their less able and less vocal fellows. The need for the teacher to have wide and varied interests is seen here in practice for if children do not enjoy cultural advantage at home their sole source of such benefit is from the teacher at school. This argument can be extended to include access to a wide and varied selection of books and other reading materials.

Early intellectual development

Intellectual growth is closely linked with the development of language. In the early years an infant learns to interpret the stimulation it receives through its senses. These explanations will subsequently lead to the formation of concepts. This is aided and developed by the parallel evolution of language. In nursery classes and early infant classes, pupils can be seen busily sorting and classifying colours, shapes and objects. We are told that a knowledge of colour and the relevant name is understood by the average child of three to five years. At that age they can understand the concept of colour and can therefore match objects on the basis of colour.

By five or six years they understand the concept of shape and can match objects on the basis of shape. At this age too they begin to classify according to kind, for example, boys, girls, cats, dogs, cups and plates. Alongside this, language is evolving. During these early years it is said that the length of sentence spoken by a child is some measure of his intellectual growth. The development of physical, perceptual and intellectual skills are interrelated. For instance a child is instructed to sit still when learning to write. To facilitate this the body must be at rest in a sitting position at a table or desk. The pencil is then held by the hand and co-ordination between hand, eye and brain is necessary, if thoughts are to be expressed on paper in written form.

Summary

This brief look at some aspects of the early sensori-motor, socio-emotional, intellectual and language development, draws attention to the individuals inheritance from the past, and the way in which this affects his future. It shows the early emergence of likenesses and differences among children and the need to use this knowledge in teaching. The student's deeper study of human development covering the full life span of individuals, during his professional training will provide the basis for a greater understanding of the learning process and how it relates to differing age groups. This knowledge also forms the foundation for selection of curriculum content and teaching methods in home economics.

Selected references and further reading
Lovell, K, *Educational Psychology and Children,* University of London Press, 1967
Lovell, K, *An Introduction to Human Development,* Macmillan, 1968.

2 External influences

An individual's development depends not only upon hereditary factors, but also upon the circumstances which attend him after birth. These are usually referred to as environmental influences. The word 'environment' can be defined as, surroundings, neighbourhood, vicinity or setting. The immediate setting into which a child is born is his family. The influences of the family are diverse. A child born into a family living in a highly developed industrialised country, has advantages which have accrued over the many years of progress from an agrarian economy. He will enjoy the benefits bestowed upon the citizens, of medical care, welfare services, controlled distribution of water, energy, housing, education and employment. When work is not available, society will cushion the family against physical hardship, by financial aid. In under-developed countries the picture is often different. These countries may be torn between warring factions jockeying for political power. Families may exist, or be extinguished, simply because there is no organised means to ensure their survival. Family environment is, therefore, a relative term, depending for its definition, upon the criteria against which it is contrasted. For the purpose of this study, we are concerned only with those families born in these islands, or those which have made their homes here.

The family in its setting has been much studied over the years and the effect this has upon the individuals nurtured within it. Studies carried out in the immediate post-Second World War period, stressed the harmful effects of poverty. This poverty was described in terms of poor housing, inadequate diet, clothing and a lack of material possessions within the home. Researchers argued at this time, that if all people lived in good quality housing and enjoyed the fruits of society which money could buy, then the overall level of the realisation of their potential in educational terms, would rise. Some thirty years later, the housing stock within the country has been increased or improved, wages have risen and educational opportunity has been extended. Yet, it is evident that much individual attainment still falls short of its potential. The reader may turn to many studies which illustrate this.

Other researchers have attributed differences in individual performance, to the context of 'class'. This word is one which evokes in some emotive feelings. The dictionary definition is a group, category, division, quality, grade or rank. For the purposes of any study, reference is normally made to the Standard Classification of Social Status Category ('The Hall-Jones Scale'), which ranks the male populace according to the occupation which they follow. Groups are numbered from one to seven: group one (the highest), contains higher administrative and professional occupations. Assistant teachers are to be found in group three; lower groups (five, six, seven) contain manual workers and the lowest group (seven) unskilled manual workers. The term 'white collared' worker, is sometimes used to differentiate between manual and non-manual, working class and middle class, employees. Different classes were said to exhibit certain characteristics relative to education, leisure pursuits and money management. These attitudes, it was stated, were a result of the family environment into which they had been born. Some felt as others before, that money was the primary cause, that differences existed because the middle classes earned more than the working classes.

This is no longer so as wage and salary levels altered. The postwar boom brought great prosperity to many manufacturing industries. Goldthorpe studied the prosperous car workers at Luton. The acquisition of expensive houses and material possessions gave the outward impression of improved status. However, attitudes to money management, length of education and leisure pursuits remained unchanged. Much effort has been made by political enthusiasts and legislators to create a classless society, in the belief that a more egalitarian community would be a happier and more successful one. Higher and more equal wages and salaries, coupled with the availability of the products of mass production have gone a long way towards making people appear to be the same. Food, furniture, fittings, clothes, cars and houses tend more and more to look similar wherever one goes. Competitively priced, mass produced clothing sold in stores with a national network has contrived to create a uniformity of a relatively high standard of dress. It is comparatively easy to reflect the sartorial habits of an idol seen in a magazine or on the television screen.

In school it is not unusual for pupils to wear a completely different outfit each day. Competitive dressing begins in the nursery class and, since few schools now wear uniform, continues right through the school years. The children of today are born into families with a greater share of a prosperous society, but those families continue to exert a powerful influence upon family members as far as the limitation of educational attainment is concerned. Parental attitudes may be a major influence upon the initial aspirations of a child and its chance to maximise educational success. For many years certain education authorities asked parents to indicate when a child was eleven years of age, how many years they would like him/her, to continue in school education. A significant number intimated that they wished the child to leave at the earliest opportunity. This decision being taken, regardless of the child's ability or performance.

Careers' teachers in school are faced with the same dilemma when neither parent nor child can see any value in staying on at school beyond the statutory leaving age. Education is seen as having no worth, either for its own sake, or as a means of entry to a satisfying career. It is on this issue that parents, holding middle class and working class values, may tend to differ significantly. The former value education highly and will often make personal sacrifices in terms of time, luxuries, entertainment and holidays, to ensure that their children have maximum opportunities. They make a greater use of the services provided locally and nationally, in the way of libraries, museums, art galleries, theatre, concerts, swimming baths and sports facilities. Education is viewed, not as being confined to a school, but as an on-going part of a way of life. There is a desire to acquire for themselves and their children an interest in cultural pleasures.

The future aspirations of such children are seen in terms of their own performance and position in society. They hope that their children will do as well, if not better, than they themselves have done. To this end they exert pressure upon children to attend school regularly and to behave acceptably whilst there. Parents try to fulfil the wishes of the teachers or school, relative to the child's dress, possessions and activities. They are, in general terms, supportive towards the school. A home with non-supportive parents can negate the efforts of the most dedicated staff at school.

I recall a situation many years ago, where the parents in the neighbourhood of a school were particularly aggrieved by a society which, they felt, exhibited great social and economic injustice towards them as workers, in a particularly industry. Unfortunately, the teachers at school, represented to them this society and its authority. As a conseqence their children refused to co-operate at school and in the short term, this made life very difficult for the teachers. However, in the long term, it was not the teachers who suffered but the children who rejected their education. One wonders whether now as parents, these same children, are supporting or rejecting their own children's education.

Summary

The environment into which a child is born exerts a powerful influence upon his attitude to education and the use he can and does make of it. Given a reasonable family income and standard of living, there are other factors which appear to determine the length and quality of education undertaken by able individuals. As wages rise and the differential between the unskilled, skilled and professional classes disappear, one may wonder if only those who value education for its own sake will pursue it to its highest levels in the future?

Selected references and further reading

Clegg, A and Megson, B *Children in Distress,* Penguin, Harmondsworth, 1968

Hoggart, R *Speaking to Each Other,* Volume one: About society, Pelican, 1970

Carter, C and Wilson, T, Discussing the Welfare State, Policy Studies Institute, 1979

Goldthorpe, J H, *Social Mobility and Class Structure,* Oxford University Press, 1980

Halsey, J H, Heath, A F, and Ridge, J M, *Origins and Destinations, Family, Class and Education in Modern Britain,* Clarendon Press, 1980.

3 Ethnic and cultural loyalties

All teachers find themselves influenced, to a greater or lesser degree, by changes within the constituent peoples in the population. This has been brought about by the immigration of substantial numbers of people from other countries.

Britain has, over the centuries from Anglo-Saxon times until the present day, absorbed large numbers of peoples from other shores. In the most recent centuries Jews, Irish and Eastern Europeans have arrived, fleeing from aggression or the threat of starvation. These peoples did not differ markedly in physical characteristics, dress, religion or social freedom from the indigenous population. Many either spoke English or had learned a smattering of it as a second language. All these factors helped them to be absorbed and integrated more easily with their hosts. In recent years large numbers of people from the new Commonwealth have reached these shores from the West Indies, Pakistan and East Africa. These peoples cannot merge like chameleons into their new surroundings. They are readily distinguishable by colour and often by dress. Their way of life is fashioned by history, religion and culture. Since what happens in society outside the classroom affects the climate inside it, some examination of these large and, consequently, more influential groups is of value.

Settlers from the Indian sub-continent

In the past, peoples from India and Pakistan have emigrated to many countries including those under British rule. It is only in recent years, that they have come to Britain. Initial emigration arose partly as a result of the abolition of slavery and partly from a need by governments abroad to recruit large quantities of cheap labour. Recruitment by host countries took place on a regional basis only. Thus emigrants retained a unity in the new country stemming from kinship, language, religion and culture. This has resulted in exclusive, independent communities in the host countries which retain close links with the regions from whence they came. Significant immigration into the United Kingdom began after the Second World War. Immigrants from India and Pakistan are openly frank about their economic motivation.

The initial settler has probably been sponsored and financed by his family. In due course he may sponsor brothers and other relatives. On arrival immigrants may work as unskilled or semi-skilled workers to pay for sponsorship and send money home for subsequent travellers. These settlers are likely to form permanent communities here. They differ from other immigrants who come on a less permanent basis such as students, doctors or other professionals. All Indians and Pakistanis encounter problems in adjusting to their new environment. These relate to problems of housing, climate, diet, language, personal and interpersonal relationships. Immigrants have responded to these by forming closely knit communities, reminiscent of their village social systems. This isolates them from the host community and even from other Indian and Pakistanis (not from their home region) who differ from them in certain codes of behaviour.

The origin of settlers

India
(i) Central and Southern Gujerat
Language—Gujerati or Hindi
Religion—Hindu.

(ii) The Punjab (principally the Jullander and Hoshiarpur district)
Language—Punjabi or Hindi
Religion—Sikhism.

Pakistan
(i) East Pakistan (Bangladesh) The Sylhet district
Language—Eastern Bengali
Religion—Islam
(ii) West Pakistan
Language—Urdu or Punjabi
Religion—Islam

Settlers from Pakistan

East and West Pakistan lie one thousand miles apart and together cover a vast area of land. They have little in common apart from their principal religion and certain traditions. Both have a significant illiteracy problem and this is reflected in the immigrants here. Although West Pakistan is more prosperous than East Pakistan, poverty is widespread among the peasant communities of both. It has been traditional to send sons abroad and a whole village may contribute to the cost of this. The emigrant knows that he must send money home from the new country, to sponsor others who will follow. This creates, not only a strong bond between the emigrant and his family and the community, but also lifelong obligations from which he cannot escape. Until the mid-sixties Pakistani households in this country were largely male. They existed as quietly unobtrusive as possible, seeking only to work, save and remit money to the homeland.

Since the sixties, wives and families have arrived. This provided the impetus to secure facilities for the practice of Islamic religious and social customs.

Islam

The word Islam is derived from Arabic. Its literal translation means 'resignation', 'surrendering' (to God). It refers to a religious system introduced by Mohammed in AD 610. Mohammed was at that time a successful trader who had lived in Mecca all his life. At the age of forty, one night he saw a vision of the angel Gabriel. The angel spoke to him and commanded him to read from the cloth which was held in front of him. Mohammed complied (although he could not read). After the vision faded Mohammed remembered the words which he had read. He felt that God had called him to be His Messenger to convey His Word to the people. Mohammed's life was changed as he undertook his new mission. Now Moslems in Egypt, Syria, the Lebanon, Saudi Arabia, Iran, Indonesia, North Africa and Pakistan are called, publicly, five times a day, in the following manner:

'God is the greatest. I bear witness that there is no God but Allah. I bear witness that Mohammed is the messenger of Allah. Come to prayer. Come to security. God is the greatest.'

At prayer time Moslems, wherever they are, look towards the now sacred city of Mecca. Every Moslem hopes to make at least one pilgrimage (Hadj) to Mecca during his lifetime. A Mohammedan temple or place of worship is called a mosque. Some have been built in this country. The most magnificent of these opened recently in London adjoining Regent's Park. Mosques are characterised externally by their dome and minaret. From the top of the tall slender tower of the latter the faithful are called to prayer by the muezzin (a public crier). This takes place at dawn, midday, mid-afternoon, sunset and two hours after sunset. The sacred book of the Mohammedans is written in Arabic and contains the oral revelations by Mohammed collected in writing after his death (which took place in AD 632. This book is called the Koran (from the Arabic, quran which means, recitation). A priest (or Imam) reads from the Koran to the faithful and explains it. Children are taught Arabic and the principle tenets of the religion which are called the five pillars of Islam. These outline the five principal duties of a Moslem.

1 Faith in Allah	–	There is no God but Allah Mohammed is His Messenger
2 Prayers	–	To be said five times a day
3 Giving alms	–	To help the poor To foster religious education
4 Fasting	–	Particularly during the month of Ramadan
5 Pilgrimage	–	To Mecca (at least once).

Fasting

All Moslems fast during the month of Ramadan. This marks the anniversary of the visit of the Angel Gabriel to Mohammed. Fasting begins at dawn and ends at dusk. Eating, drinking and smoking are forbidden. Fasting is thought to strengthen the character by helping one to resist the temptation of attractive pleasures.

Food

Moslems do not eat pork since the pig is regarded as unclean. Other meats may be eaten from animals which have been ritually slaughtered. Thus, Moslems do not usually buy meat from an ordinary butcher. They may do so from a Kosher (Jewish) butcher. Tinned meat is not usually eaten unless it has been especially prepared according to their rites. There is a reluctance to eat meals out, such as canteen meals or school dinners.

Family life

The Koran says, 'You may marry two, three or four wives, but no more . . . . and if you cannot deal equitably and justly with all, you shall marry only one.' Many Moslem states have abolished polygamy except where a first wife is barren. Marriage is a social contract arranged by the parents. Mohammed said 'I advise you to be good to women.' Moslem men are taught to respect and look after women. Girls are taught to be modest and not to flaunt or accentuate their femininity.

Islam permits male Moslems to marry outside their faith with a Jew or a Christian, but not an idolater. A Moslem woman may only marry a Moslem. The family extends to include all male relatives and their descendants. Marriages are arranged by the fathers of the bride and groom, and a woman when married remains in the confines of her family. Whilst a man's social life extends beyond the home, a woman is expected to remain within it. She depends, therefore, entirely upon her family for companionship. A Pakistani woman in Britain (particularly if without female relatives) can find herself isolated and very lonely. She rarely (if ever) works outside the home and is unlikely to have the opportunity to learn English. Consequently, she is unable to read, watch television or listen to the radio with understanding. When her children are young she will have some influence over them but as they grow older they will defer more to senior members of the family. She assumes little status until she too, becomes a 'senior'.

Pakistani children are reared in a safe, secure, caring atmosphere. They have few toys and like English children they enjoy imitating mother about her household tasks. Boys are more highly valued than girls and to the observer seem to be favoured, probably because they will later contribute to the financial status of the family and assume the dominance accorded to males. Girls are considered something of a liability. They grow up to become the corporate responsibility of the family until they marry. On marriage, a dowry must be paid and the young woman then moves into the protection of her husband's family. Should she become widowed she and any children she may have will continue to be supported by her husband's family. These close kinship ties provide a very secure environment for the individual. However, if anyone is excluded through a misdemeanour it proves a hard, lonely punishment.

Settlers from India

These have come principally from two areas in India. Firstly those from the province of East Punjab and secondly those from Gujerat which lies to the north of Bombay. Both groups share with the Pakistanis a history and tradition of migration brought about by economic necessity. Young men migrate in a similar fashion through a sponsorship by family and the village community. Close ties remain therefore, with the family, village and region of origin. Indians brought their wives and families to Britain much earlier than the Pakistanis and there are proportionately more Indian women in this country than from Pakistan.

The Sikhs

The majority of immigrants from the East Punjab are Sikhs. Their mother tongue may be Punjabi or Hindi. They are an able people who have shown over the centuries an ability to fit well into a new host country, although their country of origin has a high level of illiteracy. Sikhs have served with the army and abroad in semi-skilled or skilled occupations (and other capacities) with success.

Sikhism

The word Sikh comes from the Hindi, Sikh, meaning disciple. A Sikh is a member of what was formerly a military community belonging to the Punjab. This society was originally founded by Nanak Shah in the early part of the sixteenth century as a religious sect. Nanak was an educated Hindu. Whilst bathing one day in a stream, he experienced this vision. God held out a cup to him and bade him drink. He then spoke to Nanak. After this experience

Nanak composed the Sikh morning prayer which is said each day by the faithful. Part of this says:

'There is but one God, whose name is True, the Creator, and who does not have fear or hatred, immortal, unborn, self existent, great and bountiful.'

The principal place of worship is called the *Gurdwara* and the Holy Book, the *Granth*. The Gurdwara is the home of the Holy Book. Sikhs meet in the temple, or Gurdwara, to pray and to read the Holy Book. This lays down a code of practice for life. The Granth is placed on a platform at the front of the temple beneath a canopy. The Book is never touched with unwashed hands. Worshippers remove their shoes before entering the temple and cover their heads. The service begins with a reading from the Holy Book. This is followed by hymns, poetry, a sermon and stories from Sikh history. The service ends with a blessing and a text read from the Granth, for guidance.

It should be remembered that Sikhism developed from a rejection of the rigid caste system and ritualism of Hinduism. Its tenets are the oneness of God, the equality of all men and a common brotherhood. Sikh men show their membership of this brotherhood by having a beard, not cutting their hair and wearing a turban. On ceremonial occasions they carry a sword or dagger. Their equality as brothers is demonstrated by the assumption of a common surname. For males this is Singh (meaning, lion) and Kaur (meaning, princess) for females. This causes considerable difficulties in school.

The more educated Sikhs have emerged as significantly forceful leaders within all the immigrant groups and also within the British community as a whole. An important feature of Sikh religious tradition is the need for man to master and control his own destiny. This has made the Sikhs a forceful and sometimes militant group. This bears a likeness to Western tradition and is a hopeful sign for integration as Sikhs involve themselves within the community and national decision making.

Family life

Like the male Pakistani, the Sikh man is undisputed head of the family but the Sikh woman has a much greater freedom. Many work outside the home and this gives them a greater equality. There is less concentration upon the isolation and protection of girls than in the Pakistani family. Although marriages are arranged, the participants are allowed to express an opinion and may sometimes reject the proposition. Women attain a greater domestic influence since men normally stay in the home of the family of origin all their lives. This results in a close bond between mother and son. This power is increased further if the head of the family is away, for example, if he has emigrated. Thus a grandmother may be a formidable figure within the family unit. To Western eyes this extended family unit may appear very close knit. Sikh children (particularly at adolescence) are strongly influenced, to recognise their obligations and responsibilities, both to each other, the family as a whole and the Sikh community.

Indians from Gujerat

These people have a strong emigratory tradition. Many settled in East Africa and became a very successful commercial and middle class group. Numbers of them emigrated to Britain during the political upheavals in Uganda. Those who came directly to Britain from Gujerat had some experience of urban life, and were mainly literate. Most of the population of Gujerat are Hindus.

There are many ways in which a Hindu may suffer a loss of caste, such as by eating food cooked by a lower caste or even by sharing the same table. To lose caste is to suffer the greatest possible humiliation. The caste system was orginally based upon a strict division of labour within the community and its aim was to provide a structured and orderly society. It has no provision within it for social mobility. Indians who emigrate are on the whole those who are more willing to adapt to limited changes within the caste system. Nevertheless caste considerations do influence to some extent the choice of a marriage partner, business associates, friends, eating companions and the personal code of conduct.

Whilst strict Hindus are vegetarians some animals are regarded by Hindus as being sacred. The cow is the most sacred animal and to kill or injure one of these is a great sin. Housewives believe that any food cooked in butter or ghee is sanctified.

Family life

The woman is essentially a humble member of the family group. When she marries she must subordinate her wishes to those of her husband's family and in particular to her mother-in-law. All girls are brought up with this in mind. As in Sikh families, there is a firm bond between a mother and her son and also between a brother and sister. All children are raised with a strong feeling towards the family unit and a responsibility for it. The Hindu religion is family centred and is practised in the home with no formal community organisation. This tends to strengthen individual family bonds. Like Sikhs, Hindus are not allowed to marry a partner outside the faith. Family rejection would follow such a move. Male, social contact with a British woman would not, therefore, be welcomed.

Although Indian groups experience difficulties within their own groups and within the community, they prefer to solve problems internally. At present, therefore, they are unlikely to approach the Social Services with domestic problems. As long as family units remain extended and supportive, this is likely to remain. A weakening may occur if family units contract as young Asians are influenced by Western practice. Should this happen they will become increasingly dependent upon the social agencies.

Hinduism

In India, almost three quarters of the population adhere to the Hindu religion which incorporates many differences. These involve a great number of Gods and different Gods may be worshipped in other parts of India. The most important Gods are Brahma the creater, Vishnu the Preserver and Shiva the Destroyer. Hinduism is rich in ceremonial and the festivals provide important social occasions for its members. Hindus believe in the transmigration of the soul after death.

The caste system is the most significant custom among Hindus. This is an hereditary caste system which has long divided Indian society. Members of a caste enjoy equality with members of the same caste but do not mix socially with members of a different caste. Originally there were four castes. First and foremost were the priestly caste known as the Brahmans. Second in the social order were the military caste the Kshatriyas. Third were the merchants, the Vaisyas. Last were the artisans and labourers, the Sudras. Men married women from the same caste and children assumed the caste of their parents. Over the years the number of castes has increased as the original four became sub-divided.

West Indian settlers

The tropical islands of the West Indies consist of multi-racial societies. For their origin one must look back to the year 1665. In that year English merchant-venturers began a project in the islands designed solely to produce cane sugar on a large scale. Such a task required a large quantity of cheap labour. This was recruited by force from Africa in slave ships. So began a society comprising white and black, master and slave, from which the present West Indian community is descended. The period of time between the year 1665 and the final emancipation of the slaves in 1854 determined the pattern of family life which characterises West Indian communities, today.

Family life

During the period of slavery the African immigrants were owned by the European plantation owners. The owners gave them names, fed and clothed them. The Africans were encouraged to have children in order to maintain numbers. They were not, however, allowed to marry since this would have complicated the selling procedure. Consequently, today, marriage is seen as the culmination of achieving an economic and social goal. Similarly, white may be associated with a superior status. Some West Indian men aim to marry a woman with a lighter skin so that any children will have a fairer complexion. I recall the visit of a West Indian mother to a school some years ago. She came to complain of the appointment to the school of the first black teacher. This feeling by some West Indians that black is inferior can lead to a self-rejection which may in turn influence behaviour patterns. This is aggravated, if they find themselves in an environment in which they are (or are made to feel that they are) inferior. These situations can lead to a negative attitude to authority or an aggressive response.

It also influences attitudes towards employment. A desire to improve employment prospects for themselves and their families prompted the initial emigration from the West Indies. Emigrants were largely from the semi-skilled and unskilled groups. In the new country they wished to feel that they had risen above jobs which had overtones of master and servant. One rarely finds, therefore, West Indians working in private homes in this country. Large numbers are found, however, in the domestic areas of institutions like hospitals, schools, etc. Work in an institution is felt to be less servile than work in a private house. Unlike the emigrants from India who were initially male only, emigrants of both sexes came from the West Indies in approximately equal numbers. These were usually young. Their marital status and family life is still influenced by the breakdown of family organisation experienced during their ancestors period of slavery.

After emancipation in 1854 many ex-slaves adopted some facets of

European life, including the Christian religion. Marriage was undertaken principally to indicate a position of social and economic status. Thus a man and woman might live together and raise a family to adulthood before deciding to marry. Alternatively, less stable relationships might involve changes in partnership. Children usually stayed with the mother. A home might, therefore, include a mother with children by one or more 'husbands'. No social stigma attached to this arrangement. One consequence was, however, the emergence of a matriarchal family. Men contributed financially and authoritatively to the group but mothers and grandmothers had the most lasting influence. In the West Indies women usually worked outside the home, often in domestic situations. Here, in this country now, the women also work outside the home.

Life may, however, be somewhat different. The general loneliness of immigrant life places a new emphasis upon home and family. There is a desire to fit into the host community. Thus West Indian women feel that it is important to legitimise their children. The host community does accept unmarried mothers, but it is not the norm and West Indian mothers do not wish their children to be regarded as being outside the normal pattern of social behaviour. Besides which, a young couple can afford to marry and set up a home in this country. Youthful marriage is, therefore, a sign of an early attainment of social and economic prosperity. Young West Indians are, therefore, marrying earlier than their parents did. A limitation of family size is also apparent. No social stigma is attached to family planning in this country and West Indian mothers have been ready to adopt responsibility within the family for this. Thus there has been a significant drop in the size of West Indian families over the past few years, and family size is rapidly approaching the indigenous norm.

This is partly due to the high cost of living. Food, clothing and housing account for a major part of the family budget. If the family is limited the mother can more readily contribute to the family income. Local provision for day care of pre-school children is limited and usually priority is given to those families with a social or medical need. For example, one parent families or those where one parent is incapacitated. West Indian mothers look, therefore, to a 'child minder' for help. The latter may be registered or unregistered and vary greatly in their ability and performance in this role. Unlike English women, who often feel guilty if they leave their children to go out to work, West Indians regard themselves as guilty if they do not. They feel a responsibility to contribute to the family income to provide the necessities, as well as the luxuries, fancy clothes and a car. The West Indian woman, working alongside her English counterpart, has been quick to note and emulate the greater equality and independent approach of women in both the domestic and public scene.

Independence for the West Indian woman may lead to conflict within the home. The husband (particularly if married) may resent the erosion of what he feels to be his authority. Adjustment on arrival in this country, in living patterns, is necessary by both men and women. As the manager within the home the woman may be responsible for paying the bills and deciding what furniture, furnishings and fittings are to be purchased. She also buys the food and clothing. I have often watched West Indian women bargaining in good humoured, friendly fashion with the stall holders in the nearby fruit and vegetable market. Both obviously enjoy the interchange. Life in the West Indies is very different. The climate makes for luxuriant growth of exotic foods for the table and allows the minimum of thin clothing to be worn.

Early settlers tended to dress in this country in thin brightly coloured clothing. Babies in prams could be observed in thin dresses with little covering in the cold of mid-winter. Perhaps the school uniforms (which were usually worn at this period) indirectly educated West Indians to unfamiliar changes in clothing to meet seasonal need. Few schools now use a uniform and some mothers still need guidance in choice of clothing for the intemperate, often chilly weather, experienced in these islands. The transition from a tropical climate to a temperate one also brings health hazards. The reduced amount of sunshine in Britain cannot readily penetrate a heavily pigmented skin. Coloured adults and children may lack sufficient vitamin D within the diet. Medical researches indicate that anaemia, vitamin and iron deficiencies are more prevalent among West Indian children than English children. West Indian mothers are not always able to buy cheaply many of the foods normally eaten in their homeland. Guidance in choosing and acquiring the taste of English alternatives to achieve a nutritional balance is therefore needed.

Employment patterns among immigrant women

More West Indian women go out to work on average, than do women in the indigenous population. It is roughly the same among Pakistani and Indian women living in London. In other parts of the country this is much lower. A large number of West Indian women are employed in hospitals, the service industries, light engineering, textiles and clothing industries. Within the West Indies probably most of them would have been in domestic employment. They are reluctant to do this in Britain since this has such a low status in the 'home' country. As emigration is viewed as a social and economic improvement in status, the employment which follows, must be seen to mirror this rise in fortunes. This is also why second generation immigrants who have not been successful within the school system, reject the offer of unskilled and what they regard as low status work.

A significant number of immigrants from India and Pakistan have found employment within the textile industries, especially where run by their fellow countrymen. Where this does happen, for example in the service industries or a factory, the knowledge of this may well be concealed from the relatives at home in India, since this would be regarded as evidence of a lowering of status. Both men and women indulge in only a minimal social contact with their non-Asian fellow workers. They prefer to eat and talk apart. Perhaps one could say that the more educated an immigrant is, the more likely he is to mix with the host community. Indeed, those with professions, the doctors, teachers, lawyers, accountants, etc, tend to live in 'white' areas, rather than to settle in districts, densely populated with their fellow countrymen. The educated immigrant seems to mix with his neighbour, both at work and at home, on a more relaxed, confident basis.

For the average Indian woman arriving in Britain as a bride, a very lonely life may be in store. She leaves the very close knit security of her own family to join the unknown household of her husband. The early years of her married life will be devoted to the upbringing of her own family. She will have few contacts, if any, with the English speaking world. When the first child enters school, he will act as interpreter between home, the school and other social agencies. He will learn to read and write in the language of a host country, an experience which she cannot share. In due course, he will watch television and read the daily press with understanding. Both he, and, more controversially his sister, will grow up with the expectation and realisation, of a wide range of work within the new community. In the years to come they will share their time between an English speaking world, in which they work and spend their leisure time and their home, in which as far as the mother is concerned, time may well have stood still. For the Indian woman, the future may well be viewed with apprehension. The price she has paid for education, which will open up opportunities for the children, will be greater loneliness and isolation in old age.

Aspects of teaching home economics in a multi-racial society

This brief insight into some of the new groups of settlers illustrates the difficulties confronting those who teach in schools. Departments of Education have been encouraged to prepare student teachers in training to cope with these problems. This is an almost impossible task to do with any sense of comprehensiveness or thoroughness. The Chief Education Officer of an English city, commented recently upon the European Economic Community (EEC) funded project to 'promote' teaching of the mother tongue to immigrant children. It had cost £150 000 for four years, to teach either Italian or Punjabi to 150 children. This represented two per cent of the 9000 immigrant children from 70 different nationalities in this particular city. When this project ended, 'the county cannot afford to continue it'. This situation places the problem in perspective. It is neither economic nor practicable to teach the mother tongue to children of immigrant parents.

Teacher training departments also face difficulties in preparing students adequately in psychology and sociology. Most research in these fields has been carried out by Europeans studying Europeans. Much of this data relates specifically to the physical, mental, emotional and social characteristics of Europeans. Scholars agree that man is moulded by his environment and that there are comparative differences between the races. Studies attempting to analyse these differences are fraught with problems. With physical development a body of knowledge is already known, but studies which relate to mental, emotional and social development are difficult, since they may be construed as discrimination, or racial provocation.

Home economics teachers have in the past adapted their teaching, to accommodate pupils from the Roman Catholic and Jewish faiths. Now it is necessary to adjust to immigrants with many differences. Apart from the strictures imposed by religious differences, there are those of language, social and moral values, diet, views on education, marriage, status of the sexes, etc. The list is endless and teachers face the insuperable problem of trying to become an authority upon each and every one. This is impossible and a teacher has to set goals, within this compass, which are possible to achieve. It may be that a student or teacher will begin, as the writer has done, by choosing the three main immigrant groups within a particular geographical area as a starting point.

All home economics teachers seek to know the home background of their pupils. They have to deal with the task as it is seen. From the pupils' standpoint, life in the home economics room can be complex too. Often it is lavishly equipped with the products of an apparently wealthy, industrialised nation. These are the rewards, which they hope they too will enjoy, as education opens up the opportunity for the prosperity which accompanies a well paid job. It is for this purpose, that their parents emigrated from their homeland. Yet life in this new country is not easy either. They look different physically, they may dress differently, they speak differently and they know that things at home are different, too. The decor, furniture and furnishings are often different. At meals, different food is served and the manner of its serving, and the manner of its being eaten, is often different. Within the home, the division of labour, the rewards and punishments, and the status of male and female may well be unequal.

These and other differences may lead to a feeling of alienation among pupils. Many teachers believe that this sense of estrangement lies at the heart of many behavioural problems. Some teachers take great care to ensure that pupils work within their own known experience in the food and clothing areas, at least. Other teachers believe that it is of most value, to teach pupils of immigrant origin as much as possible about the country of their adoption. It has been my pleasure to train many teachers whose parents' country of origin lies outside these shores. Some were born here and educated at school, college and university within these shores. Among these, were those who had been raised in a non-English speaking home. Culturally, the home was a world apart. As far as teaching home economics was concerned, such students were gravely disadvantaged when viewed alongside their fellows of indigenous extraction. Even if their goal had not been to teach home economics, these students would have benefited enormously from an ongoing education in school which taught them how the host population lived. Perhaps indeed, this would have helped them to understand some of the British eccentricities.

Is it possible, perhaps, that a parallel may be drawn with the educational arguments which prevailed some ten or fifteen years ago? At that time there were those educationalists who argued that pupils from working class homes should be taught according to their own idiom. It was said that such pupils experienced difficulty in understanding teachers who came from middle class stock. Others argued that a principal aim in education was to enable pupils to achieve a social and economic mobility. In order to achieve this aim, a familiarity with language and behaviour, associated with middle class norms, was therefore essential. For immigrant pupils also, a principal aim in education should be for them to attain social and economic mobility. It is essential, therefore, that priority is given to teaching them how to achieve this.

If they are to participate on equal terms with the indigenous population at every level of prosperity it is necessary for immigrant pupils to know as much as is possible about the British culture, its shades of religion, social habits, food and so on. Their future public life will be a British one and ultimately their knowledge of this will enable them to attain economic and social success. They have then, the additional bonus of fulfilling a dual role, in enjoying with pride the cultural heritage of their ancestors, which teachers can support and encourage. The organisation of education in this country, runs counter to

Asian and West Indian beliefs. Parents are familiar with a more formal approach in the classroom which is supported by a strict discipline within the school. Many show concern at the apparent informality within school, which spills over into the home.

Parents are made aware that their children are being taught to reason, to question and to make their own decisions. Children so educated will of necessity question a lifestyle at home which has been derived from years of habit, tradition and custom. Girls are educated alongside boys to expect equal opportunity. Immigrant girls see their Western sisters contemplating (if they wish it) a full working life outside the home, with the added interest and economic reward which will ensue. Teenage Asian girls see their Western sisters enjoying the company of young men of their own choosing, far from the watchful eyes of parents. They observe that this freedom extends to the choice of a marriage partner. Both boys and girls desire a part in the youth culture of their own peer group, in matters relating to dress, speech, entertainment and politics. They are just as vulnerable as their British counterparts, to the wiles and persuasion of advertising, radio, television and the press.

Parents, however, expect sons and daughters to accept ethnic and cultural, traditions and customs with enthusiasm and unquestioning loyalty. The gulf already forged by education, widens in the home. Parents see the dominance of elders within the family, being undermined and destroyed. In an industrial society of relative prosperity there is no reason for families to cling together to ward off hunger, starvation and ensure economic survival. Second generation immigrant families will probably adopt the Western lifestyle of the nuclear family. Furthermore, in a country pledged through its social agencies to care for its people from 'the cradle to the grave', there is not the same sense of urgency within a family to care for older family members, including parents and grandparents. It is of little wonder that many immigrant parents view the future with apprehension and fear. Have they, in opening up new vistas for their children, endangered or even engineered the destruction of the way of life which they hold most dear?

What of the children? On the one hand, education will, if they choose to take advantage of it, open the doors to jobs and professions, on an equal footing with their British peers. But can these children become fully Anglicised? What is certain is that they can never go back and be as their parents were. Are they then trapped, in a no man's land, between the Eastern and the Western world?

Dietary considerations

West Indians speak (if not read and write) fluent English. Because of historical circumstances they have adopted British customs. Families have adapted readily to buying and eating the foods available in this country. They have no religious customs or traditions which prohibit them from working and eating alongside their British counterparts. This provides the opportunity for observing British behaviour, diet, dress, personal and public relationships. They also read newspapers, magazines, books and watch television. Gradually by selection, much of the British way of life becomes a part of their own lifestyle. Children eat school lunches and participate fully in food classes in home economics. Although West Indian families still eat many foods related to their home islands, they enjoy a wide and varied diet, selected from the wide range of foods available here. As a rule, adults and children appear to be healthy and well nourished.

Among Asian families, unhappily, this is not the case. Anaemia, of nutritional origin, is reported in significant numbers of Asian women, particularly in the child-bearing age group. These are most likely to be found among the orthodox Hindus, who follow a strict vegetarian diet. Such a diet may be deficient in the total protein intake, iron, folic acid and vitamins B12 and C. Osteomalacia, of nutritional origin, may be found among Moslem women. This may be due partly, to the lack of sunshine in our temperate climate, which is exacerbated by overdressing, to screen women from the eyes of men and strangers. It could also result from a lack of calcium in the diet. This has given cause for concern in schools, where Asian children, and in particular girls, have been found to be suffering from rickets. This may arise also during the 'teens.

Local health authorities have tried to come to terms with the problem by distributing leaflets to Asian mothers, explaining (in their own language) how rickets are caused and how they may be treated. Some schools, which are sited in Asian communities, serve Asian dishes at lunch time to encourage the eating of well balanced meals. Health education centres are also being set up to educate adults in these and other matters. It is very difficult, however, to persuade women to leave their homes to attend these. Whilst a language barrier exists, this will lead to a lack of knowledge and understanding on the part of Asian mothers. They reject many tinned and pre-packed baby foods because they cannot read the labels and misinterpret the pictorial message on the labels.

Among the Moslem community, fasting during the feast of Ramadan means no food or drink is taken during the hours of daylight for a whole month. This causes problems both in school and at work. Concentration flags at school as the day progresses. At work lack of concentration increases the risk of industrial accident. Adults and children may sometimes faint from exhaustion. Apart from nutritional deficiencies, the temperate climate may prove a hazard to those from warmer countries. A dark skin proves an excellent barrier to irradiation by the sun in a hot climate. It may also totally exclude the weaker rays in a temperate climate, particularly if the body is effectively covered.

Positive teaching to overcome dietary deficiencies

The aim is to teach the enrichment of the existing diet rather than to change it. The group most at risk are the Hindus. Animal protein can only be taken in the form of milk or milk products, for example, curds or yogurt. Two pints of milk would have to be taken daily, in order to satisfy the adult requirement of vitamin B12. Non-orthodox Hindus could substitute in part, by taking cheese or two eggs. For meat eaters, like the Moslems or Sikhs, 300 g of meat could be taken, and the milk content reduced to 250 ml. Wheat foods will also help in increasing the daily intake of riboflavin, thiamin, nicotinic acid and calcium. Vegetables like spinach, watercress, spring cabbage, other varieties of dark green cabbage, broccoli, will, if taken, increase the iron, folic acid and calcium intake to the body. Vitamin C is not usually lacking in immigrant diets, since plenty of fruit is normally taken. The Vitamin A and D intake could substantially be improved, if vegetable margarine was substituted for butter or ghee. This would not be popular with the Hindus, since they believe that butter or ghee sanctifies anything cooked in it. Explore the possibility also of using evaporated milk, and sardines or other tinned fish in the diet. Nuts and vegetable protein, for example, soya, peas, beans, lentils, may also be used.

There is no blueprint for either content, or method of teaching dietary enrichment and control. Each teacher has to follow the same path of investigation according to the circumstances, in which teaching must take place.

Strategy

1 Define the exact problem.

2 Use your knowledge of nutrition to work out possible solutions.

3 Try out these solutions with the pupils.

4 Retain those which work, discard those which don't.

5 Amend those retained in the light of experience.

It is well to remember that changes in eating habits are more likely to be achieved in younger subjects, but even with them it is a lengthy process, requiring sustained effort over many years, on the part of both the teacher and pupil.

Selected references and further reading

Department of Education and Science, A Language for Life (The Bullock Report). London: HMSO, 1975

Bhatnagar, J *Immigrants at School,* Cornmarket Press London, 1970

Derrick, J *Language Needs of Minority Group Children,* NFER Publishing Company, 1976

Rosen, H and Burgess, T *Languages and Dialects of London School Children,* Ward Lock Educational, 1980.

4 Resources for looking and listening

These include:

Books (specialist text, supplementary reading, literature)

Magazines, newspapers

Reference materials for independent study

Live animals, plants, fish, etc

Display materials (models, specimens, pictures, charts, photographs)

Flannelgraph, magnetic board

Films

Slides

Overhead projector

Tapes

Television (live or videotape)
Radio
Records
Programmed instruction
Prepared information sheets
Computers, calculators
The blackboard.

This list in not exhaustive, but it does illustrate the significant number of aids which are available for learning and teaching. Most professional courses for teachers encourage the use of all the above. The majority of these are in use in schools. They may be kept in a central resource library, or divided between a library and specialist departments. In larger schools a specialist (assisted by a technician) is responsible for the control and servicing of these resources.

Books

An intending home economics teacher should be familiar with the wide variety of books currently available for the study of the subject and its component and related disciplines. This includes text and reference books and narratives in literature, whether fictional, autobiographical or biographical, which can be used to illustrate and enrich home economics studies, at all ages. These should be classified and listed under categories. Those texts covering course work should be in the departmental library. Others for reference and supplementary readings may be sited in the central library. I have visited many schools richly endowed with space, furniture, furnishings, fittings and equipment, which are sadly lacking in books.

Studies of schools from the earliest times emphasise that books are tools for the teacher and the principal source of enlightenment for the pupil. It was said earlier that Alcuin and Erasmus 'scoured Europe for books'. Their task was more difficult than ours, since books were then individual, costly, handmade and few in number. Modern mass production has ensured that copies of even the most treasured of scripts are available to students in school, university, local or national libraries. Yet in some schools, books seem less sought after than more eye catching expensive equipment. Indeed, with the onset of severe economic restrictions and cutbacks, some schools may have to rely more and more upon parental help, even for some essential texts.

Substantial libraries can only be built up systematically over a number of years. They provide essential reading for relevant studies and provide the means for developing interests which will live on, long after school days have ended. Pupils should be taught that books are to be used and valued. This is an essential part of social education. Vandalism directed against books should be actively discouraged and punished. Attractive books, magazines and newspapers in the home economics department, in an atmosphere which invites one to linger and explore, encourages pupils to enjoy reading. Through reading one can enter the private and public lives of others. For instance, Toad, greedy Toad, licking his lips as he experienced the delight of eating toast, oozing and dripping with butter. The mysteries of bath night in 1900 as portrayed in *Larkrise to Candleford*. The tribulations of Victorian young ladies in polite society, as mirrored in *Cranford*. Experiences of twentieth-century school life, not in the vast supermarket of education, the comprehensive school, but in the sanguine peace of Miss Read's village school.

How wonderful to escape reality for a while and to enjoy the fantasy of another place, another age, or another time. Perhaps one might be glad to return to the present, after reading about the privations of Nicholas Nickleby and the pupils at Mr Squeers' school, Dotheboys Hall. To this day, the local graveyard bears witness to the many boys of tender years whose stay there was only transitory. Perhaps, life on a modern housing estate and days spent in the local comprehensive school, might seem more attractive and inviting after such reading. Literature can tell much about the physical, emotional, political, social and economic climate of an age. Looking back and looking forward, through literature, is at one and the same time, an object lesson in the realisation of truth, joy, pain, relief and escapism through fantasy.

Learning to enjoy reading

For the able child, reading presents no problems. A few children arrive at school already able to read. Most pupils master the elements of reading in the first two years in the relaxed, unhurried atmosphere of the primary school. As seen earlier, pupils concentrate their efforts during these years, in reading, writing and number. Because all children do not appear to progress with ease after the initial two years, much research is currently focussed on methods of teaching reading. It is thought that less able readers do not fully comprehend what they see in the early stages of reading. They cannot then apply the necessary knowledge and experience to the more complex subsequent words and sentences. Practice in seeing, hearing, speaking and writing at this stage is critical and teachers should concentrate upon this.

Pupils profit, too, if they consolidate this experience at home. Parents who talk, read and listen to their children, bestow great benefit upon them. The child whose parents are disinterested, less able or non-English speaking, may suffer severe handicap. How then can the home economics teacher help in this situation? In the majority of schools, pupils attending home economics classes are in mixed ability groups. Classes will, therefore, comprise a wide range of reading ability and comprehension. This necessitates a range of text books covering the same subject area at differing levels of depth. Where an appropriate easier text is not available, then a teacher can construct one. In cases of severe difficulty, a taped, spoken account may accompany the text to be read, so that a pupil can test the accuracy of his own reading and understanding. It is important that a pupil does read.

Where a great deal of practical work is done there is a temptation for a teacher to demonstrate and pupils' subsequent work is an imitation of what has been seen and heard. If this is then followed by copying from the board, a pupil can attend class, go through the lesson and depart, almost without having to think at all. Resulting practical work may be perfect and book neat, but all the planning, reasoning and application, is the teacher's and not the pupil's. This is the opposite of good educational practice.

Guidelines on choosing textbooks

Know what is needed, ie the content needed for the job which the book is to fulfil. Examine the author's credentials for writing the book. For example, if he states that he has based the text upon experience gained in preparing pupils for the GCE 0 level examination over a number of years, a teacher occupied with the same task can identify with him and feel that they share common problems. A glance at the text will show whether the book fulfils the task of tackling such problems. Is the content up-to-date? Is the data accurate? Books dealing with textiles, food, nutrition, social policy, etc, readily date because of technological developments, research findings, or changes in legislation. Does the text cover the viewpoint and values which you wish to foster? Is it clear visually and likely to be understood? Are sufficient examples given to clarify the content? Where experiments are set, do the expected results follow and are conclusions drawn? Could pupils use the book on their own? Does it cover what is usually taught by you? Is that teaching extended?

For younger pupils, illustrations are very important. They serve to arouse and sustain interest and give clues to the text for less able readers. A study of a range of dictionaries prepared for pupils' use at different ages will illustrate key stages in progression through primary and middle school. Stage one dictionaries, contain one picture plus the relevant noun on each page. Stage two dictionaries, contain some pictures plus the relevant noun and also some verbs, adjectives, etc. Stage three, has a full range of words but no pictures. Photographs and pictures give a clear visual image which extends knowledge, by showing a particular thing, place, person, activity or process, etc. As pupils grow older, pictures become less important and may be regarded as a bonus or window dressing. When abstract thought is used with ease, much pictorial representation gives way to diagrammatic presentation.

School book illustrations are also altering to reflect social changes. For example, portrayal of family members shows people of varying racial origin. Recent trends in equal opportunity for both sexes are mirrored in school book illustrations which refuse to show toys for boys and girls. Men and women are sometimes shown engaging in non traditional roles, for instance, a woman bus driver, or a male nurse. It is important that teachers are non-emotive and balanced in their approach to these matters. This is also necessary when assessing the validity of books relating to socio-economic conditions. Some books are used to express a very biased, political platform by a writer. Even if teachers feel drawn towards a particular political viewpoint they should put a balanced selection of books before their pupils, otherwise a school becomes an instrument of political engineering.

Where charts or diagrams are used, check the presentation for accuracy. Presentation is particularly important in clothing textbooks, since pupils use these continually for reference when learning how to sketch the processes required for answering examination questions. The presentation of the general layout of the book is important too if pupils are to 'find their way about it' easily. Check for a table of contents, index, bibliography, suitable print, clear print, diagrams, illustrations and durable binding. Pupils need to be taught how to use a book and the library from which it comes.

Using a library

Primary schools have a library and pupils learn how to borrow a book. This is often followed by enrolment at a public library and regular visits there with the class teacher. At high school the internal process becomes less intimate and more complex. Large schools have their own tutor librarian whose sole task is to manage and run the school library. He is responsible for co-ordinating the choice, ordering, classifying, indexing of books and operating an efficient loan scheme. It is his task to familiarise staff and pupils with the siting of categories of books, the organisation of the library and the loan system. Thus pupils should know how to find a book on the library shelves and how to borrow it.

The home economics departmental library

The head of home economics acts as librarian. Books will be recorded on arrival and covered with adhesive covers to prolong their life. The name of the department and school will be stamped inside. Books will be classified and indexed to allow for borrowing. A record is kept of all loans.

Using books

Pupils need guidance in finding their way about a book. Explain the significance of the table of contents, index, referencing and bibliography. Illustrate the difference between scanning, reading and studying. Allow time for practice in all three. Show the significance and use of each. Teach pupils how to paraphrase, summarise, precis and make notes. Show how information can be tabulated. Discuss what has been read. Explain the usage of technical and unfamiliar words. Discuss viewpoints given by the author. Encourage pupils to select not only books which they can easily understand but those which provide some challenge. Set work which demands the use of several books at once, for example, topics and projects. Provide a variety of books. Show, or remind pupils, how to use a dictionary and thesaurus. Encourage the use of these in accompanying writing. Endeavour to have in the department thesauri and dictionaries of differing levels to provide for the needs of pupils of wide ranging ability.

Magazines and newspapers

These add colour and topicality to the life of the department. It isn't necessary to have a regular subscription to be able to use these. Individual copies may be bought when they include something of particular interest. Friends and pupils' parents may contribute discarded copies to the department. Aim to cover a wide range of interests. Research indicates that publications usually reflect a particular shade of values which will appeal to a given audience. Purchasers choose those which most nearly reflect their own particular value choices. Such choices may be determined by age, morality, sex or socio-economic factors. It is therefore educationally sound to put before pupils a broad range of the publications of the day. Older pupils may profitably discuss relative qualities of differing publications. Discussion can focus upon cost, frequency of publication, presentation, visual appeal, content, use of advertising space, language, reflection of current social values, contributors, etc. Items felt to be of particular interest to pupils in general can be prominently displayed to engage their attention.

Miscellaneous materials

Additional materials for reading can be obtained from a multiplicity of sources. These include the energy industries, Gas, Electricity and Solid Fuel.

Food, textile, equipment and detergent manufacturers are a few of the many sources which may be approached. Local and National Government sponsored agencies are also helpful. Home economists are employed by widely diverse agencies, designing and developing a wide range of educational materials for the use of pupils and teachers. Large companies and business concerns are able to combine the expertise of the home economist, advertising and marketing experts in the production of posters, charts, booklets, leaflets and sometimes films. These supply an up-to-date, accurate and often specialised source of information on a wide variety of subjects, products and resources.

They provide also a valuable source for use in consumer evaluation of products. Pupils can test for themselves the claims made by manufacturers for those products which find their way into the majority of homes. Since most firms have continuous research programmes it could be argued that their published material is far more up-to-date than books, which are printed at infrequent intervals. The home economics department could establish its own consumer bureau with senior pupils being responsible for sending for new materials, receiving them, filing and organising a loan system. The same team could assist the head of department by arranging for visits, by representatives from the organisations already visiting the school on a regular basis. Such activities would develop and extend intellectual and social skills among the administrative, pupil team.

Assessing the value of resource material from commercial sources

Ask the following questions:
Is it suited to the age and ability of the pupils?
Does it accord with or supplement material already in school?
Is it thought provoking?
Will it add interest to a particular lesson?
Is it clear visually, well written and accurate?
Does the information given, appear biased?
Can it be used to develop balanced, critical assessment and decision making?
Will it promote positive attitudes to health, management of resources, time or leisure pursuits?
Does it encourage reading?
Does it extend pupils' knowledge of practice outside school, for instance, about banks, home buying, careers, alternative patterns of living at home or abroad, etc.?
Does it extend pupils' knowledge of labour saving techniques?

Establishing a personal collection of resource material

It is wise to begin collecting materials from various sources as soon as possible. These can be classified and stored in boxes or files. They will prove invaluable both during teaching practice and later in a first teaching post. Aids to learning and teaching are many and varied and come from widely differing sources. They include specimens, models, slides, photographs, posters, charts, leaflets, tapes, pictures, etc.

Criteria for selection of materials

Many materials will be chosen against a time when they will be needed. The following points will help in deciding whether such a choice is justified.

Can they be transported easily? (weight, size, shape)

Are they expensive or irreplaceable?

Can they be handled and passed around a group? (durability)

Are they too small to be seen, other than by individuals?

Will they fulfil a specific function? (arouse interest, extend knowledge, increase understanding, sustain interest).

Choosing visual materials for a specific lesson

Objective of lesson, to show the positioning and working of a handstitched buttonhole, on the centre front opening of a blouse.

Visual materials

Finished Blouse (the real thing) Illustrating fabric used, centre-front opening, number and siting of buttons and buttonholes, choice of button, size of buttonholes, thread used, finished buttonholes.

Specimens (actual size) Illustrating in stages the marking, cutting, button-hole stitch, round end, barred end, finished buttonhole. (Fabric size 18 cm x 24 cm, to allow for each stage to be handled separately.)

Specimens (large scale) To enable each stage to be worked by teacher, so that the whole group can see. Contrasting thread is used. Stages can then be loosely pinned up in an accessible place. Pupils can then borrow and use them if they forget the process. (Fabric size 46 cm x 30 cm, buttonhole size 23 cm, stitch depth 4 cm.)

Charts Showing diagrams of positioning, marking, cutting, fastening on, working stitch, round end, barred end, fastening off. Pupils can readily see these whilst they work. They will use these to provide a model for sketching diagrams which are a necessary part of examination work.

Books Giving written instructions and diagrams. Valuable discussion can be undertaken here on the relative value of different publications.

Needle Appropriate type, size.

Thread To suit fabric of blouse in nature, colour and thickness.

Further guidance on resource selection

Specimens These are usually the 'real thing', and are used to illustrate specific points.

Models May be made by the teacher or pupils, such as a scale model of a kitchen layout in card and balsa wood. This can be used to illustrate the use of space, the location of kitchen fitments, storage, work-top surfaces, appliances, access, circulation, internal finishes, decoration and accessories. Careful mounting is necessary on a suitable board and storage facility provided for after use.

Pictures and photographs Present these carefully mounted on card, with or without a finished border. Use economically, to maximise visual impact. Question viewers on what they see, directing questions to achieve the desired effect. Be responsible in mounting and displaying, since a principal aim throughout, is to nurture the development of aesthetic appreciation.

Charts These are used to show a logical progression of an activity, thought or purpose. They depend for effect upon visual impact and may include pictures, diagrams, graphs and words. Charts take various forms according to the information to be communicated. For example, a 'flow' chart will illustrate the steps in the full sequence of making a cup of tea. A 'flip' chart, however, shows only one stage at a time. This is used on an easel. As each stage is finished, the page is 'flipped' over to reveal the next.

Diagrams These are symbolic drawings, which are designed to illustrate an abstract concept. For instance, the wiring of a plug, or a simple circuit. Diagrams can be built up gradually upon a chalkboard, with an accompanying explanation. Alternatively, they can be pre-arranged and presented large scale on charts, or small scale as photocopied handouts. The 'build up' and 'pre-prepared' principle is employed when using the overhead projector. Diagrammatic representation, is used extensively on clothing pattern envelopes and pupils need careful and systematic help, in reading and interpreting these.

Graphs Pupils are introduced to these in primary school when they consider comparative numbers of boys and girls in the class, numbers staying to school dinners, etc. High school pupils should, on entry, already be familiar with line, bar and circle or 'pie' graphs.

Display areas and interest boards

These are a part of the internal wall decoration in the primary school. Part one stressed the importance of a stimulating environment, as a background to learning in the early years. In the primary school, the message is largely visual. Its import is clear, and supported by only a few words, for instance, road safety, hand washing, foods for health. In the high school immediate impact is still necessary, but this can be achieved with less emphasis on a pictorial message. There will be a greater verbal content and both the choice of language and use of words, need the utmost care. Presentation requires good, clear lettering and an overall pleasing design and colouring. Adopt short cuts by using stencils, felt tip pens, or *Letraset*. Displays can be a mixture of personal, commercial and topical exhibits, according to the objective of the exercise. Remember that one does not 'notice' a familiar environment, so change displays frequently.

Flannelgraph and magnetic board Both work on the same principle, which extends the 'flash' card approach, used in the teaching of reading. The flannelgraph consists of a board covered with felt or flannel, to which cut outs, backed with a rough surface, will adhere. The magnetic board is made of steel and is expensive in initial outlay. It relies upon the magnetic attraction of items placed upon it. These adhere only if small magnets are attached to them. Both the flannelgraph and magnetic board are used in a 'build up' situation. For example, they can be used to show steps in laying a table, or building up a diagram of the principal food groups. One food manufacturer, for instance, has designed a kit to demonstrate the management of a domestic refrigerator.

The chalkboard This has already been discussed in another context. Its value lies in the fact that the visual image can instantly reinforce a verbal explanation. New words can be recorded, discussion points listed, timetables built up, prior to practical work, etc. Impromptu diagrams can clarify explanation, for instance where to 'snick' turnings on a collar, or faced opening. Pupil participation can take care of lists of dishes borrowed, marks achieved, etc. Social education is fostered, when a pupil is responsible for looking after the board, ensuring that it is ready for use, by the teacher and class.

Handouts   The decline in the number of chalkboards in school, is partly responsible for the rapid escalation in reprographic representation. Spirit duplicating machines have largely been replaced by photo-copiers. These may be used for circulating question papers, answer sheets, diagrams, notes, work schedules, questionnaires, assignments, etc. The principal advantage of 'handouts' lies in the content being restricted to the exact framework of what is required. For example, a teacher may collect and collate information on a given subject, from a number of sources. This is economic in the use of time and books. Nevertheless it can be argued that it robs the pupil of the valuable exercise of seeking out the sources, sifting the material and selecting the relevant information to be used. In short, it reduces pupil initiative. It can also lead to a decline in the number of books purchased in school and in their use by pupils. Where all staff in school use photocopying extensively, it does prove very costly.

The overhead projector   This consists of a rectangular glass plate, about 23.5 cm x 25 cm, upon which transparencies are laid. Mirrors are positioned overhead. The image is magnified and projected onto a large screen, positioned behind the speaker. It is inexpensive to operate, since transparencies are prepared upon a plastic sheet, with a stylus pen and sheets may be cleaned and used again. Diagrams can be built up by overlaying transparencies. A speaker can point to exact features of the diagram, as needed. Transparencies are simple to make and easy to use and store. Older pupils can prepare their own transparencies for group report-back sessions or seminars.

Tape slide programmes   Slides may be prepared by the teacher, or some can be purchased in sets, dealing with a particular theme, for example, the development of housing over a given period of time. Slide projectors are synchronised so that a taped commentary can accompany the visual sequence. I have found this a valuable technological exercise for students to undertake. They learn the technique of photography and slide preparation. Each programme demands an economical and appropriate choice of subjects for viewing. Scripts are written, recorded and synchronised with the visual presentation. Audience response (using adults and children) to quality of presentation and content, is noted. It was mentioned earlier that a tape slide programme was being marketed by student midwives aimed at teaching correct infant feeding procedures to non-English speaking mothers. Apart from uses in teaching, tape slide programmes can form a focal point at parents' evenings, or exhibitions.

Filmstrips   These are made up of a sequence of shots (like slides). Their use is simple. The strip is wound into the projector and rewound after use. The film may be stopped at any point for as long as required. It is usually accompanied by a sound track. To be effective, pupils must be adequately prepared before viewing and the film suited to their age and ability.

Films Sound and motion pictures provide immense possibilities for use in education. They may bring to life a literary work, or show the sequence of major events in history, or the evolution of social change. Specialised films may bring into the classroom, the production and marketing of well-known commodities, like sugar, margarine, bread, soap or a bale of cloth. Films dealing with controversial aspects of education (birth, family planning, sexually transmitted diseases) enable these subjects to be dealt with in an impersonal and non-emotive fashion.

Television Much of what has gone before relates also to the showing of television programmes. However, proposed programmes for schools reach teachers each session before term begins so that forward plans can be made for viewing a single or a series of programmes. In reviewing the possible use of television, radio, films, film strips, tape slide programmes, the same general principles should be observed:

Ensure that the content of the programme fits in with the work being done.

Satisfy yourself (if possible by pre-viewing) that the quality of the programme is good.

Check that the information is accurate, up-to-date and such that the chosen pupils can understand it.

Consider whether the presentation is likely to appeal to the pupils.

Does the length of programme time exceed the length of time pupils can reasonably be expected to concentrate?

Will the length of programme fit into the normal class time?

Has the programme a balanced viewpoint?

Read any explanatory notes.

Preparing the class

Tell the class briefly about the content of the programme, directing their attention to specific features to be noted.

Give the length of the programme.

Explain that notes cannot be taken, but that follow-up work will be done later.

This could take the form of a discussion followed by some visual or written presentation of what has been seen. Alternatively, oral or written questions could be set and answered. The programme may raise other questions which may need answers, for which further research is necessary.

Organisational procedures

Order the particular piece(s) of equipment from the central source.

Book an appropriate room.

Check the 'blackouts' work and there are sufficient chairs.

Collect equipment from source in good time.

Check that it is working.

Ventilate the room.

Arrange slides in carousel in order, erect screen, thread film or make whatever other preparation is necessary.

Show programme.

Re-wind film, box slides or whatever is appropriate.

Check that room is tidy.

Return equipment to store.

Part 5 has examined some aspects affecting the quality of pupils' learning. The final part looks at the school curriculum and the contribution which home economics can make in the primary, middle and high schools.

Selected references and further reading
Department of Education and Science, The use of books, Pamphlet No. 45, HMSO, 1964
'Miss Read', *Village School,* Michael Joseph, 1956.

Part 6

The schools' curriculum

1 The structure

'Education should enable the individual to formulate his own philosophy on life and enable him to enter society at the end of his schooldays on the road leading to its fulfilment.'

The first part of this book examined schools as they are. This section looks at some of the reasons why they are so. Education adds to the knowledge of each individual and serves to enrich him. It develops within him, understanding, insights, attitudes, and enables him to perform skills which he could not do before. Schools are the recognised institutions where this learning takes place. The curriculum is a plan for learning. This has evolved as a reflection of tradition, our cultural heritage, and the current social pressures of society. Teachers are the instruments of implementaton. The present society is one which is demanding and competitive. This is reflected in the national and international scene. Our society is based upon an industrial economy. It has seen a century of unparalleled technological change. The development of communications by land, sea, air and satelite has drawn the world into a common forum for dispensing ideas. If sown in fertile soil these germinate and produce great wealth for those who reap.

Technological change has reduced the demand for manpower. This has led to a greater competition for the available work. Schools reflect this scene in a pre-occupation with leaving certificates and the growing tendency to defer the age of leaving to enter employment. Education is vital to the development of the individual and to sustain a healthy national prosperity. The schools' curriculum therefore should seek to:

1 direct individuals towards society as it is seen to be and to equip them with the necessary skills to cope with living in a world which is rapidly changing;

2 offer a suitable range of knowledge and experience to the learner at each stage of his physical, mental, emotional and social development;

3 include, where appropriate, a range of subject disciplines;

4 present subject disciplines in such a manner as to ensure mental, emotional and social development of the individual.

Broad aims embodying the purpose of a school are drawn up and these provide the basis for the philosophy upon which the thinking is founded.

Formulating a curriculum
Summary

1 Decide what is necessary in the light of:
  (i) Pressures from society (economic, social, religious, political)
  (ii) Tradition (custom, cultural heritage)
  (iii) Particular needs of pupil group (age, ability, sex)
2 Formulate aims (broad areas of determination)
3 Formulate objectives (list specific outcomes desired)
4 Select content
5 Organise content
6 Choose learning experiences
7 Organise learning experiences

8 Decide what to evaluate in light of (3)
9 Decide how to evaluate (3)
10 Build in the means for amending programme according to results of evaluation.

Note
Numbers 3, 5 and 7 will illustrate the chosen patterns of learning and teaching. Numbers 4 and 6 will show the sequential progression of the curriculum planned in accordance with the current knowledge of human development.

These principles are followed whether a curriculum is being planned for a whole school, that is the general school curriculum, or a curriculum planned within any given subject specialism. We have seen that a school curriculum is based upon the needs of people. Much research (which is ongoing) has been directed towards identifying the nature of those needs. One such framework is shown in Appendix 1. This framework clearly identifies the physiological needs and experiences necessary for an individual to develop his full physical, mental, emotional and social potential. These are provided in part by the home, school and other agencies, such as church, clubs and associations. It is to the provision of such experiences that the school curriculum is largely addressed. The years spent in school are designed to equip an individual to embark upon the next stage in life's journey whether this be employment, further education or higher education. It is important for pupils and teachers to view the education received in school as incomplete and representing only a stage in a continuing process which is life long.

A look at the framework in Appendix 1 will show that school 'subjects' are not mentioned, nor do they immediately spring to mind. Further thought will suggest certain areas of human experience. These are identified in Appendix 2 as language skills, human skills, science studies and expressive arts. This definition is merely for convenience of thought and translation into curriculum action. In Part 1 section 1, it was noted that the curriculum was not expressly divided into ˙these areas within the primary school, although experiences were designed for pupils which would fall into these categories. The sections which followed, dealing with the middle years and later years, saw the emergence of a more exact grouping. This led to a categorisation into what are familiarly known as subjects, for example, home economics, English, mathematics, science, etc.

All subjects can be studied to give individuals experiences necessary for development.

1 The study of any subject can provide a wide variety of experiences and behavioural outcomes.

2 It is probable that the study of no single subject will provide a complete range of necessary experiences and behavioural outcomes.

Since the study of differing subjects can provide a duplication of both experiences and behavioural outcomes it would appear sensible where practicable, sometimes to put subjects together for joint study as was discussed earlier. This is what happens in integrated studies. This enables objectives within more than one subject, to be realised within a single common study. In this process pupils are brought together perhaps in a year group. Staff are brought together to teach as a team.

Content of differing subjects is brought together. This exercise requires an organisation of content, selection of learning experiences and an arrangement of those experiences which can most readily be achieved through team teaching. Teachers may in selecting their objectives in this circumstance, place a greater emphasis upon the behavioural outcomes to be achieved, than upon factual content. Much good work has been done in this field. Some has foundered, however, because teachers have not fully understood the following:

1 The reasons why the subjects were put together.

2 That common concepts had been established which were continuous.

3 That learning experiences should be planned to achieve certain designated purposes.

4 That these must be clearly defined to provide a model against which degrees of success or failure can be measured.

5 That human experience is continuous and each exercise is simply a part of a progression which increases in sophistication.

Thus whether subjects are studied separately, or integrated, teachers need to understand the factors influencing schools' curriculum:

(i) Pressures from society (economic, social, religious, political)

(ii) Tradition (custom, cultural heritage)

(iii) Particular needs of pupil group (age, ability, sex)

(iv) The aims of the school

(v) How the school achieves those aims through the framework of its curriculum

(vi) The part played by one's own subject in the realisation of those aims

(vii) One's own role within this.

Subject specialisms

Each subject:

1 has its own body of knowledge which is usually referred to as content;

2 has its own register. This is the language in which it is expressed and which enables it to be understood both by specialists and lay people;

3 has its own study techniques, that is, methods of inquiry;

4 has its own manner of presenting facts, opinions and generalisations;

5 has its own mode of asking and answering questions;

6 has particular means of evaluation;

7 conducts its own form of empirical research;

8 may show a clearly defined progression of study through school, further and higher education;

9 may have vocational outlets within a clearly defined career structure leading from studies in further and higher education.

Home economics fulfils all the preceding criteria numbering 1 to 9. Downey, 1960, page 254 argues that each subject study should therefore follow: the acquisition of skills, attitudes and *'disciplined habits necessary for the discovery of new knowledge in the field,'* and *'in the acquisition of the most useful fund of information possible of mastery within the limits of the time available for the subject.'*

The next section addresses itself to that important question. What is knowledge?

Selected references and further reading

Department of Education and Science, Local Authority Arrangements for the Curriculum (report on circular 14/77 review) HMSO, 1979

Department of Education and Science, Aspects of secondary education in England: A survey by HM Inspectors of Schools, HMSO, 1979

Department of Education and Science, A view of the Curriculum, HMI Series: Matters for Discussion No. 11, HMSO, 1980

Department of Education and Science, A Framework for the School Curriculum, 1980

Brialt, E and Smith, F *Falling Rolls in Secondary Schools,* NFER Publishing Company, 1980

Dewey, J *Democracy and Education,* Macmillan New York, 1967

Downey, L W *Secondary Education: A Model for Improvement,* from Taba, H, *Curriculum Development Theory and Practice,* Harcourt Brace and World, Inc, 1962.

2 Knowledge

The Shorter Oxford English Dictionary defines 'knowledge' as: *the theoretical or practical understanding of an art, science, language, etc.'* What then is the nature of knowledge? Much research has focussed upon this question. Knowledge of a particular subject is usually referred to as 'content'. Acquiring an understanding of that content is often spoken of as 'knowing'. The means by which that knowing is achieved is that subject's method of inquiry.

Historically, greater emphasis has been placed upon 'content' and the discipline necessary for getting to know that content. This has usually been achieved by memorising. A consequence of this was the belief that getting to know the content of a subject exerted a discipline upon the mind. Certain subjects (the difficult ones) were said to do this better than others. This led the early schools (as noted in Part 2, section 2) to place great emphasis on the study of classics and mathematics. The last century has seen a rapid decline in the study of classics. This century, with its rapid technological development, has witnessed more interest in mathematics and the sciences, accompanied, not surprisingly, by a greater emphasis upon methods of inquiry.

How much knowledge?

The question of how much one needs to 'know' (ie quantity) in order to have 'an understanding' (ie depth or quality) will probably never be answered;

hence Downey's 'the most useful fund of information possible of mastery within the limits of the time available.' The emphasis placed by Downey upon 'useful fund of information' implies that the content is subjected to careful selection. In respect of the 'mastery' about which Downey speaks there are two opposing schools of thought. Early scholars and teachers thought that it was the form of the subject which trained the faculties. Faculties so trained it was argued, could transfer this power to any other situation. Now, although it is accepted that the nature of the content determines the quality of thought processes, a greater emphasis is placed upon an analytical or scientific approach to thinking.

Implicit in the latter approach is an understanding of the methods used in inquiry; the critical estimate of the evidence collected; the use of this knowledge and understanding in the solution of relevant problems. Taken at its extreme the 'disciplining of intelligence' approach through the study of hard subjects rejects as valueless the study of the 'applied' subjects like home economics. If, however, actual content is seen to be less relevant than the amount of mental activity used for the search and use of knowledge, then it follows that almost any subject can be studied with equal advantage. A middle view would be that a study of a variety of subjects gives a balance in intellectual development. This follows, since there is a relationship between thought processes and the content of a subject and since thought systems for studying subjects differ. This is clarified in an examination of 'content' and the functions which it serves.

Levels of knowledge

Content or knowledge can be divided into four levels each with differing functions.
Hilda Taba, 1962, pages 174 to 181.

1 Specific facts and processes
2 Basic ideas and principles
3 Concepts
4 Thought systems

1 Specific facts and processes

This content includes specific facts, descriptive ideas at a low level of abstraction, specific processes and skills. Included in this category will be processes taught in dress construction and food preparation. It covers basic recipes, rules for kitchen usage, basic hygiene, characteristics of digestion, bones in the body, etc. Basic formulae used in mathematics and science are also included in this category. Teachers base their choice of material in this area upon the use to which such knowledge is to be put. It is probable that subject specialists will not agree on what should be included and what should be left out. For example, collars, openings, seams, fastenings, stitches, how many, which? Methods of cooking, how many, which?

It should be remembered that much information in this category quickly becomes obsolete or out of date. Nevertheless, facts are the basic or raw material from which ideas can be developed. Facts are to ideas what words are to thought and language. Therefore, each subject specialist must examine carefully the vast array before him. From this he chooses the most important facts, the most relevant processes, according to (a) the time available (b) the ideas and concepts which are to be developed. Remember that:

all pupils do not need to know the same facts, since facts in themselves do not constitute the fundamentals of learning;

recall of facts alone should not be the principal focus either of teaching or evaluation of learning.

2 Basic ideas and principles

These form the second level of knowledge. The structure or framework of a subject is made up from these basic ideas or principles. Easy movement, at this level of learning, demands that the student understands relationships between ideas, people and things. Mathematical principles, scientific laws and causal relationships, fall into this category. For example, man cannot constantly take and use natural resources without replacement, without upsetting the balance of nature. This is seen in agriculture where soil erosion results from overcropping. It is seen in the rapid reduction of world energy sources and resources. Unless man observes basic principles of good husbandry famine will surely follow.

In the home, good housekeeping, which makes for economic stability, is necessary if family life is to be maintained on equable terms. Physical health in family members, is sustained only if a nutritional balance is held in family feeding. Child rearing and parenting practices are influential in human development. From these basic ideas and others, the structure of home economics is formulated. Basic ideas give a wider control over subject matter. They allow for the continuity and development of ideas over a period of time. For example, the whole of a school life or the whole of one's natural life. Basic ideas and principles allow facts to be organised and relationships between them to be seen. This provides the context from which insights and understanding in learning emerge. These open up the way for the discovery of new knowledge.

Basic ideas and principles in a subject are fundamental to its understanding. They are the central ideas around which the organisation of the subject matter takes place. Basic ideas and principles, in a subject, are essential learning for everyone and form therefore, the core of the subject curriculum.

3 Concepts

The third level of content or knowledge consists of concepts. These are complex abstract ideas which emerge when experiences are repeated or when they are undertaken in a variety of contexts. Concepts are said to be infinite since they can be studied at ascending levels of difficulty, without reaching conclusion. They hold therefore, the key to curriculum planning and illustrate continuity in education. Some concepts running through home economics courses at differing levels are: health, safety, independence, interdependence, economic stability, good housekeeping, morality, ethics, aesthetics. Scientific concepts with which you will be familiar are light, heat, time, space, colour, etc. In mathematics the 'set' concept runs through the school curriculum at primary, middle and high school levels. In the early stages of education, a concept is presented to pupils in a concrete form. Development to an abstract appreciation is arrived at with growth of maturation. For example, safety is presented in the primary school in a simple cause and effect situation. If a glowing electric fire is touched it burns and pain and injury is experienced. Similarly, if one runs into the street in the path of an oncoming vehicle, pain and injury is experienced.

As the concept of safety is developed in the middle years and later at high school level, insights and understandings are arrived at which enable a more complex view to be taken. Safety is seen in relationship to health, for example, safe water supplies, sanitation, hygiene, housing, pedestrian vehicular segregation, medical care, work practice, use of tools and machinery, dangerous materials, safety of the person, security from thieves, etc. This illustrates that the concept of safety is one which is central to the lives of individuals from the cradle to the grave.

4 Thought systems

The fourth level of content or knowledge is seen in the thought systems used in the study of academic disciplines. These are the methods of study or lines of inquiry which are seen to be usual and most appropriate to the study of a particular subject. Such methods of study will embrace the three levels of content or knowledge already discussed, ie basic facts, ideas, principles and concepts. Thought systems are simply the manner in which each subject organises its thinking, relative to the levels of content within it. It is seen to be of most value if it has a disciplined way of asking questions, logical ways of relating ideas and a rational method of inquiry.

Applications to teaching

A technological age requires that people are able to use their minds and apply knowledge to new situations. This is perhaps the most difficult task facing teachers. They constantly seek ways in which learning may lead to disciplined thought. Mere attendance at school does not teach anyone to think. Attending classes for X number of years in a particular subject does not necessarily teach an individual to think in a disciplined way. Covering a particular area of content does not teach the learner how to study that subject effectively or how to use the facts, ideas, principles or concepts, constructively.

'Covering' is a word frequently used by teachers in school. To 'cover' a subject has long been seen to be a desirable objective, but 'covering' in itself has a very limited application. Teachers should address themselves to the problem of teaching the learner to develop systemised thought in a particular subject. From the examples of concepts given above, it can be seen that differing subjects may have concepts in common. For example, health may be seen in terms of food and nutrition, hygiene, medicine, microbiology, biology, chemistry, physics, housing, textiles and clothing; the list is endless. This illustrates the inter-relationship of subjects and suggests their integrative possibilities.

The last section discussed integrated subject studies and possible pitfalls. Avoid the 'squirrel' syndrome where pupils are set to collect endless facts. Pupils need an active involvement finding out the answers to questions, discovering new questions related to the answers. Remembering the levels of content and knowledge; facts should be used to throw up ideas and to reflect on problems to be solved. The teacher suggests the path to follow. If success is not achieved, change the question. Perhaps the solution to the original problem will then suggest itself.

This is the approach much enjoyed by 'gifted' children. They have, seemingly, a superfluity of curiosity and interest which spurs them on in such a way as to suggest a mind so direct in its application to the task in hand that it excludes every outside distraction. As some businessmen pursue riches with ruthless determination, so the gifted child pursues knowledge. The teacher will observe that this single minded approach may exclude all personal relationship and contact with others. At times it may suggest a self which is completely insensitive to others.

For those with a limited curiosity and interest the teacher's task is more difficult. It is his task to grade the steps along the way so that each child can just see the goal within his grasp. This requires careful planning by the teacher. It is not uncommon for pupils in high school (particularly those with little or no aspiration) to reach a point where they lack motivation and assume a position of complete indifference. This is a problem for teachers which appears to be increasing. Teachers encounter few problems with those who are interested, able and have aspirations which can only be satisfied by work and the attainment of the relevant certificates.

For those who have no interest, no aspirations, combined sometimes with a lack of ability, school is seen to be an unnecessary chore. Such a chore, indeed, that it is difficult to persuade some pupils even to enter the school building on a regular basis. For these young people the statutory requirement to attend school seems an unnecessary invasion of their time and liberty. Sadly, I am told, some pupils consciously aspire to a life of unemployment, which if realised, represents a reservoir of unused work potential and a burden on the national economy. It also represents an undesirable face of a social security system which was designed to cushion those members of the population who, in times of hardship, were in need, as a result of ill-health, unemployment or old-age. Where the school curriculum is rejected by youngsters such as these, local education authorities seek to provide alternatives. This may be offered in centres away from school. At these, pupils who have rejected school, are taught in very small groups, by specialist, experienced teachers. The latter aim to rehabilitate the pupil by encouraging him to adopt a disciplined approach to living in a society where pupils attend school and adults follow a job of work. From these centres, pupils either return to the mainstream of the high school system or leave on reaching the statutory school leaving age.

Section 3 will examine the formulation of educational objectives. These are the targets, or goals, along the educational continuum, set for learners, by teachers. They serve as a model against which the quality of learning by individual pupils may be measured. It follows from this that an evaluation of the quality of pupils' learning will also provide a measure of the quality of a teacher's teaching performance.

Selected references
Taba, H *Curriculum Development Theory and Practice,* Harcourt, Brace and World, Inc, 1962

Hall, OA and Paolucci, B, *Teaching Home Economics,* John Wiley, Second
  edition 1970
Dewey, J, *Democracy and Education,* Macmillan New York, 1967.

3 Formulating objectives

*'A satisfactory formulation of objectives which indicates both the behavioural
aspects and the content aspects provides clear specifications to indicate just
what the educational job is. By defining these desired educational results as
clearly as possible the curriculum-maker has the most useful set of criteria for
selecting content, for suggesting learning activities, for deciding on the kind
of teaching procedures to follow.'*
Ralph W Tyler, *Basic Principles of Curriculum and Instruction,* 1950

*'A statement of an objective is useful to the extent that it specifies what the
learner must be able to* DO *or* PERFORM *when he is demonstrating his mastery
of the objective . . . , the most important characteristic of a useful objective is
that it identifies the kind of performance that will be accepted as evidence that
the learner has achieved the objective.'*
Robert F Mager, *Preparing Instructional Objectives,* 1962

It is the task of all teachers to prepare clear, exact objectives for their pupils.
These describe the precise performance expected from them. Benjamin
Bloom et al have made the teacher's task simpler by the development of a
taxonomy which arranges educational objectives according to their properties
and relationships.

Classification of educational objectives

(See Benjamin S. Bloom, *Taxonomy of Educational Objectives,* 1956)

A *Cognitive* (relating to knowledge, intellectual skills and ability)

B *Affective* (concerned with interests, attitudes and values)

C *Psychomotor* (dealing with manipulative skills and abilities)

A *Cognitive (relating to knowledge, intellectual skills and ability)*

1 *Comprehension*
2 *Translation*
3 *Interpretation*
4 *Extrapolation*   *levels at which intellectual ability*
5 *Application*   *and skill may be demonstrated*
6 *Analysis*
7 *Synthesis*
8 *Evaluation*

Objectives in the cognitive realm place emphasis on the mental processes of
organising and assembling material to achieve a given purpose.

1 *Comprehension* The ability to give a literal (re)presentation of a communication. This is the lowest level of understanding.

2 *Translation* The ability to translate a communication into other words or another form without sacrificing accuracy.

3 *Interpretation* The ability to grasp the meaning of a communication and represent it in differing ways or in differing contexts.

4 *Extrapolation* The ability to deduce from given data implications, trends, consequences, which are in accord with that data.

5 *Application* The ability to use ideas, principles, procedures, to solve an abstract or concrete problem.

6 *Analysis* The ability to understand, implicit and explicit form, structure and interrelationship of ideas within a communication.

7 *Synthesis* The ability to produce an original communication from given information and material.

8 *Evaluation* The ability to form judgements about the value of qualitative and quantitative material, using given or one's own criteria.

B *Affective (concerned with interests, attitudes and values)*

1 *Receiving*	
2 *Responding*	*levels at which objectives*
3 *Valuing*	*in the affective domain may be*
4 *Organisation*	*demonstrated.*
5 *Value complex*	

'The ordering of objectives ... is of prime importance in the affective domain . . . The entire domain proceeds from categories which are relatively simple, requiring very little from the student, to categories of objectives which require a fairly complete internalisation of a set of attitudes, values, and behaviors. We imagine that the learning of the more highly internalised objectives must start with the more simple and perhaps superficial behaviors specified in the first few categories of this domain. It is entirely possible that the learning of the more difficult and internalised objectives must be in the form of a 'loop' which begins with the simple and more overt behaviors, gradually moves to the more complex and more internalised behaviors, and repeats the entire procedure in new areas of content and behavior until a highly internalised, consistent, and complex set of affective behaviors is finally developed.'

David R Krathwohl, Benjamin S Bloom and Bertram B Masia, *Taxonomy of Educational Objectives*, pages 79 to 80, David McKay Co. Inc., New York 1964

1 *Receiving* (or attending) In its simplest form is awareness. The pupil is conscious of receiving stimulus but does not consciously identify it or direct it. The next step is a willingness to be aware. The pupil does not consciously 'turn off' but is willing to look and listen. The third step is controlled attention. The pupil consciously controls his attention and focusses it towards the stimulus. We say that he is showing interest or giving his full attention.

This is the state required for teaching to be effective and the reason for the maxim; don't begin until you have the full attention of the class. If the objectives state, 'to arouse interest', this is the point where an initial evaluation of whether this has been achieved, takes place.

2 *Responding* The first stage shown by pupils is acceptance. The pupil obeys non-commitally; neither willingly nor unwillingly. It is a neutral state. The second stage is a willing response. This is a chosen action. The third stage is a response which is evoked because of the enjoyment which accompanies it.

3 *Valuing* This is an abstract concept signifying worth. It is a product of socialisation and arises only after practised behaviour. Valuing is shown at three levels. Firstly acceptance. This is a non-commital acceptance. For example, to wash one's self, to write neatly. The pupil accepts it in a state of neutrality, neither liking or disliking it. The second stage is preference. The pupil washes because he likes the feeling of well being it produces rather than because it is anti-social not to do so. He writes neatly because he wants to, he prefers it, not because he has to. The third stage is commitment. At this stage a person is fully committed to a certain viewpoint, he holds a belief or conviction. This decision may be taken on rational or irrational grounds. At this stage a person identifies with others who hold the same views or beliefs. He joins a group, works for a cause and is said to hold certain ideals.

Classroom implications This third stage can be turned to advantage in class control. It is illustrated in the old adage—'birds of a feather flock together'. One can use this phenomena in two ways. It may be felt to be desirable to put those holding the same values together for ease in management. Conversely, if a pupil exhibits anti-social tendencies, it may help if he is attached to a person or persons holding different values, in the hope that either he will accept that other values are desirable, or that the strength of the alternative peer group will prevail.

We have seen that values are established as a result of practised behaviour. They are acquired from the people with whom one associates most. Therefore, even before entering school, pupils have already acquired values from living in the close knit proximity of their families. When they enter school and exhibit these values, some may appear desirable, others undesirable. For example, a pupil may already hold the view, 'what's yours is mine, what's mine is my own'. Such a pupil in primary school is a problem both to his teacher and to fellow pupils. Unless his viewpoint can be changed, he will, in a very few years, also represent a threat to the well-being of the wider society outside school. The ease with which children adopt anti-social values from their peers, is a common concern among many parents.

4 *Organisation* As adults they hold certain views, believe in certain values and have organised these values into a framework which determines for them the way in which they live. Parents wish their children to hold the same values and beliefs as they do themselves. These are significant requirements to them when trying to select schools for their children, in which the philosophy of the school and teachers, resembles their own beliefs. For example, parents holding certain religious beliefs, wish their children to be brought up in the company of others who share the same faith. Rapidly this is becoming a luxury few can afford for their children. Some parents will actually move to another home in order to be in the catchment zone of a school which values good behaviour, diligence and success. In a wider context, Britain has, for

generations, been a refuge for families fleeing from the oppression of other lands where man is not permitted to hold certain values and beliefs.

Parents know that children acquire the values of their peers. Where the peers are anti-social in outlook and behaviour, many parents strive to ensure that their sons and daughters do not keep 'bad' company. There is a good deal of evidence to support this view. It also focusses attention upon two things:
   (i) the need for care in the selection of teachers
   (ii) the responsibility placed upon teachers to ensure that school is not a breeding ground for the acquisition of socially undesirable values, ie those values which are harmful to the well-being of the individual, family and society.

How values are organised into a system or framework

It was said earlier that valuing involved a practised, consistent mode of behaviour. Before values can be organised into a system, they must first be conceptualised. The conceptualisation of a value, means that the value is viewed as a mental image. Values are said to be organised when the practice of them is consistent, and when they are grouped together to form a picture of behaviour from which known characteristics can be recognised. For example, earlier this century those values associated with the working class and middle class were grouped to form a picture of the way in which members of these social classes behaved. It was claimed that individuals could be identified by their behaviour (according to the values which they held) and were placed in the appropriate social classes, or categories. Scholars sought also to correlate this with occupation and education.

The Education Act of 1944 provided opportunity for secondary education for everyone. This opened the way to higher education and the professions. Since then the correlation between education and social grouping has altered considerably. Recent research findings by Goldthorpe indicate that, of those men studied, seventy per cent of those now in class one of The Standard Classification of Social Status Category (The Hall-Jones Scale), had fathers who followed manual or semi-skilled occupations. These seventy per cent were, therefore, of working class origin. Dahrendorf expressed the view that education had, in Britain, since the 1944 Act, provided a ladder for social mobility. Britain could no longer be divided rigidly into classes as before. But, he stressed, people could still be grouped according to their behaviour, as shown by the values which they held. This meant that although class division, based upon education and occupation, had gone, the organised frameworks of working class and middle class values remained.

So, it can be said that values have been organised and internalised, when behaviour is clearly identifiable, according to the characteristics which the individual exhibits. The reasons why individuals hold the views they do, is more difficult to explain, as is shown by the last example. Does parental and family influence far outweigh that imposed by education? The previous example suggests that this could be. Nevertheless, the acquisition of values is an ongoing process and values held can be changed, although this is a slow process. Where values held are expressed in behaviour, which may be described as prejudiced, or discriminatory, relative to education, race, religion, etc, a change in these values is a slow, long and often painful process. Such values are often the sum total of centuries of thinking and practising by groups of people, both here and overseas.

5 *Value complex* The organisation of our value system into a recognisable behaviour pattern is usually referred to as our code of behaviour. This means that behaviour is clearly recognisable, consistent and predictable. As maturity approaches, it is seen as an expression of our philosophy on life. It will be seen in Appendix 1, to be a prime need for each individual, that he develops what is for him an acceptable philosophy of life. This is essential for mental and emotional stability and happiness.

C *Psychomotor (dealing with manipulative skills and abilities)*

1 *Perception*
2 *Set*
3 *Guided response*   *levels at which psychomotor*
4 *Mechanism*   *response may be demonstrated*
5 *Complex overt response*

1 *Perception* This is the process of becoming aware. It is experienced at three levels:

(i) Sensory stimulation
(ii) Cue selection
(iii) Translation

(i) *Sensory stimulation* is recognised by one or more of the sense organs, ie

Visual – images or mental pictures experienced through the eyes

Auditory – hearing through the ears

Tactile – relating to the sense of touch

Taste – experienced through taste sensitive areas of the tongue

Smell – experienced through the olfactory nerves of the nose

Kinesthetic – felt through the muscles, joints and tendons.

The act of perception accompanies the first stage of receiving or attending in the affective domain. Interest may be aroused in the pupil, therefore, by a delicious smell of baking bread, or the sight and smell of fresh strawberries. In learning, seeing is the most dominant of the senses. Hearing is the next. Teachers endeavour to strengthen perception by presenting stimuli through several of the senses. This is particularly important with young pupils and those who are poorly motivated, or less able. Objectives may be chosen which require pupils to directly identify, sensory stimuli, for example, smells, tastes, sounds, etc.

(ii) *Cue selection* This involves the selection of cues which require response if a task is to be satisfactorily completed. Home economics teachers teach pupils to recognise and respond to cues, appropriate to particular situations. For instance, to identify smells which accompany changes in food during cooking, or to listen for sound cues, like hissing, spluttering, rhythmic bubbling, to savour food and identify when more salt or sugar is required, or to feel when buns are cooked, etc. When pupils are incapacitated in one or more of the senses (blind, deaf), cue selection in the remaining senses becomes even more important and should be stressed in teaching.

(iii) *Translation* This is the mental process of determining the meaning of the cues received and deciding upon the necessary action. A recipe is read and the appropriate action is taken to prepare the dish. In this, full use is made of knowledge previously acquired and experience. This example might well form the basis of a specific objective.

2 *Set* This relates to personal adjustment to carry out a task. Three aspects of set have been identified:

(i) Mental
(ii) Physical
(iii) Emotional

(i) *Mental* This is a readiness in a mental sense, to carry out a motor act. Firstly, the three levels of perception must be satisfied. Judgement or discrimination is necessary in selecting the action to be taken. Objectives to evaluate this might be, a knowledge of the steps in preparing a cup of tea; a knowledge of tools appropriate for specific tasks; a knowledge of the steps in making up a gored skirt.

(ii) *Physical* This is a bodily readiness for the required task. Sitting, or standing in the appropriate position, with limbs correctly positioned, for rolling pastry, for machining, for writing, etc.

(iii) *Emotional* Having the right attitude, to attempt the task with success, ie a willing disposition.

3 *Guided response* This is the selected response given under the guidance of the teacher. Conditions of perception and set, must be favourable for success.

There are two categories of response

(i) Imitation
(ii) Trial and error

(i) *Imitation* This is a direct response to having seen the teacher perform a task. For example, setting on a collar, lining a skirt. Objectives would relate to the completion of the task as demonstrated.

(ii) *Trial and error* This involves the selection of the most appropriate response, from a group of responses, by performing the task in different ways. An objective set would require a most efficient, appropriate, satisfactory method to be used for completing a specific task. For example, making a dart, finishing a seam, pressing a skirt.

4 *Mechanism* This is the level at which a learned response has become habitual. The learner has acquired a degree of skill and confidence in the act. Objectives may be set which evaluate that skill. For example, individual hand stitches, machining, drafting, etc.

5 *Complex overt response* At this level, a high degree of skill has been attained, in movements which are of considerable complexity. There are two categories of response:

(i) Resolution of uncertainty
(ii) Automatic performance

(i) *Resolution of uncertainty* Although the skill is complex in nature, the individual is able (without a mental picture) to carry it through with confidence. For example, setting up and using a sewing or knitting machine.

(ii) *Automatic performance* This demands finely co-ordinated motor skill, with fine muscle control. For example, fine stitching on delicate fabrics, complicated icing design, fine brushwork in painting, intricate detailing in embroidery.

Selected references and further reading
Tyler, R W, *Basic Principles of Curriculum and Instruction,* Chicago: The University of Chicago Press, 1950

Bloom, B S, et al, Taxonomy of Educational Objectives, The Classification of Educational Goals, Longmans, New York, 1956

Mager, R F, *Preparing Instructional Objectives,* Palo Alto. Fearon Publishers, California, 1962

Taba, H, *Curriculum Development Theory and Practice,* Harcourt, Brace & World, Inc, 1962

Hall, O A and Paolucci, B, *Teaching Home Ecnomics,* John Wiley, Second edition, 1970

Schools Council Home Economics Team, Home and Family 8-13, Forbes, 1979

4 Choosing objectives

This brief examination of the taxonomy of Benjamin S Bloom indicates that learning is viewed as being both continuous and hierarchical, with clearly recognisable steps in progression, in each of the areas of cognitive, affective and psychomotor skills. It is the teacher's task to arrange learning experiences for pupils, in sequential fashion, with the simplest at the beginning and continuing them in a pyramid of attainment to the top. It is important to understand the relationship between the cognitive, affective and psychomotor levels of progression.

Behaviours in the cognitive, affective and psychomotor domains

Level of behaviour	Cognitive	Affective	Psychomotor
5 Integration and control	Evaluation	Characterisation by a value complex	Complex overt response
4 Relationship of parts; a system	Analysis synthesis	Organisation	Mechanism
3 Action	Application	Valuing	Guided response
2 Readiness to react	Comprehension	Responding	Set
1 Awareness	Knowledge	Receiving	Perception

*Hall and Paolluci, 1970, page 186

The hierarchical progression is illustrated in the table above. Time is required to accomplish long term aims, relative to behaviour in all three areas (cognitive, affective, psychomotor). It is important, therefore, to think through a sequence of learning (daily, weekly, termly, yearly, see Part 2, section 2). The objectives for this learning will serve as a guide for the evaluation of achievement. The achievement will be seen in much narrower terms than the objectives from which it stems.

Stating objectives

Describe:

1 the *kind* of behaviour expected
2 the *content* to which that behaviour applies
3 the *context* to which that behaviour applies

Avoid general statements like: to develop an ability to think and express one's self clearly. Such a statement does not specify: what is to be thought about, what is the content of the expected expression, whether the expected expression is to be oral or written. Instead, state clearly whether:

1 facts or opinions are required
2 information is to be recalled
3 content is to be learned
4 knowledge is to be applied to the solution of a given problem, *or* to the assessment of a given situation.

Continuity in the curriculum

The principle of continuity in the curriculum is illustrated as certain concepts are studied at greater depth, with the increasing maturity of the individual and the higher the level of course undertaken. It is important to note that new content need not always be added for learning to be increased, or enriched. By a more limited coverage a deeper understanding may result from a more detailed analysis, or a more rigorous examination, of ideas. It is also possible to use the same content to achieve different objectives.

Complex objectives

If objectives are complex, analyse them. Then state each required component, specifically. For example: understanding, competence, appreciation, discrimination, an awareness, clear thinking. These are all complex. Let us examine one of these, 'competence'. 'To demonstrate *competence* in meal planning.' Questions which arise are:

1 Does this relate to theory or practice?
2 For whom are the meals to be planned?
3 Which meals, one meal, a day's meals, a week's meals?
4 What are the conditions for planning? (Number of people, ages, occupations, cost, equipment, occasion.)

It is soon apparent that the objective given is open ended and subject to many interpretations. The more intelligent the reader, the greater the number of variables will be found and the outcome will be confusion. It is not possible to interpret the objective as it stands, accurately. One often meets the following objective, at all levels in education: 'to develop good hygienic practice'. What exactly does this mean? Does it mean the same to primary school and high school teachers? Does it mean the same to general subjects' teachers and home economics teachers? If certain practices are to be encouraged, then spell them out. If these practices recur week by week, detail them at the outset of the course and indicate that they will be evaluated at each lesson.

Different kinds of learning

Plan objectives to cover different kinds of learning (cognitive, affective, psychomotor).

Remember:

1 An increase in knowledge will not, in itself, lead to a change in attitude. For example, a knowledge of Islam (Part 3, section 3) will not in itself, make British pupils more tolerant of their Moslem neighbours. If it is desirable that attitudes be changed, then specific experiences to bring this about must be planned.

2 Experiences planned to develop manual skill will not necessarily develop thinking. Thus, if thinking is to be developed, the lesson must include appropriate experiences for this to be done.

3 Content, presented by the teacher in logical form, does not in itself, teach logical thinking. If pupils are to develop logical thinking, specific experiences must be planned for them to practise this for themselves.

4 Objectives are intermediary only in the continuum of learning. They should be planned to increase in difficulty. This is based on the assumption that a teacher has a knowledge of the full range of expectation in his subject within the school (an argument for specialist teachers) and of the aims, implicit in the philosophy of the school. It also assumes that the teacher has a knowledge of the maturation process in pupils to enable appropriate experiences to be planned accordingly.

Relating learning experiences to objectives

The stating of objectives serves only to chart the path for a teacher and pupil to follow. The teacher has then to select the most appropriate means by which the pupils can achieve the objectives.

Criteria for determining the means

1 *Continuity*
2 *Sequence*
3 *Integration*

1 *Continuity* Concepts within a subject area may extend vertically through courses at all levels (section 2). It is necessary, therefore, to precede new learning with a review of what has already been done (Part 3, section 2). This provides a firm foundation on which to build. As maturation of pupils increases, learning experiences of greater difficulty are planned, which promote development in cognitive, affective and psychomotor skills.

2 *Sequence*   By grading the difficulty of learning experiences, concepts may be explored at greater depth and breadth.

3 *Integration*   The relationship of the different parts of the home economics course should be clear to the learner. The relationship of home economics to other subjects within the school curriculum should be made clear.

In conclusion, it is well to note that Tyler said:

'The term "learning experience" refers to the interaction between the learner and the external conditions in the environment to which he can react. Learning takes place through the active behavior of the student; it is what he does that he learns, not what the teacher does.'

Selected references and further reading

Taba, H, *Curriculum Development Theory and Practice,* Harcourt, Brace and World, Inc, 1962

Hall, O A and Paolucci, B, *Teaching Home Economics,* John Wiley, Second edition, 1970

Schools Council Curriculum Bulletin 4, Home Economics Teaching, Evans/ Methuen Educational, 1971

Schools Council Home Economics Team, Home and Family 8-13, Forbes, 1979

5 Home economics in schools

The name

Home economics is now the name most widely used to describe the area of study embracing the particular concerns of the home economist. Although this name was first adopted on the other side of the Atlantic, it has its roots firmly set in the English language. My search for a logical reason for its adoption led to the Shorter Oxford English Dictionary. The word 'home' originates from the Old English ham, meaning a village or town, with its cottages. It has come to mean, a dwelling which shelters a family, or an institution which houses many people, related only by their reason for being there. For instance, age, infirmity or lack of parental support.

An alternative word used in the above contexts, is 'house'. This is derived from the Old English word hus. House also refers to the shelter afforded to a small group of people living together as a family, or a much larger group, brought together by circumstance or design, to fulfil a common purpose. The following are some of the uses of this word accrued over a long period of time; boarding house, House of God, Religious House (convent or monastery), legislative house (parliament), playhouse (theatre), school house (pupils grouped together for common activities, sports, games, leisure or academic pursuits).

The person who managed the hus or household is described as a hus wif. This dates from the twelfth century (Middle English). By definition, 'Often, a woman who manages her home with skill and thrift, a domestic economist.' It follows, therefore, that if the person who manages the affairs of a house is a domestic economist, then, since an alternative word for house is home, the person who manages the affairs of a home, is a home economist. This line of reasoning can be carried further to suggest a logical reason why the early institutions trained teaching and institutional management specialists under one roof.

It has already been established that home and house are interchangeable in use and meaning, relative to the shelter which each afforded to a single group of people (a family), or a larger group of people, brought together by circumstance, in an institution (religious, charitable, or educational). Home and institution, represent the micro and macro, aspects of daily living. It has been argued that the person who manages the former, is a home economist. In a like manner, it can be argued that the person who manages an institution of the kind described, is also a home economist.

Historical perspectives

We have looked at those influences exerted on curriculum planning by contemporary society and tradition, in Part 6, section 1. All home economics syllabuses reflect, in part, the historical reference of the subject and the contemporary view held of it, both nationally and internationally. As a teacher in school, you will provide the mouthpiece for the current position, as you see it, feel it, interpret and present it. In Britain we are influenced, particularly, by two separate groups of pioneers. Those working in the nineteenth century in this country, and their sisters across the Atlantic, in America.

In this country the home economics teaching profession originated from small groups of socially conscious women who were concerned for the plight of the poor, of whom there were vast numbers. The birth of the industrial revolution brought to this country vast wealth, power and prestige. Poor agricultural workers were drawn to the heart of the industrial development. Small villages became towns, towns became cities. The railways spread like a spider's web, outwards from the industrial cities of the north. Between the railway lines, poor, mean dwellings, hastily mushroomed, to house those arriving from the depressed agricultural areas. Local records in Yorkshire show that workers walked to Barnsley, Leeds and Bradford, from Somerset, East Anglia and the South-east coast, in search of a better life.

South Yorkshire was already an active mining area. Men, women, boys and girls, worked beneath the green fields, in the wet, darkness of the pits. Contemporary writings tell of women and girls (barely in their 'teens) hewing coal and hauling it to central collecting points. They had not yet achieved the dignity now accorded to animals. Others worked in the mills which sprang up alongside the river valleys. Whole families spent the hours of daylight, imprisoned at the looms. Infants crawled between the machinery, cleaning those parts inaccessible to a bigger child, or adult. Threat of starvation brought workers, too, from overseas. Thousands from Ireland swelled the populations of Liverpool, Leeds and Manchester. It was against this backcloth that Home Economics Education in this country, was born.

The premier colleges which were to train home economics teachers for over a hundred years, took root in the major industrial cities of London, Leeds,

Leicester, Liverpool, Manchester, Glasgow and Edinburgh. The story of their foundations are remarkably similar and make fascinating reading. All began as small voluntary bodies, seeking to help the poor and unfortunate to survive. Florence Nightingale said, in a nursing context, that *'Health begins in the homes of the people'*. The early home economists based their teaching on this premise and placed priority on thrift, feeding and clothing the family and attempting to curb, through clean houses and personal habits, the spread of infection. Housing was poor and infection, due to ignorance, a lack of clean water and sanitation, was rife. Tombstones in a local Leeds churchyard, bear testimony to whole families being wiped out within days, during outbreaks of cholera.

When W E Forster (the Bradford politician) introduced compulsory national elementary education in 1870, it was, he said, *'to bring elementary education within the reach of every English home . . . .'* Later in the speech, he said, *'Upon this speedy provision of elementary education, depends our industrial prosperity.'* Some might argue that such a measure had been introduced to promote Britain as an industrial nation, rather than a provision to educate the masses. From this need for an educated work force, grew, in 1913, the junior technical schools. These provided a two year course for thirteen to fifteen year olds. Such courses combined a general education with a specialised industrial training. Many girls, completing courses directed towards domestic economy, took jobs as domestic servants, or were employed in shops, hospitals or service institutions.

These two historical views of the origins of home economics, have coloured the contemporary view, both of the subject and its possible vocational outlets. Those with extreme egalitarian beliefs regard home economics teachers as descendants of nineteenth century middle class ladies. An opposite view flees from the image of 'the domestic', the technical, and the servile aspects conjured up by domestic service. It is a pity some do not clarify a distinction between service and servility. Many schools do not advise pupils in the later years to study home economics, either at school, or as a vocation. Parents, ambitious for their child's success, may take the same view. In consequence, there is a dearth of well-qualified, female home economists to fill top posts—a situation which men have not been slow to alleviate. The only University in this country with a Chair in Home Economics, is Surrey, held by Dr Roger Irving, a chemist.

The development of home economics in America seems to have followed a different path. Early pioneers appear to have concentrated from the start, in the nineteenth century, on a scientific approach to home making. Such knowledge and resources, as were available at the time, were focussed on any area seen to be a vital part of family life, or an adjunct to it. The aim was to enrich the quality of enjoyment of life by the individual and the family, of which he was a part. As a result home economics seems to have grown up with a wider, deeper involvement, in the business, social, industrial and educational life of the nation. It may be studied in many universities at initial and higher degree levels. Higher degree studies reflect a well developed system of research work in industrial, social, business and educational fields. Some initial degree courses in this country reflect the influence and philosophy of American teaching.

The position of home economics in the school curriculum in this country is influenced also by the view taken of it by institutions of higher education. University entry requirements have played a significant role in the development of the schools' curriculum. Technical subjects, like home economics, art, craft, design and technology, have not enjoyed a parity of esteem with non-technical subjects, in acceptance for university entrance. Some universities now accept one technical subject at General Certificate of Education Advanced Level, for entry to some degree studies. The attempted goal of academic recognition has led to a significant part of these studies at Ordinary and Advanced levels being devoted to theoretical studies. In home economics courses one finds a greater emphasis on one or more of the following; physical science, biology, nutrition, social science and history.

This trend is reflected in courses studied later, in further and higher education. One consequence of this is a narrowing of craft course provision, within the school, in home economics. At a time when unemployment is rising rapidly, particularly among early school leavers, there is urgent need for technical provision within the curriculum for those with modest academic achievement.

Current thinking in home economics, also, owes much to those who have in recent years, pioneered the entry of home economists into wider areas of employment. This too, has influenced the content of courses at degree, sub-degree and school levels. Much of this has been done by the National Council for Home Economics Education (formerly the Northern Union of Schools of Cookery, the original validating body for the first teacher training courses). This validating body drew together those interested in the development and advancement of home economics. This resulted in a pooling of the skills and talents of those in industry, commerce, the professions, the social agencies and education. Together they formulated courses at sub-degree level which prepared students to enter areas of work, as home economists, at levels commensurate with their ability, attainment and interest.

The Home Management and Family Care Certificate course draws students from the forty per cent of the population, who leave school at sixteen years of age, with modest academic achievement. Leaving students are employed as residential care assistants, house parents, hospital aides, nursing auxilliaries, assistant matrons/housekeepers in residential schools, home helps, mother's helps, etc.

The Certificate in Home Economics Course draws students at post sixteen, who have achieved good results in the General Certificate of Education Ordinary level, or the Certificate of Secondary Education. Successful leaving students find employment as home economists in industry, commerce and the social agencies.

The Diploma in Home Economics was designed for the eighteen year old Advanced level General Certificate of Education student. This was developed in the late sixties. It gives entrants a broadly based education, in the contributory disciplines of home economics. Diplomees leave with a high level of expertise in food preparation and nutrition. They have a sound knowledge of physics and chemistry, combined with a study of materials science. Home management studies focus upon the choice and use of materials, equipment and services. Behavioural studies include psychology, sociology, economics and law. Professional studies focus on the roles undertaken by home economists in business, commerce, industry and the social agencies. The home economist is seen primarily as a communicator, who bridges the gap as a skilled professional, between the housewife (the consumer) and industry (the producer). It is the role of the home economist to interpret and communicate the consumers' anticipated and current needs, to the producer. Where design factors originate problems for the house wife, the home economist explores the source and suggests possible solutions to the manufacturer. Affluence has brought the fruits of highly complex technology within the grasp of the ordinary person. It is the home economist who shows the consumer how to use domestic equipment to derive the greatest benefit from it; whether this is in terms of performance, or conservation of energy consumption.

It is in these areas of human interaction that the roles of the home economist in industry, commerce, the social agencies and education come together. The architects of the Diploma Course in Home Economics, saw a need for a study of the physical, emotional, mental and social development of individuals. These are used as a backcloth to nutritional studies, communication, marketing and business methods. Within communication studies, students learn to talk to a wide range of individuals, conduct interviews, script and present radio and television programmes and prepare reports on industrial practice. During the course they initiate, manage and present demonstrations to small and large audiences. Diplomees from this course have pioneered many new employment areas in business, commerce, the social agencies, marketing, consumer advice, as well as the more familiar areas in the service industries and food and equipment companies.

In the early seventies, it became apparent that these home economists, enriched by two to three years of working experience in industry, would be an asset in schools and establishments of further education, as teachers. Since then, a few each year, have undertaken a year's professional training and entered the teaching profession. These early entrants brought a new and exciting dimension to the home economics scene in schools. Pupils enjoyed engaging in taste panel work. They examined and measured the amount of pressure required to crush the potato crisps in their lunchtime packet. The respective weights of beans and liquid were reported in differing brands of baked beans. Pupils compared the quality and quantity, money for money, of own brand commodities, with well known brand lines and 'best buys' emerged. Costs of branded commodities, were priced in the corner shop, market and supermarket, etc.

There is no doubt that this highly successful Diploma course has exerted a powerful influence on the acceptance of home economists in new areas of professional outlets. It has greatly influenced the content and direction of the new degree courses in home economics and prepared the way for those graduates entering new fields of employment. The already established path of diplomees moving from industry into education, will encourage a greater flexibility among employment patterns, for home economists in the future. This will serve to bring a more practical view of life to the teaching of home economics in schools and promote a more realistic approach to the planning of vocationally orientated courses, in both schools and further education.

The next section examines home economics in the schools curriculum, partly as it is and partly as it could be. It attempts to illustrate the principles outlined in sections 1 to 4.

The structure of home economics

Home economics may be studied in all three phases of education in primary, middle and high schools.

Aims

Home economics supports the aim underlying the general school curriculum, which seeks to maximise the means by which each individual can, in adulthood, live his life to its full potential (physically, mentally, socially and emotionally) in the realisation of his own philosophy (see section 1). This can only be done by using the relevant knowledge, experience and resources. To be effective each individual must be able to relate to the element of chance which has determined his birth, in respect of hereditary make up, race, religion, culture, the economic prosperity of his native homeland and his family circumstances. This requires a basic knowledge, understanding and expertise, in the three key areas which comprise the core of home economics:

A Human development   Fulfilment of a
B Aspects of family life   personal philosophy on life
C Outer environmental influences

Structure

The subject can be so structured as to realise, and be seen to be realising, the aims outlined above. It offers the student knowledge of facts and principles, ideas and concepts, within the field of physical, mental and emotional health and social well-being. Opportunity is given for the practice of these in everyday life and, for the knowledge and experience so gained, to be applied to new and more demanding situations. Within each area, concepts can be identified which, through their development, illustrate the linear nature of the subject. (See pages 170-172)

Structuring courses

Generally, courses are structured in one of two ways. First, the area of study is defined. Home economics is said to be multi-disciplinary. This means that it is made up of a number of recognised subject disciplines, such as physical science, biological science, nutrition, social science, psychology, philosophy, art and design, clothing, textiles, food studies and housing, etc. To form a field of study, knowledge is selected from the component disciplines, following two basic principles:

(i) that sufficient knowledge is chosen to give an understanding of the originating discipline itself

(ii) that appropriate knowledge will be selected to give enlightenment and understanding of the three key areas, which comprise the core of home economics, namely:

A Human development
B Aspects of family life
C Outer environmental influences.

The structure of home economics

A   Human development
B   Aspects of family life
C   Outer environmental influences

A   Human development

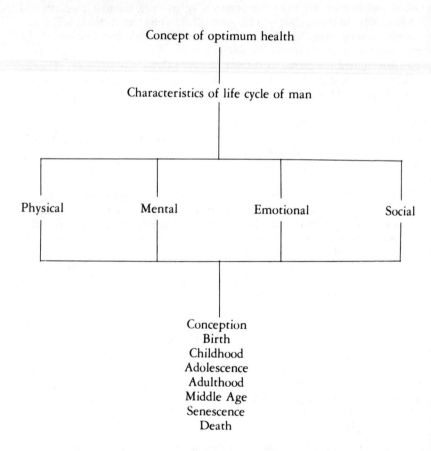

Concept of optimum health

Characteristics of life cycle of man

Physical   Mental   Emotional   Social

Conception
Birth
Childhood
Adolescence
Adulthood
Middle Age
Senescence
Death

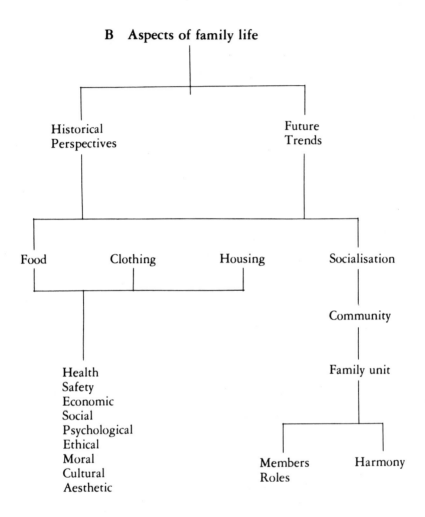

B Aspects of family life

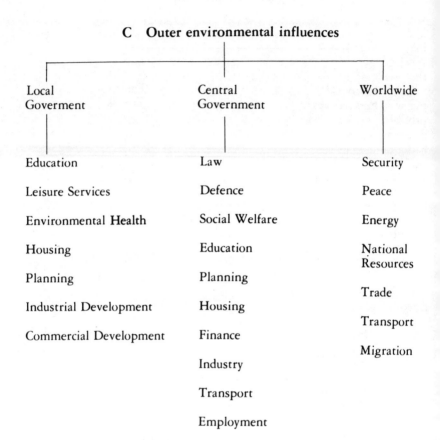

C   Outer environmental influences

Local Goverment	Central Government	Worldwide
Education	Law	Security
Leisure Services	Defence	Peace
Environmental Health	Social Welfare	Energy
Housing	Education	National Resources
Planning	Planning	Trade
Industrial Development	Housing	Transport
Commercial Development	Finance	Migration
	Industry	
	Transport	
	Employment	

For example, scientific studies may be described as applied science. This means that the specific items of course work are chosen to illustrate stated scientific principles related directly to the home, such as the working of a refrigerator, wiring an electric plug, detergency, food spoilage, etc. In selecting material, course planners will consider the general aims of the course, the age and ability of the students, before deciding which experiences will provide a good background knowledge to fulfil those aims.

Alternatively, courses may be planned from a problem solving base. This may be accompanied by a problem solving means of implementation. Thus, specific knowledge is chosen from the component subject disciplines to enable the problems set to be solved.

This method highlights the interrelationship of concepts to each other, and the way in which they merge to form a synthesis, in the solution of the problem. It is called the derivative approach. In the first method, the basic discipline approach, the student is required to select for himself, from his background knowledge, that which is appropriate for the solution of given problems. Whichever method of course structuring is chosen, it is the teacher who is the instrument of implementation. The pupil is the problem solver, and it is in his ability to apply the knowledge at his command that assessment can be made of the level of his understanding.

Planning a syllabus
Guide lines

1 Decide what it is reasonable to expect pupils to learn, relative to their age and ability.

2 Plan content and learning experiences, in relation to previous knowledge (acquired both at school and at home).

3 Provide opportunity for practice, in what is being learned.

4 Use learning outcomes to plan further work and experience (continuity).

5 Plan, so that pupils can apply their knowledge and experience to further work.

6 Give opportunity for pupils to reason out additional uses to which their knowledge and experience can be put.

7 Plan, for opportunity in observation and recording.

8 Build in an element of the pupil's own appraisal, of what has been learned and why it has been learned.

Defining limits of choice

In deciding what takes place in the classroom, the teacher defines the pupil's limits of choice, thus imposing constraints. In real life, outside the classroom, there are restrictions too and choices are limited. These constraints may be money, time, equipment, family commitments, job, sex of individual, conventions, social milieu, etc. There are also constraints upon the teacher and pupil, imposed by each pupil's individual differences. Provision of content and learning experiences, must differ for children with special needs, for example, slow learners, the culturally disadvantaged and those with special gifts. Planning must also take account of present trends, which place an emphasis on course content and skills, leading to a school leaver being 'more employable'. In this context, particular mention is made of practical skills, business skills, social skills, basic literacy and numeracy.

Implementing a syllabus

For many the choice of syllabus planning is narrowed by the influence of examining boards. Syllabuses may be already prescribed and a teacher then implements them. This means that the person implementing is not involved in the actual planning. However, although syllabuses may be written by unknown planners, they do reflect those influences, stated earlier, ie the historical perspectives of the subject and the current interpretation of the age. When a number of syllabuses for a given course are studied, it will be found that there are more likenesses within them, than differences. A teacher has, therefore, ample opportunity to show ingenuity and creativity in the scheme of work prepared from a set syllabus and the means chosen for its implementation. The way in which this is done will reflect the education, interests and skill of the teacher. (See page 175)

The early school years (5-9)

The overview of the primary school (Part 1, section 2) clearly indicated that the curriculum was not divided into separate subjects. In considering the role and content of home economics in this area of the curriculum one must first study what is already being taught.

Many of the activities which take place in the primary school are the forerunner of what is, later, a part of the home economics curriculum at middle and high school. It is, therefore, essential to examine these against the model of the structure of home economics outlined earlier. By setting them in context, it is possible to add to these activities, those elements which can, with profit, be undertaken by primary school pupils and teachers.

Aims underlying the primary school curriculum

To provide opportunity within an appropriate environment, experiences which will enable individuals to develop:

(i) co-ordinated muscular skills
(ii) emotional self-control
(iii) mental alertness, a desire to learn and acquire knowledge.

The means by which this is done is through:
(i) handling materials and tools
(ii) playing with, or beside others
(iii) language, spoken, written and read
(iv) calculation
(v) physical exercise
(vi) musical appreciation.

Within that context consider:

The aims specific to home economics in the early years

To lay the early foundations of knowledge in the three key areas comprising the central core of home economics:

SUMMARY

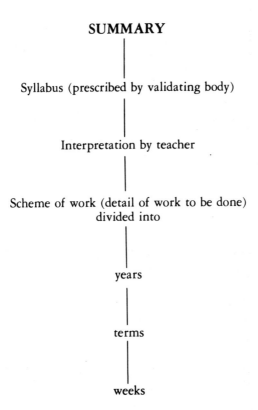

Syllabus (prescribed by validating body)

Interpretation by teacher

Scheme of work (detail of work to be done)
divided into

years

terms

weeks

A *Human development*
B *Aspects of family life (food, clothing, housing, socialisation)*
C *Outer environmental influences*

Within the primary school, pupils' activities are chosen which will develop within the learner, competences in speaking, reading, writing, numeracy and socialisation. Such activities include knowledge, experience and skills, known to be necessary for the healthy development and maturation of all children. Additional elements normally associated with home economics, may be included to supplement, strengthen and enrich this learning. Some examples have already been given in Part 1, section 2. The following will illustrate further those elements already taught by primary school teachers, which lay the foundations of later home economics teaching, together with some suggestions for additional content.

A *Human development*

The life cycle – the concept of the continuity of life (links with religious education), birth, baby, child, adult, old age, death

Sexuality – boy, girl, man, woman

The family – brother, sister, father, mother, aunt, uncle, cousin, grandparents

Relationships – inside family
– outside family: friends, neighbours, teachers, policemen, minister, doctor, dentist, librarian, shopkeeper, bus conductor, etc

View of self – in relation to: parents, brother, sister, grandparents, friends, teacher

B *Aspects of family life*

Role playing using the Wendy house:
Mother, father, doctor, nurse, patient (including dressing up)

Family activities – shopping, cooking, serving meals, eating meals, washing up, cleaning, making beds, looking after baby, sewing, the family wash, keeping clothing tidy in drawers and on hangers, sweeping, dusting, arranging flowers

Decision making – shopping, buying a dress, furniture, car, etc

Entertaining – friends for tea, phoning relatives

Illness – doctor, nurse, patient

Leisure pursuits

Holidays and visits

Good health – towards personal responsibility for:
– clean hands (Appendix 3), nose, hankie
– clean habits, toilet, washing, bathing, hair, teeth
– exercise, sleep and rest

Choosing food – a varied diet, including milk, eggs, meat, fish, cheese, fruit, vegetables, bread, cereals
– *limit* sweets, crisps, biscuits and cakes

Safety and security

Control of infection – clean personal habits (hands, nose, hankies)
– clean utensils (washing up, Appendix 4)
– food handling and preparation

Use of water, gas – correct use of cooker, fires, kettle, pans, solid fuel, electricity

Tools – knife, fork, spoon, scissors, pins, needles

Labelling – reading labels

Unknown substances – avoidance of unsafe bottles, jars, pills, etc

Storage – keeping cleansers, detergents, etc, in initialed, labelled containers, away from food and children

Clothing – hanging coat, hat
– looking after boots, shoes, gloves, PE gear and pumps.
– dressing and undressing
– eating and drinking carefully to avoid spills
– respect for own clothes and those of others

C *Outer environmental influences:*

Leisure services – use of libraries, parks, swimming bath.

Roads – safe usage, crossing patrol, community policeman.

Transport – use of school bus, train, bicycle.

Safety of person – avoidance of invitations to accompany strangers or enter a stranger's car.

The examples which follow this and those in Appendixes 3 to 7, illustrate ways in which elements of home economics practice may be readily incorporated into the existing framework of the primary school curriculum. Teachers will find that it is simply a matter of extending and developing existing practice. The examples chosen may be used with five, six or seven year olds. According to the age, ability and experience of the pupils, so appropriate language, narrative, visual materials and means of recording will be chosen. The 'top infants' can be introduced to the four basic tastes of sweet, sour, salt and bitter. This leads to discussion on the role of the tongue, teeth and saliva, in the appreciation of food and in the process of eating and digestion. The writer has found that once children are able to understand how to taste and savour food, they derive far more enjoyment from it. By using simple foods like raw fruits, raw and cooked vegetables, children may be introduced to the 'real' taste of many foods for the first time.

I followed up the apple topic, which had been done in the autumn, with one on new potatoes in the spring. Potatoes from different parts of the country were chosen to illustrate that the soils adhering to them were different. Taste panel work was carried out to show that flavour, appearance and texture is different in different varieties and flavour is also affected by the soil in which the vegetable is grown. One boy was loathe to participate, as, he informed fellow pupils, he had never eaten potato without the addition of pickle or sauce (commercial). He discovered that unadulterated potatoes were enjoyable. This incident illustrates the need to teach pupils, not only food choice, but also how to eat in order to derive the maximum pleasure and benefit from food. It also shows that by the time pupils arrive in school, their palates are already in bondage to titillating tastes.

The illustrations given have been selected from B. Aspects of Family Life (food), but could have been taken from other areas. In choosing, use for guidance the three Ss: *Sound, Safe, Simple.* When applied to food studies, choose examples which have a sound nutritional base and which will give early education in scientific principles. The concept of safety is ongoing throughout the eleven years of compulsory education. As seen earlier, it relates to the *safe* use of gas, electricity, water, tools, etc, as well as hygienic practice to control infection. Selected activities within the primary school must be *simple,* to allow for the age and ability of the pupil and the usual scarcity of equipment, money and facilities.

The reader will find that some pupils in the primary school have already assumed, what to most people would seem to be, adult responsibilities. These pupils handle surprising sums of money in the purchase of food, not only for themselves, but other family members. They are responsible for choosing, buying, preparing and serving food, on a regular basis. The following is an example of a boy, at present aged eight years. John aroused my immediate interest since his movements were so deft and his manipulative skills so well developed. He showed enormous interest in any food preparation and always said that it would be repeated that night at home. Early discussion revealed that the family ate fish and chips five nights a week, which John collected from the shop. The household is an all male establishment, with John, three brothers and father. John visits his mother in another household, each Sunday. John was responsible within the home for most of the food purchase, preparation (if any), serving and washing up.

Everything learned at school in food class, was written down and incorporated into the family diet. So far milk, eggs and raw fruit have been used in class. John now prepares regularly at home, scrambled eggs on toast, sandwiches with chopped egg filling, baked puddings with an egg custard base and other simple milk dishes. Raw fruits are used to supplement a diet lacking in vegetables. John is an able pupil and learns quickly. Circumstances have decreed that he is to be responsible for his own diet and so will determine his own health. Money is not a problem in the home and he is not unloved. For pupils like John, food education is essential in the primary school, for his need is immediate.

The middle years (9-13)

Part 1, section 3, showed that the curriculum in middle schools is designed to consolidate and continue the knowledge and learning acquired by pupils in the primary school. Methods of teaching continue to be informal, with pupils enjoying the security of working, for the most part, with their own class teacher at least for the first two years. Specialist teachers may be at a premium in school and generally fulfil a substantial general teaching commitment. The later years in middle school prepare pupils physically, mentally, emotionally and socially, for transfer into a larger educational establishment, which is generally committed to specialist teaching. The last two years in middle school may, therefore, include some specialist teaching.

Any home economics component within the middle school curriculum must, therefore, fit (at least at first) as it did in the primary school, into a generalist teaching programme. This means that elements of home economics may be taught through this general programme and, sometimes, by general subjects' teachers. What is important is not the name that the programme is given, but the content of the teaching. This should be looked at against the structure of home economics, outlined earlier.

The aims specific to home economics in the middle years are:

To consolidate and extend pupils' knowledge and experience (derived from school and home) in the three key areas comprising the central core of home economics.

A *Human development.*
B *Aspects of family life* (food, clothing, housing, socialisation).
C *Outer environmental influences.*

A Human development
The life cycle
This builds on the knowledge acquired in the primary school, relating to conception, birth, adolescence, adulthood, old age and death. Particular attention is paid to the developmental characteristics of changes in the human body experienced between the ages of nine and thirteen. This includes growth patterns in male and female. Pupils will consider height, weight, shape of body, size of hands, feet, puberty, etc. Physical, mental and emotional characteristics are studied.

B Aspects of family life
Good health
This concept is developed from the knowledge and experience gained in primary school. Pupils learn sufficient, in physiological terms, to understand the working of the body, to enable reasoned nutritional choices to be made. This includes the identification of parts of the body, sufficient to give an elementary understanding of digestion, absorption and functions of food in the body. Physical growth is considered in terms of muscle, bones, blood, teeth. The concept of personal responsibility for good health is continued from the stage reached in the primary school. This relates to hygienic practice and control of infection, as well as nutritionally sound eating habits. This includes the care of hands, hair, teeth, feet and skin. Food is considered, according to its bodily function, within the main groups—body building and repair, energy giving and protection. Nutrient groups are identified, ie protein, carbohydrate, starch, sugar, vitamins and mineral salts. The choice of food to satisfy bodily needs is extended, including an appreciation of the need for adequate dietary fibre. A more serious consideration begins of the social, economic, cultural and aesthetic factors in the choice, purchase, preparation and service of food.

Clothing and home accessories
Craft techniques build on those acquired in the primary school. Since much of the curriculum is shared by boys and girls, there is little emphasis on clothing construction (other than for dolls or puppets) and more on craft skills. Girls may make a simple skirt in the third or fourth year. Boys and girls may instead

make shorts for physical education. In years one and two, pupils are taught to select fabric and thread for a task in hand and to handle the tools appropriate for its completion. Fabrics may include canvas, felt, hessian or cotton. Threads include cotton, sylko, Anchor soft embroidery cotton, Coton a Broder, wool or nylon yarn. Tools include pins, needles, scissors, tape measure, thimble and iron. Pupils use hand stitching to join fabric pieces or for embellishment. Stitches include tacking, running, hemming, oversewing, blanket, chain or cross. Finished articles include pictures, wall hangings, shoe bags, oven gloves, simple toys, etc.

In years three and four, pupils begin to use a sewing machine. Simple patterns are made and used. Fabric work moves gradually from coarse to medium weight material. Thickness of thread, size of needle and choice of stitch are related to these. A more serious approach to colour appreciation and texture begins. Tie dye techniques are introduced. Pupils incorporate new and earlier skills into the making of pictures, puppets, patchwork items, aprons and a skirt or shorts as mentioned earlier.

Housing and socialisation

In the middle school, curriculum studies will concentrate on the individual child and the view he has of himself within his family, his home and the constraints of what is still seen to be a limited community environment. This area of the curriculum should, therefore, focus a pupil's attention upon his own home and those within his immediate locality. Sometimes this involves an historical surveillance of the development of houses in the district. This looks at changes in family life over a given period of time. It introduces pupils more seriously to some of the 'outer environmental influences', which determine safety, convenience, aesthetic quality, comfort and amenity, within the home and its surroundings.

It is important to develop an understanding that man is not an island, but lives as he does, partly as a result of what has gone before and partly as a result of a highly complex organisation of man's skill and ingenuity, to which each succeeding generation contributes. At a personal level, no one lives by his own efforts alone, but is supported by a vast number of his fellows. They produce food, clothing, housing and a wealth of services on which his comfort, amenity and survival depend. The historical perspectives may be made more alive by visits to museums, art galleries, combined with the often enthusiastic support of local historians, conservationalists and older people in the community. A study of the development of ancient and modern equipment may illustrate how the same task can be done with a saving in terms of time and energy. One may then ask what has man done with the extra time? This then relates to leisure pursuits, patterns of living and socialisation. There are many interesting aspects of housing which may be developed in the middle school. In practice, a teacher will choose those which his own education and interest enable him to do well.

The later years (13-18)

The later years in school see a widening and diversification of studies within the curriculum. Broad areas of study beginning in the primary school and continuing through into the middle school, have gradually split into a number of specialist subjects. It is because of a sometimes common ancestry, that some knowledge is common to a number of subject syllabuses. For example, some knowledge in the home economics syllabus will be readily discernible in syllabuses in physiology, biology, physical sciences, art and design, sociology, religious education and environmental studies. This knowledge has, at its roots, that which is seen to be essential learning for everyone, as part of their general education. This indicates the integrated nature of the general school curriculum and the part which it fulfils in the ladder of progression within the formal education process.

This ladder has a number of 'stepping off' positions. The first rung, at sixteen, to enter the work place or institute of further education. Some pupils, however, will remain at school until eighteen, before stepping into a labour market. A smaller number will continue their education, into institutions of higher education, thus deferring still further the point at which they begin their chosen career.

The influence of examinations on the curriculum

It could be said that examinations fulfil the role of selecting individuals for their future niche in life. It is this role which causes so much concern to pupils, parents and teachers.

The General Certificate of Education

This was established in 1951 as a single subject certificate at two levels. Ordinary level, normally to be taken at sixteen years, and Advanced level at eighteen years. The General Certificate of Education replaced the School Certificate which was a grouped subject Certificate. All these subjects had to be passed at the same sitting. The School Certificate was also offered at a Higher level. The General Certificate of Education is designed for the top twenty per cent of the whole ability range. The General Certificate of Education examination is managed by independent boards, administered by the universities. This Certificate is used as a means of selection for entry to universities and other institutions of higher and further education.

The Certificate of Secondary Education

This was established in 1964 in response to an increasing demand for a school leaving certificate for those pupils for whom the General Certificate of Education Ordinary level, was unsuited. The new certificate resulted from a thorough investigation carried out by the Schools' Council, into the needs of pupils in the forty per cent band below those catered for by the General Certificate of Education. The needs of these pupils and the areas of study were researched principally by teachers. The resulting examination was planned and administered by the independent Regional Boards. These were constituted, with a membership, including a majority of practising teachers.

'Each Board must offer external examinations on syllabuses produced by the Board (Mode 1 examinations), must examine work based on a school's own syllabus (Mode 2), and must provide a means of checking standards so that, subject to this checking, a teacher may use his own syllabus and examine his own candidates (Mode 3). In this way the examination can be sensitive to the needs of the schools.'

G E Whalley, *The Certificate of Secondary Education,* The University of Leeds Institute of Education, 1969.

The present position

Some fifteen years have now elapsed since the inception of the Certificate of Secondary Education and its progress can be reviewed. At the outset, schools taught the GCE O level and the CSE candidates separately. Some still do, but others teach candidates together and may enter pupils for both examinations. This is economic of staff time, but a study of the respective syllabuses, indicates the difficulties presented.

The Domestic Science 1981 (Ordinary) syllabuses A and B. Syllabus A (Food), Syllabus B (Clothing) of the Northern Joint Matriculation Board state:

'In all papers candidates will be expected to show that they have knowledge of the elementary science necessary for the proper understanding of the processes involved, but questions dealing with scientific principles will have particular reference to their practical application.'

Syllabus A indicates the following:

1 An emphasis on siting, planning, construction, function and relative underlying principles, applied to kitchen equipment, including gas and electrical appliances.

2 Sources of energy, the heating effect of a current and the meaning of electrical terms in relation to applicances.

3 Human hygiene and physiology. Sufficient knowledge to understand the functioning of the body. For instance, nutrition, digestion, absorption, circulation, respiration.

4 Cleanliness in relation to the supply and handling of food.

5 The principles of nutrition and the effects of cooking processes on the principal constituents of food and as an aid to digestion.

6 Processes of decay (fermentation, souring and putrefaction).

From this selection of content it is possible to illustrate an intention by the Board to evaluate levels one, two, three and four of learning, shown earlier (section 2).

Level — one   Specific facts and processes.
— two   Basic ideas, including scientific principles and laws.
— three   Concepts (eg light, heat, time, etc).
— four   Thought systems, problems and their solution,
application of knowledge to new situations.

The Yorkshire Regional Examination Board CSE syllabus, 1980, illustrates the following.

Aims 1 and 2 of the examination place priority on the recall of basic facts and definitions in the written paper. The syllabus outline indicates a similar area of study to the GCE outline, in terms of home, family, house, furniture, furnishings, kitchen planning, services, money management, food and nutrition. The knowledge included is, however, broader, more general and less demanding. Candidates are not asked to give basic facts and definitions based on scientific knowledge. They are not asked for a knowledge of basic principles or concepts. Basically, candidates are asked 'how', rather than 'why'? A review of question papers will show that the GCE O level questions demand a deeper knowledge, focussed on an individual question, whilst CSE papers demand less depth of knowledge over a range of sources. A grade one CSE award is usually acceptable in lieu of a GCE O level pass for entry into further education. This does not mean that the two awards are the same, but simply that the CSE candidate has shown that he is of such a calibre that he would have achieved a GCE pass, had he followed the appropriate course.

How then does a teacher come to terms with teaching both CSE and GCE O level candidates together? At extremes it would appear that either the CSE candidate is required to study at too great a depth, or the GCE candidate is working at too superficial a level. No doubt a compromise is reached, but is this acceptable to teacher, pupil and educational principles and practice? The recent report by Her Majesty's Inspectors (1979), indicated that ninety per cent of pupils were entered for examinations, designed for sixty per cent of the school population. The Inspectors felt that too many examinations were being taken, by too many pupils, in schools. Children were attempting examinations beyond their capabilities. The effects of this could be measured in terms of truancy, or absenteeism from schools, both during a year and on the actual day of examination. Apart from the number of pupils rejecting school and what they were asked to learn, other effects could be seen. The media reports disquiet among the public, employers and teachers themselves, about the minimal standards of attainments by some pupils.

This concern is reflected by Her Majesty's Inspectors. In a report (1979), they propose a basic core curriculum. They cite too many examinations, too many subjects, from which to choose at 14+, resulting in a lack of balance in the curriculum studied by individual pupils. The only subjects common to most pupils at 14+ were found to be English, mathematics and physical education. This report clearly indicates that examinations do have a dominating influence on the curriculum. This does not mean that examinations in themselves are bad. They are an effective means of evaluation. What is bad, is forcing those who are not able to cope, to take them. 'Force' is exercised by teachers, parents, employers and the demands of further and higher education. These are demands of 'society' which play such an important part in shaping the schools' curriculum (Part 6, section 1). This society has never been more competitive. This is reflected at home, nationally and abroad, internationally.

In their wisdom, Her Majesty's Inspectors recommended that the lower forty per cent of the ability range should be relieved of the necessity of entering the examination contest. Advanced forms of evaluation could be employed, they advised, which would give a profile of pupils leaving school, in terms of character, as well as accomplishment.

After 16+

Those who choose to stay in full-time education may do so in school or in an adult college of further education.

Further education

Colleges of further education attract mainly those who wish to enter vocational courses, with a GCE O level or CSE entry requirement. Others may wish to pursue the two year GCE A level course in a college of further education, in the context of an adult environment.

Towards a National Award System

The Haslegrave Committee was set up in 1967 to review the provision of sub-degree level courses, in particular those associated with the training of craftsmen, technicians and those who worked in business and public administration. The report, published in 1969, recommended the setting up of two new bodies, the Technician Education Council and the Business Education Council.

The Technician Education Council

This was set up in 1973 to review, plan, administer and co-ordinate all technician courses. The report (1969) envisaged that existing courses would be replaced by a co-ordinated scheme of awards.

The Business Education Council

This followed in 1974 and dealt in a similar manner, with courses and awards, for those working in business and administration.

The City and Guilds of London Institute

At the time of the Haslegrave enquiry, this independent foundation, was already the world's largest examining body for craft and technician courses. It, therefore, volunteered to take the Technician Education Council and the Business Education Council under its wing. The Department of Education and Science grant-aided the two new bodies. The DES envisaged that, between them, the three validating bodies would cover the full range of sub-degree level courses. In due course, it was hoped that courses validated by other bodies would be drawn into one national structure of awards. Within that structure, it was also hoped, a ladder of progression to the highest awards would be possible, using alternative routes. The achievement of this goal will take many years but progress is being made.

Home economics in the national structure

The vocational courses (referred to earlier) presently validated by the National Council for Home Economics Education, will, in 1981, be drawn into the national structure. Craft courses will be validated by the City and Guilds of London Institute. The Technician Education Council will validate the present Certificate and Diploma Courses. This will make it possible for students to achieve a a Higher Diploma in Home Economics. Entry to this course will initially be direct for candidates with a minimum of five subject passes in the General Certificate of Education, of which at least one must be at Advanced level. In due time it is hoped that a ladder of progression, via lower level courses, will provide an alternative route.

Education after 16+ in schools

Provision falls into two categories. Firstly, Advanced level GCE courses, for those wishing at 18+ to enter higher education and secondly, for those wanting to leave at 17+ to enter work.

The Certificate of Extended Education (17+)

The Schools' Council working paper, number 46, discussed the needs of an increasing number of sixth form pupils, who had no clear vocational aims and who had probably achieved CSE, with grades two to four. The CSE Boards were encouraged to set pilot examinations for this age group. Successful candidates received a CSE Certificate, appropriately graded, with an accompanying letter of credit, recording the experimental and so far unofficial, grades received. The Keohane Committee of Enquiry was set up to survey the current scene and to make appropriate recommendations. Surveys of pilot CEE exams in 1977 and 1978 (when there were more than 20 000 candidates) found that more than two thirds were taking one subject only. Most others took two subjects. About two fifths were also taking CSE. One fifth went on to take A level GCE subjects. It was found that two thirds of sixth form colleges entered candidates whilst only one quarter of schools with a sixth form, did so. More girls than boys presented themselves for examination. The Keohane Report (1979) said;

'It appears that over two thirds of those taking CEE pilot examinations expect to seek employment on completing their studies at 17+. It is therefore crucial that CEE, if it is officially introduced, should be able to prepare people effectively for employment.'

It went on to recommend:

'To ensure that communication (including oral) and numerical skills are covered, all CEE certificates should record performance in appropriate proficiency tests in English and mathematics.'

It suggested that schools should not require every CEE candidate to follow a quasi vocational course but, nevertheless, schools should consider combining the single CEE subject in courses containing basic skills, vocational preparation, and personal and social skills, relevant to possible work outlets. A final significant suggestion, that:

'The Schools' Council and the Further Education Curriculum Review and Development Unit, should act jointly, to bring closer together, the structures and content of CEE and FE courses and to investigate flexible approaches to certification, which would allow national validation of a variety of course elements, eg through the use of CE as a component part of FE courses.'

This may herald a much closer working liaison between schools and further education colleges, offering courses for students of 16 to 19 years.

Examinations at 18+

The General Certificate of Education (Advanced level) may be used as a school leaving certificate, but is usually taken as a means of entry to higher education (university, polytechnic, college of higher education). The Certificate is designed for those candidates who attain 'grade C' or above in the GCE at Ordinary level. Readers will be aware of the debate which has ensued over a number of years, about its possible replacement. This probably began with the concern expressed by the Crowther Committee (in its report published in 1960), about the content of Advanced level syllabuses. The Council and Standing Conference on University Entrance, agreed in 1966, that the reasons for disquiet were that:

'the sixth form curriculum was too narrow, pupils were forced to make subject choices too early, Advanced level, GCE courses, were not appropriate for many students in now expanding sixth forms.'

Still, in 1980, no alternative award, acceptable to institutions of higher education, schools, parents and employers, has been devised. As a result, students from different schools vary enormously in the extent of their general education and maturity, on leaving at eighteen years of age. Some schools offer sixth formers a curriculum narrowly based on Advanced level choices. Others include mathematics and science for 'arts' students, a language and literature for 'science' students. Often such schools manage to include current affairs, religious education, community work, physical education, and choices from home economics, art and music. It can be concluded that examinations do dominate the sixth form curriculum. The degree to which this may disadvantage a student, will depend upon the individual school's policy.

Home economics examinations at 18+

The syllabuses of the Northern Joint Matriculation Board, Domestic Science (The Home, The Family and Society) (Advanced) and, Domestic Science (Fashion and Fabrics) (Advanced), represent excellent sixth form studies for any student. From the aims of the syllabuses, it is clear that course content has been thoughtfully prepared, taking into account the needs of the subject, the potential interests of students, and the needs of schools, in the identification of the contemporary needs and expectations of society (Part 6, section 1). Both courses are rigorous in their demands upon the student and teacher. The means of evaluation have been chosen with due regard to an intellectual level, appropriate to students at Advanced level GCE standard. The award of marks is a fitting recognition of the four levels of learning outlined previously (Part 6, section 2).

These courses have been planned by representatives from schools and higher education, having a wide compass of knowledge and expertise. Syllabuses are regularly reviewed and amended to provide excellent guidelines for inexperienced and experienced teachers alike. Individual teachers are free to interpret these through their own schemes of work and teaching strategies. Students benefit in taking these courses, from an already established, national view of parity and esteem. Teachers gain by involving themselves in this ongoing subject and course development. They are able to measure their own performance and that of their students, against others, nationwide. Teachers may further involve themselves by suggesting questions to the Board, appropriate for inclusion in final papers. Examining Boards advertise regularly in the national press for practising teachers willing to join examiners' panels. The way is open, therefore, for teachers to participate in a system of national evaluation which, if not perfect, is the fairest method yet devised.

Selected references and further reading

Department of Education and Science, Secondary School Examinations (a single system at 16 plus), HMSO, 1978

Department of Education and Science, Proposals for a Cerificate of Extended Education (Keohane Report), HMSO, 1979

Department of Education and Science, Aspects of Secondary Education in England: A survey by HM Inspectors of Schools (1975-1978), HMSO, 1980

Department of Education and Science, Choice of Careers Series 117 (Careers and Occupational Information Centre of the Manpower Services Commission), HMSO, 1980

Central Office of Information, Britain 1980, An official handbook. London: HMSO, 1980 (describes the machinery of government and other institutions together with necessary physical and social background and the part played by government in the life of the country)

Lovell, K, *An Introduction to Human Development,* Macmillan, 1968

Hall, O A and Paolucci, B, *Teaching Home Economics,* John Wiley, Second edition, 1970

Schools Council Curriculum Bulletin 4, Home Economics Teaching, Evans/Methuen Educational, 1971

Schools Council Working Paper No. 55, Curriculum for the middle years, Evans/Methuen Educational, 1977

Schools Council Occasional Paper 1, Standards in public examinations: problems and possibilities, 1979

Schools Council Home Economics Team, Home and Family 8-13, Forbes, 1979

General Certificate of Education (Domestic Science 1981) (Universities of Manchester, Liverpool, Leeds, Sheffield and Birmingham)

Domestic Science (Ordinary)

Syllabus A: Domestic Science (Food)

Syllabus B: Domestic Science (Clothing)

Domestic Science (Advanced)

The Home, the Family, and Society

Fashion and Fabrics

Certificate of Secondary Examinations 1980 (Yorkshire Regional Examinations Board)

Home Economics

Conclusion

The reader has, through the pages of this book, glimpsed the many faces of teachers, the infinite variety among pupils and the complexity of schools. An individual teacher plays but a small part in the whole continuum of a pupil's learning. Nevertheless, each teacher fulfils a major role in a pupil's life at a given point in time. In the fulfilment of that role, an awareness is necessary of the stages in the maturation process, to enable teachers to provide appropriate experiences for pupils that they may develop those skills suited to their age and ability. Without the right skills, pupils will find difficulty in adjusting to life after school, in a demanding world governed by the constraints of technological advance.

The text illustrates that much knowledge and many skills relating to the teaching process are common learning for all intending teachers. Thus, with a subject specialism, studied to an appropriate level, a home economics teacher can climb the career ladder to success on equal terms with other subject specialists. As a home economist, there is the bonus of prospective, flexible, vocational interchange between teaching, industry, commerce and the social agencies.

For those who study home economics in schools, each will find elements from which benefit is drawn in daily life. Pupils who derive a special interest and pleasure from home economics (whether of modest or outstanding ability) can proceed by additional study, to a rewarding vocational goal, via further and higher education. What more can be asked of a subject in the schools' curriculum and what better reason for ensuring that home economics has a continuing place in a pupil's general education?

Appendix 1

Diagram 1 The individual's needs

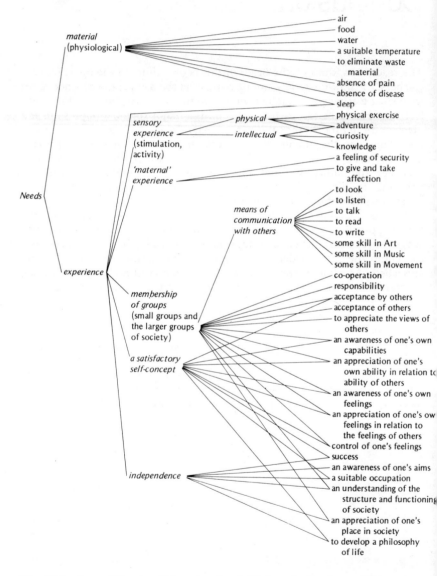

The Objectives of Teacher Education, Leeds University Institute of Education.
Published by the National Foundation for Educational Research 1973.

Appendix 2

Diagram 2 Development of the school curriculum

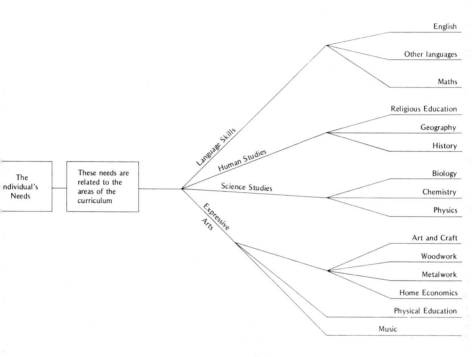

The Objectives of Teacher Education, Leeds University Institute of Education.
Published by the National Foundation for Educational Research 1973.

Appendix 3

The early years (5-9)
Washing hands

Hands *(action)*   tap - turn on, off, open, close; towards, away; anti-clockwise, clockwise

Water *(action)*   run, flow, trickle, gush; slow(ly), very slowly, fast, very fast; rush, splash, spray

(temperature)   hot, cold, warm, lukewarm, cool, tepid, very hot, very cold, ice cold, freezing, boiling, steam, scald

(quantity) how much   a little, not much, a lot, fill, full, half-fill, half empty, bowl-full, basin-full, sink-full, washbasin – full, overflow, run over, run out

Manual skills

Washing hands   Wet hands

Drying hands

1 Rub on soap	6 Rinse, remove soap, clean, cleanse
2 Rub hands together	7 Pull out plug
3 Dip hands ⎫	8 Rinse bowl
4 Plunge ⎬ in water	9 Shake hands
5 Put ⎭	10 Dry

Sensory perception

Visual – clear, white, pink, froth, foam, lather; bubble, big, bigger, expand, burst, shiny, silvery, glassy

Hearing – splash, plop, gurgle, swirl, glug

Smell – scent, nice, pleasant, pleasing

Touch – soft, smooth, slippy, slippery, sliding, slithering

Washing hands

Why?   To remove dirt - seen, unseen - germs

When?

Appendix 4

The early years (5 - 9)
Fruit drinks (Milk)
Milk shake
Milk as a: drink, food

Hunger, hungry, stomach, empty, rumble, eat, full, satisfy

Milk only food for young babies, young animals, puppy, kitten, cows, farm, dairy, milkman, bottle, baby, suck, bottle, sleep; family, mother, father, brother, sister

Milk — food for all. Drinks, hot - tea, coffee, cocoa; cold - milk shake

Milk Shake
Collect, gather: Equipment - Measure, beakers, tray, teaspoon, screw top jar
 Ingredients - Milk, Fruit flavoured instant dessert powder

Skills
Manual
1 Wash hands	4 Measure powder	7 Screw top on jar
2 Measure - milk	5 millilitres	8 Shake well
150 millilitres	5 Add to milk	9 Unscrew jar
3 Pour into jar	6 Stir	10 Pour into beaker

Social
1 Take to table	4 Drink - follow tasting procedure
2 Sit with group	5 Discuss
3 Wait for all to be ready	

Shared group work
1 Washing up	5 Measure detergent	8 Dry
2 Collect beakers	6 Wash	9 Put away
3 Wipe table	7 Drain	10 Wipe table
4 Collect water		

*Sensory perception

Visual – milk, white, not clear; can't see through; milk shake, pink, pale, frothy, bubbly, foamy

Hearing – stirring – less noisy than water; shaking – swish, splash; pouring – plop; drinking – plop

Smell – nice, pleasant, raspberry, not as strong as raspberryade; like jelly, like sweets

Touch – on tongue – smooth, silky, soft – in stomach – satisfies, not hungry

Taste – nice, pleasant, raspberry, milky, sweet, sickly

*All words in this section derive from pupil responses (age six years).

Appendix 5

The early years (5 - 9)

Apples
Fruit – Orchard, tree, farmer, pick, pluck, harvest; basket, box, lorry, market, stall, shop, buy, greengrocer, supermarket, buy, mother, basket, ripe, unripe

Eat – Raw – at meals, after meals, between meals

Skills – For health, keep fit, well, healthy

Manual
Wash hands
Collect: Equipment – board, cloth, plate, vegetable knife
 Ingredients – apples, two kinds, sorts, varieties
Wash apples – clean, dirt, germs, sprays, insecticides
Wipe
Cut, share, four, quarter, seeds, pips, brown, white, ripe, unripe, slice, bite, front teeth, cut, chew, back teeth, crush, grind, squash, break up

*Sensory perception

Visual – red, green, orange, yellow, stripes; big, small, round, ball, top, bottom, brown, stalk, stem
Hearing – crack, crunch, munch
Smell – apple, sweet, sour
Touch – juicy, hard, soft, chewy, tough, crunchy, munchy, crisp
Taste – sweet, sour, sweet/sour, apple, fruity

*All words in this section derive from pupil responses (age six years)

Appendix 6

The early years (5 - 9)

Fruit salad

Fruit - Raw

Orchard, tree, farmer, pick, pluck, harvest, basket, vox, lorry, market, stall, shop, buy, greengrocer, supermarket, mother, basket, ripe, unripe, home, abroad, overseas apple, banana, grape

Health   Healthy, fit, well

Fruit salad   Sweet, pudding, dessert, second course, dinner, lunch

Skills   Wash hands

Manual   *Collect:*

Equipment   board, cloth, plate, vegetable knife, spoon, measuring jug, dish

Ingredients   two eating apples, two bananas, six grapes, one small orange

Measure water into jug
  (560 millilitres)
Add instant fruit drink crystals
Mix well
Peel and slice orange into dish
Quarter apples
Core
Slice
Add to dish
Pour over fruit
Half grapes
Take out pips
Add to dish
Stir well
Leave for one hour
Serve for dinner, lunch or at tea time
Eat with blancmange, cream or ice-cream

Skills

Writing
Individual pieces of work to incorporate key words used

Appendix 7

The early years (5 - 9)
Fruit drinks (water)

Raspberryade
1 Collect, gather: *Equipment:* Jug, spoon, beakers, tray
Ingredients: Water, powder
2 Measure water
3 Add powder
4 Stir
5 Pour into beakers

Skills
Manual
Wash hands
Measure using spoon, powder
measuring jug, water
Stir
Pour
Washing up

Social
Share equally between group
Hand round
Wait till all are served
Drink quietly, slowly to experience taste
Conversation, learn to: listen to others, contribute within group
Share work entailed by group in: clearing up, washing up

Sensory perception
Visual – water clear, see through; becomes pink, dark, can't see through; tones – light, pale, dark, bright

Hearing – spoon on jug, bank, clink, stirring – swish
pouring
drinking   plop

Smell – water – none – like swimming bath; raspberryade – like jelly, raspberry

Touch – water – wet, slippy; drink – sticky, washes over tongue, refreshes, no longer thirsty

Taste – water – none; drink – sweet, raspberry

*All words in this section derive from pupil responses (age six years).

Appendix 8

The story of milk

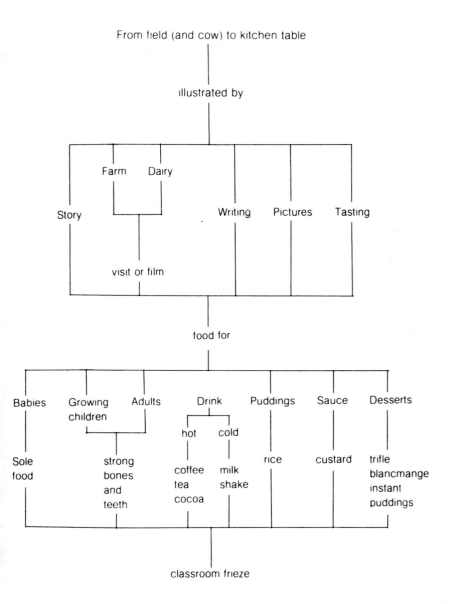

From field (and cow) to kitchen table

illustrated by

Story   Farm   Dairy   Writing   Pictures   Tasting

visit or film

food for

Babies   Growing   Adults   Drink   Puddings   Sauce   Desserts
          children

                        hot   cold

Sole   strong   rice   custard   trifle
food   bones   coffee   milk   blancmange
                    and   tea   shake   instant
                    teeth   cocoa   puddings

classroom frieze

Appendix 9

Fruit for Health

Illustrated by **Apples** (Appendix 5)

Narrative	seed, variety, growing, blossom, fruit, orchard, harvesting, packing, marketing, shop, greengrocer, customer.
Visual	visit/film, pictures, blossom, fruit.
Varieties	Cox's organ pippin, Worcester Permaine, Granny Smith educe differences in appearance and smell tell the story of each kind
Raw	pupils act as taste panel, commenting on appearance, smell, taste, texture. exercises teeth, massages gums fruit salad (Appendix 6)
Cooked	stewed apple - wet heat baked apple - dry heat apple jelly - collect tiny pots so each pupil can take one home sensory evaluation to educe effects of cooking
Record of Learning	writing pictorial representation

Index